This book is to be returned on or before
the last date stamped below.

Also by David Sinclair

The Pound: A Biography
Hall of Mirrors
Shades of Green
Two Georges: The Making of the Modern Monarchy
Edgar Allan Poe

SIR GREGOR MACGREGOR

AND THE LAND
THAT NEVER WAS

The Extraordinary Story of the Most
Audacious Fraud in History

DAVID SINCLAIR

First published in 2003
by HEADLINE BOOK PUBLISHING

10 9 8 7 6 5 4 3 2 1

ISBN 0 7553 1079 9

Text design by Jane Coney
Typeset in Castellar and Granjon by
Palimpsest Book Production Limited,
Polmont, Stirlingshire
Printed and bound in Great Britain by
Mackays of Chatham PLC, Chatham, Kent

HEADLINE BOOK PUBLISHING
A division of Hodder Headline
338 Euston Road
London NW1 3BH

www.reviewbooks.co.uk
www.hodderheadline.com
Author's website: www.dsinclair.net

CONTENTS

PART THREE – STATE OF CHAOS

ACKNOWLEDGEMENTS

The origins of this book lie with the Knight of Glin, Desmond FitzGerald, a man as charming as he is cultured and as inquiring as he is knowledgeable. It was Desmond who first awoke my interest in the fantastic story of Gregor MacGregor, with which he has a peculiarly personal connection, as he explains in his foreword. During my subsequent researches, Desmond's advice and practical help were invaluable. I am grateful, too, for the courteous and professional assistance of staff at the British Library, the British Museum and, in particular, the National Library of Scotland. My thanks are also due to my old friend Alan Plews, who was involved in unearthing some of the obscure original material on which I have drawn.

There are few more impressive sights in the world than a Scotsman on the make.

J.M. Barrie

FOREWORD

Family history is now the most popular hobby in Britain and America. People crave to discover their personal and group identities. When the Public Record Office in London opened its genealogy website in 2001 the system instantly crashed with an over-burdening of 1.2 million hits and when the Ellis Island immigration records went online, also in 2001, they registered 50 million hits on the first day. Genealogy is more popular than pornography!

I have always been fascinated by the subject, in a thoroughly amateurish way, though I agree with Hugh Massingberd's suspicion that 'anyone interested in investigating their roots, must be barmy, boastful and a bore'. He continued: 'Unfortunately, the pursuit of ancestors has attracted more than its fair share of cranks, charlatans and crackpots.' He concludes his review of a book on the missing heirs of Bonnie Prince Charlie by quoting Anthony Powell, a dedicated genealogist, who said somewhere that family history 'teaches much about the vicissitudes of life; the vast extent of human oddness'.

David Sinclair's account of the story of Gregor Mac-Gregor came about by fortuitous chance. David married a glamorous County Limerick girl and they came to live in these parts, near Adare, for a few years. At a party, he told me of his interest in economics and gave me a copy of his book *The Pound: A Biography*. I then recounted my long fascination with His Highness Sir Gregor MacGregor, the so-called Cacique or Cazique of Poyais, and his amazing financial scams in London and Paris in the 1820s, not to mention his military adventures in South and Central America during the South American struggle for independence under Simón Bolívar between 1811 and 1821. It was then that he hatched the plan for the colonisation of Poyais on the Mosquito Coast with its mythical capital of St. Joseph – a tropical mirage if ever there was one. David looked at my notes and material, collected as a schoolboy, and immediately fell for the idea of a biography of the extraordinary MacGregor.

What is the connection between my own family ancestor-worship and this exotic charlatan? While at school at Stowe, I spent many hours of my spare time trying to put some bones on the Glin FitzGerald family tree. Considering the antiquity of the family there was then comparatively little known about what they did and what they were like. Their medieval story, with the fall of the family during the Elizabethan wars culminating with the well-known siege of old Glin Castle in 1600 by Sir George Carew, was occasionally mentioned in history books. But most of our family papers had been destroyed in the 1860s by my eccentric and erratic ancestor 'the cracked Knight', or 'cracked Jack' as he was sometimes known, and very few letters or documentation survived this Victorian holocaust. It was only in the early twentieth century that the folklore associated with the family was diligently collected by a Glin man, Thomas F. Culhane, then living in Australia, which revealed many a fascinating tale. More recently, a deep trawl through eighteenth- and nineteenth-century newspapers by two local scholars, Thomas J. Byrne and Tom Donovan, revealed a chronicle of horse-racing, duels, a debtors' prison and other financial disasters which gave considerable life to the dry catalogue of the births, marriages and deaths of the FitzGerald family as set out in successive editions of *Burke's Landed Gentry*.

Seated on a high ladder in the coffered and coved library at Stowe, I used to comb the *Gentleman's Magazine* for mention of the English families that the Glin FitzGeralds had married into during the late eighteenth and early nineteenth centuries – the Fraunceis Gwyns of Forde Abbey and Combe Florey, the clerical Eyres and, finally, the Hippisleys of Abbotsleigh Court, near Bristol. It was this last family that provided the link to the tale of the bizarre life of the Cazique.

In *Burke's*, Ellen, third daughter of Thomas FitzGerald, 23rd Knight of Glin, is recorded wrongly as marrying in 1791 Colonel Gustavus Matthias Hippisley, son of Robert Hippisley Trenchard Esq., of Cutteridge and Abbotsleigh, Somerset. However, according to two Irish newspapers, they were in fact married in early December 1789, at Tarbert (a few miles from Glin) and then again at Lucan, County Dublin on 15 December. Why they were married twice is unclear.

Although *Burke's Landed Gentry* (1843) records both Robert's second marriage to Anne Priddle of Basingstoke and the children they had, *Burke's Commoners* (1838) has no mention of this marriage and it would appear that Gustavus was born out of wedlock as he did not inherit any of the family estates in Somerset and Wiltshire. *Burke's Royal Descents* (1848) shows the Hippisley family's royal Plantagenet descent from Edward I.

Gustavus's birth date is unclear but he went to St. Paul's school in 1778 and joined the army in 1787, purchasing a cornetcy in the 9th Dragoons, so he presumably met Ellen FitzGerald when his regiment was stationed in Ireland. The Trenchard and Hippisley families had landed interests near Glin at Mount Trenchard, so there may have been a local connection.

In 1796 Gustavus's army career took him and his wife to the Cape of Good Hope, the same year that the Irishman Earl Macartney was appointed Governor. As Lady Macartney did not accompany her husband there, Lady Anne Barnard acted as his hostess. Mrs Hippisley seems to have been friendly with the Governor for Lady Anne wrote to Macartney on 17 February 1801, the Governor having returned to Europe in 1798 because of his health: 'But let me tell you a little news of your friends here. Your adorer Mrs Hippisley has given the world another little one.' Later that year, on 7 December 1801, Lady Anne complained, 'It is impossible for me to count up all the Court Marshals now on the stocks (I fib – there are five); the affronts which have been offered by the officers to each other; the scandals which have grown out of nothing ... General Hall has been sent to Coventry by his regt. as has Mr Hippisley ...'

Hippisley had acted as Major of Brigade at the Cape, but Lady Anne's Cape diaries paint a scandalous picture of Mrs Hippisley's behaviour in the small civic and military establishment of Cape Town. On 25 April 1799 Lady Anne wrote in her diary, showing surprise that her husband had brought Mrs Hippisley to a breakfast and describing her as 'the greatest Trollop in Africa – she must feel awkward in Colonel C's [James Crawford] company considering the present she made to him of what he did not soon get the better of – but I believe that he was not the only one present which owed her as much', obviously a comment on the shocking state of her health (it would appear she had the pox!). On 25 July Lady Anne noted with distaste that she had come unasked with 'her present lover Colonel Hall' and elsewhere, a year later, she described the Hippisley ménage: 'the mad ill behaved peacock Mrs Hippeley [sic] who I found with her lover and husband in the new house – everybody's house and nobody's house – she mistress but two masters there'.

This scandal led to a court martial in the Cape on 12 January 1802 when Hippisley charged a brother officer, Lieutenant Thomas Amory of the 8th Light Dragoons, of 'causing him – publicly – at the mess – a personal hurt and dishonour to his regiment'. Amory is reported to have described Hippisley as 'a pitiful fellow, to live by the prostitution of his wife'. Various other evidence was given, including one report that Mrs Hippisley was caught more or less in flagrante with Brigadier General Hall in the block house at Hout Bay and said of her husband, 'look at the contented cuckold'. Hippisley is quoted as saying to Hall, 'Is it for this that you have lent me money, to debauch my wife?' Amory was let off with a public reprimand.

These dramatic events did not prevent Mrs Hippisley from producing four children between 1798 and 1803 – one wonders about their paternities! The marriage must have endured, as their youngest child, Jane Augusta, was born in 1809, by which time the Major was back in England in the West Mendip local militia. We will meet with Jane Augusta later in this foreword.

Gustavus retired from the army in 1815, at the end of the Napoleonic wars, as a Lieutenant in the 17th Foot on Irish half pay. After thirty years of campaigning, Hippisley, like many others, sought another country where his military experience might be utilized. This led him to the great adventure of his life, which was to enlist in the cause of he liberation of Venezuela, Caracas and New Granada from Spain under the leadership of Bolívar. Bolívar's army agent in London, John Luis Lopez Mendes, arranged for Hippisley to raise a regiment of Hussars for the Republic of Venezuela with Hippisley as Colonel Commandant. He had to procure transports, provisions, uniforms and other necessities, the cost of which was to be repaid to him by the Venezuelan government on his arrival in South America. The uniform of the Hussars was dark green with scarlet collars, green sleeves, red cuffs with an elegant Austrian knot on the arms, dark green trousers with red stripes and wellington boots.

The newly raised regiment sailed from London at the end of November 1817 with two of Hippisley's sons, Gustavus Butler and Charles, as Captains. The expedition went badly from the start and the combination of the tropical climate and the lack of military discipline and commissariat led to the death by fever of many men. Others deserted and rivalries with other regiments made poor Hippisley's life a despairing one.

None of the promises made in England were kept and Bolívar prevaricated about the promised payment. Hippisley threatened Bolívar with an account of the treatment he had received in contrast to Don Luis Lopez Mendes's promises in London. Bolívar replied that the gallant Colonel could do what he liked, neither he nor the government was to be intimidated by these threats.

Hippisley returned to England and, in 1819, John Murray published *A Narrative of the Expedition to the River Orinoco and Apuré, in South America; Which Sailed from England in November 1817 and Joined the Patriotic Forces in Venezuela and Caracas* by G. Hippisley Esq., late Colonel of the First Venezuelan Hussars, in the service of the Republic, and Colonel Commandant of the British Brigade in South America. This solid book of over 600 pages was as long winded as the title but received some attention in the press. Poor Hippisley had lost £500 in the Venezuelan cause and only recovered £60. His litany of moans and groans was amusingly pilloried in *Blackwoods Magazine* of September 1819:

This is an extremely comfortable book to look at and touch, but an extremely uncomfortable one to read. It is excellently well printed – and the hand slips smoothly over the wire-wove hot-pressed paper, as over a lady's arm, with or without a glove. Indeed it does one's heart good to dally with so comely an octavo – fat, fair, and forty – and we absolutely fell asleep with it in our arms. On awakening from our slumbers, we began to converse a little with our Spanish mistress, but to our unspeakable mortification found her not only tiresome to a degree, but unhappy herself unless she could make us equally so . . .

Colonel Hippisley keeps so constantly before our sight in one attitude of distress after another, that our feelings of sympathy are so worn out that we wish that either he or ourselves had never been born – and feel at last as we could not long survive his narration of all the miseries of human life.

These sentiments were reiterated some years later, again in *Blackwoods Magazine*, in January 1834, in a review about a book on Lord Byron's travels to Greece which mentioned the soi-disant Colonel Hippisley's volume on his service with Bolívar and his retirement 'in disgust on not finding port wine and beef steaks to be always procured in the other hemisphere . . .' The volume was

invariably asked for by Lord Byron at dinner and at length Fletcher, his valet, brought it regularly with the tablecloth. Its soporific qualities, he amusingly remarked, were truly astonishing, surpassing those of any ordinary narcotic; perusal of a few pages sufficed to lull him to sleep and obtained him a comfortable siesta even when ill disposed or in bad humour with himself.

Hippisley must have left his promiscuous FitzGerald wife by the time he came back from South America as we find him living, presumably bigamously, in Guernsey with Anna Maria

Newman, a widow. He had one son, William Theodore, born there in 1817, and three daughters. The Colonel was buried in St. Sampson in Guernsey in 1831. His legitimate wife lived on in London for another decade until 1841 when she died, according to a death notice in the Limerick Chronicle of 26 June, in Gower Street, Brunswick Square 'in her 61st year', which clearly could not be true as this would have meant her marriage at the age of eight! She was described in that notice as 'the widow of Colonel Hippisley, and aunt to the Knight of Glin'.

Gregor MacGregor is only mentioned once in Hippisley's book, as a Major General on furlough on the staff of the Venezuelan army. This would have been in about 1817 or 1818 when MacGregor and his wife and child were in Dublin and later London, where MacGregor called on Lopez Mendes to raise a loan for an expeditionary force for the Venezuelan service. Hippisley had sailed to Venezuela late in 1817 so he would have probably missed MacGregor in London. However, this was a time when many young British officers, idle after the Napoleonic wars, were selling and buying commissions for the cause of South American independence. According to General O'Leary, an Irish soldier in South America, in 1826 Hippisley wrote a long and ingratiating letter to Bolívar retracting much of the content of his book. His effusions 'show repentance enough for errors which he had incurred at another epoch, take away all authority from any point of view, of the unjust concepts of a book whose testimony has been invoked often as impartial and discreet by the slanderers of Bolívar'. Hippisley was probably looking for a handout!

Colonel Hippisley's eldest son, Gustavus Alexander Butler, so named after his pretentious Ormonde and Plantagenet descent from Edward I, had, as already noted, gone to South America in his father's Venezuelan Hussars. He seems not have returned with his father but became a Lieutenant Colonel in the Republic of Columbia. He wrote a long poem in three cantos, *The Siege of Barcelona*, published much later in 1844. In the preface he talks of 'the false enthusiasm and fancied glory of aiding an oppressed and struggling people in the endeavour to cast off these galley chains which ages of despotism had apparently so securely riveted' and recalls the money both he and his father had lost in the cause.

Hippisley Junior may have crossed paths with MacGregor in South America as a number of stanzas enthusiastically record his bravery and glory in the victories of Alacran and Juncal, though MacGregor himself did not take part in the siege of Barcelona. These engagements took place in 1816 so much of the poem must have been based on hearsay. However, Gustavus was soon to become deeply involved with MacGregor and this connection is chronicled in Hippisley's booklet, *Acts of Oppression Committed Under the Administration of M. De Villèle, Prime Minister of Charles X, in the Years 1825–26. In a Series of Letters*, which was published in 1831. In the preface he recounts his five-year participation in the arduous struggle for South American independence and his return to England, in broken health but with the consolation that he had been engaged in a glorious cause. This brings us to 1824–5 and he continues:

It was with the extreme pleasure therefore, that he [Hippisley] hastened to avail himself of an invitation from General MacGregor (now President of the Poyaisian Republic) to join him in Paris, where he anticipated benefit from the change of climate, as well as the gratification of a personal introduction to a man, with whose character he had been a long time conversant – it has been remarked, that no man is a prophet in his own country – this assertion was verified in respect to the General, for at the same instant, that the English journals were impugning his conduct, and casting unmerited obloquy upon his name, the inhabitants of a large portion of the Southern Hemisphere, were singing the praises of one of the earliest and most intrepid defenders of their freedom!

This suggests that Hippisley was a naive dupe to MacGregor's lies and the book is a panegyric honouring MacGregor. It is written in a jovial and jaunty style and he comments on Paris:

the modern Athens, the emporium of the arts and sciences, the grand mart of fashion ... where virtue in rags crouched in a hovel, while vice inhabits a palace, and parades her unblushing front in the broad glare of daylight.

Gustavus complains about the food and the discomfort of French town houses, and notices the 'blushing effrontery and the conduct of the licensed filles de pave'.

The booklet contains a long account of the Cazique, swallowing all the spurious grand Scottish and English family connections, not to mention his glorious military exploits in the Peninsular war and those more genuine successes in South and Central America. Poor Hippisley was totally swept up in the Cazique's tissue of lies and eventually he spent an uncomfortable time in two French prisons. The story of their French sojourn is fully chronicled in the text of this book.

Another character must finally be woven into the genealogical tapestry: a certain William John Richardson of Oak Hall, Wanstead and Gloucester Place, Portman Square. Nothing seems to be known of his origins, though one of his last surviving descendants once told me she thought he was a bastard son of either the Duke of Wellington or of his brother, Richard, Marquess Wellesley – hence Richard-son! He owned, it is said, docks in London and Liverpool and a painting of Princes Dock is mentioned in a will, more of which later. Relevant to our story is that Richardson was a pawn in the career of our confidence trickster and arch impostor Gregor MacGregor.

In 1823 a pompous proclamation was issued ('We, Gregor 1st, sovereign Prince of the State of Poyais, to his most gracious majesty George IV') appointing Richardson as his highness's Chargé d'Affaires at the Legation of the Territory of Poyais in the United Kingdom of Great Britain. Richardson was also invested as a Commander of the Most Illustrious Order of the Green Cross and gazetted Major in the Royal Regiment of Horse Guards. So the charade continued and much of the activity took place at Oak Hall, which became the centre of the planned Poyais operations combined with the office of the Legation at Dowgate Hill in the City of London. It is unclear what Richardson's connection with Hippisley Jr.

was at this time, for it was not until 1834 that Richardson married Hippisley's youngest sister, Jane Augusta, by his father's marriage with Ellen FitzGerald. Richardson remained loyal to MacGregor for many years, but he and Hippisley fade out of this exotic tale by 1831, after Hippisley published his book on his experiences with MacGregor in Paris. Though MacGregor tried to raise another loan, by 1838 his wife had died and he was virtually penniless. He did, however, return to Venezuela where he died in 1845 as a hero, having been reinstated as General of Division with a pension. He was given a full national and military funeral in Caracas.

Gustavus Hippisley's literary effusions continued with a book of privately printed poems, *Hours of Idleness*, published sometime in the mid-century. It is dedicated to his sister, Mrs Richardson, and no fewer than seven poems celebrate her beauty and charms:

In vain the painter's hand essays to trace
Those nameless beauties that adorn thy face . . .

His poetry has very little merit, but in the book he includes a long and spirited poem celebrating the union of England, Scotland and Ireland, entitled *The Shamrock, Thistle and Rose*, by his mother Ellen from Glin.

In the library at Glin a framed sepia photograph of a watercolour portrait of Mrs Richardson hangs by the chimneypiece. Obviously, the original was painted at the height of her beauty in the 1830s. The legend in our family was that she was the great friend, supporter and even mistress of my great-grandfather, the 'Big Knight'. The Richardsons later moved to a large house at 15 Portland Place and were considered extremely wealthy in their day arising from Richardson's interests in the docks. He was a founder member of the Reform Club in London, but he still remains an elusive figure. He died in 1883. He had four sons and one daughter, Geraldine Augusta, who in 1859 married Lieutenant Colonel Sidney Burrard who served for 25 years in the Grenadier Guards. He was a younger son of Sir George Burrard, 4th Baronet of Wallhampton, near Lymington, Hampshire. His sons and grandson became the last Baronets and the title is today extinct. They were all in the army, one becoming Surveyor General of India and another an expert of firearms. The Burrards' only daughter, May, married Henry Pakenham Mahon of Strokestown, County Roscommon in 1890. It was their redoubtable daughter, Olive, who remembered something of Richardson's supposed Wellesley origins. A watercolour of Mrs Richardson and her daughter, Mrs Burrard, still hangs at Strokestown, which is now open to the public and has a splendid recently restored walled garden. Geraldine Augusta Richardson lived in her widowhood at 42 Brunswick Square, Brighton until 1900. She entertained lavishly and an old newspaper cutting records one of the fashionable lunches that she gave there. When she died in 1900 she left to my grandfather, the Big Knight's son, FitzJohn, a silver tea pot and service commemorating a speech made in Perth by her husband and an oil painting of Princes Dock. These items never seem to have come to Glin, but my grandfather must have set great store by this link with Mrs Richardson for one letter survives from her daughter, Geraldine Augusta Burrard, prescribing a diet of turtle soup and strong beef for her mother. Another, from a Brighton neighbour, the Countess of Munster, to my grandmother, Lady Rachel, describes Geraldine's death throes with sympathetic condolences and memorials of friendship.

When I was a schoolboy in 1955, investigating these by-paths of family history, I corresponded with Colonel H. G. Burrard and Sir Gerald Burrard, the 7th and last Baronet, the son and great-grandson respectively of the old dowager. They both remembered Mrs Richardson and Mrs. Burrard's generosity and extravagance. Geraldine Augusta inherited a considerable fortune after her mother's death in 1900 and in 1901 married a penniless spendthrift James Nairne Smyth Pigott from a well-known Somerset county family who went through the last of the Richardson money. She died in 1908. One can only speculate on the source of this fortune and the docks that must have been its origin. It seems fairly certain that William Richardson invested no money with his friend, the exotic Cazique of Poyais, the subject of this picturesque story. Again, the words of Anthony Powell can be quoted, for this chronicle shows 'the vast extent of human oddness!' Such are the curious by-paths found in my family history, which link in turn to the ensuing amazing story. Read on!

Desmond Fitgerald, Knight of Glin
Glin Castle
Co. Limerick, Ireland

AUTHOR'S NOTE

THE VALUE OF MONEY

Money plays a central role in this story, but it can be difficult for a reader transported back to the early years of the nineteenth century to appreciate the significance of the sums involved without reference to what would be their equivalent value today. Rather than providing footnotes, or equivalent figures in parentheses – which I am sure would be irritating – I should like to use this note to advise readers that multiplying the amounts in pounds sterling quoted in the story by 55 will give a rough equivalent of their modern values. That means every £100 mentioned in the story would represent approximately £5,500 today.

For this deceptively simple calculation, I am indebted to Mr Robert Twigger of the Economic Policy and Statistics Section of the House of Commons Library, who produced a detailed research paper in February 1999 designed to provide a long-term perspective on the change in the purchasing power of the pound between 1750 and 1998.

With 1974 as the base year, at a value of 100, the average price index for the years 1820 to 1830 works out at 10.7. The index for 1998 is computed at 592.3 and when that figure is divided by 10.7, it yields the number of pounds now required to have roughly the same purchasing power as £1 between 1820 and 1830 – that is, £55.35.

The importance of the multiplier will become obvious as the story progresses and the reader encounters sums of a few hundred thousand pounds, which, it must be remembered, would be worth several million pounds at today's prices.

Of course, all sums are given in the pounds, shillings and pence of pre-decimalization days, so for those who have forgotten how the 'old money' worked – or readers too young ever to have dealt with £.s.d. – it may be worth recalling that there were twelve pence to a shilling and twenty shillings to the pound.

PART ONE

A FARAWAY COUNTRY

THE PROMISED LAND

The new year of 1823 announced itself in violent fashion with a vicious storm that battered the east coast of Britain for a fortnight. Scotland suffered the worst of it, lashed by gales and snow that trapped people in their homes, brought mail deliveries to a halt, and made travelling by coach too dangerous even to think about. At sea, the weather was lethal. The American ship *Elizabeth*, out of Boston, running for shelter off the Scottish coast, sank with all hands, while just a single survivor was washed ashore from the Russian vessel *Eolus* when she went down. A local packet boat, the *Betsy Crook*, almost made it to the Firth of Forth, but was blown on to rocks and wrecked at the entrance to Crail harbour, below Fife Ness.

In the comparative calm of the port of Leith, on the Firth a mile from Edinburgh, Henry Crouch watched the weather with anxious eyes. He was the captain of the *Kennersley Castle*, an armed merchantman, due to sail on 14 January carrying nearly 200 passengers and a year's supplies. They were destined for a new colony in South America but with just a week to go before departure, it seemed unlikely that the loading of the ship could be completed in time unless the storm abated quickly. In the event, it grew worse. Tuesday 14 January was the very day on which the tempest unleashed its full force on Edinburgh. Virtually nothing moved in or out of the city; the roads were impassable under the swirling snow.

For the emigrants booked on the *Kennersley Castle*, quartered at the inns and boarding houses of Leith, it was a frustrating time. They had arrived at the port in a state of high excitement, impatient to embark on new lives full of promise and, they were sure, of prosperity. Theirs was not a flight of the dispossessed, an escape from rapacious landlords, a deliverance from the poverty and hardship that accompanied the economic upheaval of the industrial revolution. It had been a conscious, carefully planned decision founded on the ambition to better themselves, to improve their standard of living, and to be pioneers in a land that they had been assured would amply repay their courage and enterprise.

Among the party was a small group of professional gentlemen – doctors, lawyers and even a banker – who had been encouraged to see themselves as the future elite of the new colony. Others were farmers, some in late middle age, who had sold their holdings or relinquished long-standing tenancies and used their savings to buy perhaps a hundred acres of what was, by all accounts, astonishingly fertile ground, and might even contain the bonus of rich gold or mineral deposits. Then there were shopkeepers, who saw the opportunity to develop a whole new market, or artisans attracted by wages better than they could hope to obtain in Scotland. Clerks had been lured from behind their desks by the promise of posts in the civil service of their new country, and one young man with artistic inclinations looked forward to becoming a theatre manager.

Small wonder that, like Captain Crouch, these eager emigrants chafed at the delay imposed by the storm. As the women struggled to keep bored children amused indoors, and the men watched the blizzard from the grimy windows of some gloomy alehouse, they dreamt of what life would be like in the sunny, gentle climate of their new South American home which, they had been told, was 'one of the most healthy and beautiful spots in the world', where 'Europeans do not suffer by any of those disorders so dangerous in the West Indies; and live to a very old age.'

Indeed, the settlers had been furnished with so much information about the country they were to adopt that they almost felt as if they knew it already. They could hardly wait to see with their own eyes the scenes that had been painted for them in promotional leaflets, in newspaper articles and advertisements, in ballads they heard in the streets, in a handsome, 350-page guidebook 'chiefly intended for the use of settlers', and by the representatives in Scotland of the government of a land which – according to a senior British naval officer who had spent many years in the region – 'is excelled by no country under the influence of the British dominion'.

This earthly paradise was called the Territory of Poyais, and it was described as 'a free and independent state situated on the mountainous side of the Bay of Honduras; three or four days' sail from Jamaica; thirty hours from the British Settlement of Balize [sic] in Yucatan; and about eight days from New Orleans, in the United States of America'. The Territory lay between the Spanish South American provinces of Honduras and Nicaragua, from which it was separated by a chain of almost inaccessible mountains. Its natural defences had preserved it from Spanish domination and, in fact, the country had been sporadically settled by British people since its discovery by West Indies pirates in the late seventeenth century. For political reasons, Poyais had never been officially claimed as a British colony, in spite of close links between its native rulers and the British West Indies, and several approaches by Poyaisian kings to the government in London with offers to attach their country to the Empire. As a result, the immense natural resources of Poyais – its extremely rich and fertile soil, its luxuriant forests, its gold and its abundant marine life – had been left largely undisturbed.

As the official guidebook put it, under the heading of 'Commerce':

The Geographical position of this hitherto neglected

country, being in the vicinity of some of the richest provinces of Spanish America, at nearly an equal distance between the southern part of the United States on the one hand, and the new Republic of Columbia on the other, being also within a convenient distance of the West India Islands, and close to the British Territory in Yucatan; together with the immense variety of exceedingly valuable commercial commodities, which are the natural production of the soil, present of themselves, even independent of the operations of the planter or cultivator, a rich field for successful commercial industry ... It has been computed that, even in the uncivilized state of the country, and independent of the native consumption, manufactured goods to the value of upwards of fifty thousand pounds pass annually into the Spanish American provinces through this territory alone, yielding, under every disadvantageous contingency, a very large profit to the adventurers; and there is no doubt that this trade, protected by a wise and liberal policy on the part of the Government of Poyais, may be carried to an extent, much beyond any calculation which can at present be formed, and that it will amply remunerate those who may become interested.

Best of all, however, for the prospective settlers waiting impatiently in Leith, was the understanding that the risks of emigration to Poyais were negligible. Apart from the fact that the natives – known, apparently, as Poyers – were Anglophiles, after more than a century of contacts with the British, there was the reassurance of knowing that their new land was governed by one of their own: a distinguished Scotsman who had been given the responsibility by the

Poyer king. Some of them had even met the man, General Sir Gregor MacGregor, a veteran of the Napoleonic wars and a hero of South America's struggle to liberate itself from Spain, who had subsequently been honoured with the title of His Highness Gregor, Cazique of Poyais (*cazique* being equivalent to 'prince', from the Spanish-American word for a native chief).

His Highness had travelled to the United Kingdom for the specific purpose of recruiting officials for his government, and encouraging immigration by people with the sense of adventure and the skills to exploit the riches of his territory and nurture in it the roots of European civilization to which the natives aspired. And, as he told the members of the Leith party who had been introduced to him at his Edinburgh lodgings, they would not be the first. A group of seventy colonists had already arrived in Poyais to begin the work of developing the country.

For those trapped in Leith, though, paradise continued to be postponed. The blizzard raged along the Firth of Forth throughout Wednesday and Thursday, and it was not until the weekend that Captain Crouch could begin to complete the loading of his ship. By Monday, the hold of the *Kennersley Castle* was filled with enough beef, pork, flour, rice, oatmeal, pot-barley* and other provisions to sustain the colonists for twelve months, together with 'good English' horsehair mattresses, blankets, pillows and an extensive

---

* Barley reduced to small, round grains for cooking, otherwise known as pearl-barley.

selection of tools for house building and agriculture – but the emigrants' hopes of departure suffered another blow as the weather closed in again. It was not until Wednesday, 22 January, that the passengers could finally bid emotional farewells to hundreds of relatives and friends gathered on the dockside and board the boats to take them to the ship, now riding gently at anchor in Leith Roads.

His Highness the Cazique came aboard to wish them well, and to ensure that their accommodation was comfortable. He delighted many of them by announcing that, since this was the pioneering voyage from Scotland to Poyais, he had decided to give free passage to all the women and children. As MacGregor was rowed back to shore, the colonists broke into spontaneous, rousing cheers. Captain Crouch fired a broadside of six guns in salute, and hoisted the flag of Poyais, a green cross of St George on a white background.

At last they were on their way, with favourable winds and fair weather, and nothing more than a heavy swell to trouble them. Two days' sailing brought the ship round Duncansby Head, by John O'Groats, and into the Pentland Firth, the narrow channel that separates the Orkney Islands from the Scottish mainland. Two days more took the vessel past Cape Wrath and the Butt of Lewis, and down the north-western coast of the Outer Hebrides, so that, by 27 January, the passengers were watching the little island of St Kilda fade into the distance as they headed out into the Atlantic.

It was to be their last glimpse of land for more than a

month, yet the time passed pleasantly enough. Some of the better-off emigrants had their own cabins, but even those who travelled steerage found nothing to complain about in the space and quality of their quarters. The food on board was good and plentiful, and the captain spared no effort in maintaining the well-being of his passengers, so that when his prudent attempts to conserve the ship's supply of fresh water seemed to result in short rations for the children, he responded without demur to the concern expressed by the parents and increased the daily allowance.

There was just one unpleasant incident, when a man travelling in steerage so far forgot himself as to make improper advances to a young woman. His neighbours convened an impromptu trial in their quarters and, after considering the evidence, sentenced the man to a flogging, not only to punish him but also to warn others whose strength of character might be found wanting under the pressure of confinement and boredom.

The guilty party, however, was not prepared to accept the punishment imposed by his peers, and he appealed to the cabin passengers, whose social standing and future prospects in Poyais made them the natural leaders of the group. These worthies consulted the Captain, but he refused to become involved, merely pointing out that while he was not responsible for discipline among the passengers, he would be compelled to take action if their behaviour threatened the safety and smooth running of the ship. The gentlemen, fearing that the flogging might inflame the victim's friends, decided that it was in the interests of good order – with several weeks of the voyage still ahead – to set aside the sentence. It was a judgement that dismayed some of the self-appointed lawyers of the lower deck, who muttered darkly that such a failure of will among the leading citizens of the new colony would not be forgotten by 'bad characters' who might be inclined to cause trouble once they were ashore. For the time being, however, harmony was maintained, and the *Kennersley Castle* ploughed on uneventfully through the Atlantic rollers.

In fact, there was plenty to occupy the minds of the emigrants as each day brought them closer to their future home. They pored over the maps given to them by officials at the Poyaisian Land Offices in Edinburgh and Glasgow, and speculated about what the countryside might be like. All they had actually seen was an engraving of the port of Black River, which was where they were to make their landfall. The picture showed a peaceful lagoon, its entrance formed by two spits of land covered with palm trees and profuse vegetation. In the distance, behind a neat, well laid out little town, loomed a great mountain, known as the Sugarloaf, its lower slopes thickly forested, and beyond that more mountain ranges could be seen disappearing into the distance. As for the rest of Poyais, its appearance was left to the imagination of the colonists, based upon what some of them had read in the guidebook, what they had been told by Sir Gregor MacGregor and his agents, and descriptions published in the promotional leaflets and advertisements.

'The Face of the Country', an announcement in the

Glasgow newspaper the *Sentinel* declared, 'is beautifully varied by Hill and Valley, and likewise abounds with fine Savannahs and Plains, and in Forests of the most valuable TIMBER, such as Mahogany, Cedar, Santa Maria Wood, Rose Wood, Zebra Wood, Pitch Pine, and many others.' To which the guidebook added that the coasts were generally flat, and surrounded with reefs, while the interior was 'full of large rivers, that run some hundred miles up into a fine, healthy and fruitful country'. The climate was described as 'mild for those latitudes, and being continental, not nearly so hot as the islands in the same parallel'. The guidebook went on:

> The great salubrity of the air of this delightful and most valuable country, supplies a constant fund of health and activity to the European settler, a blessing which is seldom enjoyed in the same degree in any other part of North or South America. With the exception of a few months in the year, this country is constantly refreshed by regular sea breezes, accompanied by an average of heat that may be taken at the temperature of 80 degrees. The temperature of the air varies indeed considerably according to the elevation of the land, but with this exception, the medium degree of heat is much the same throughout the country.

At this point, the author of the guidebook – Thomas Strangeways, a captain in the 1st Native Poyer Regiment, and an aide-de-camp to the Cazique – seemed to forget the practical purpose of his work and his language soared as he described the seasons of the year. The travellers, who were refugees from the Scottish winter, read it over and over again:

> The Spring or vernal season may be said to commence with the months of April and May, when the foliage of the trees evidently become[s] more vivid, and the savannahs begin to change their russet hue, even previous to the first periodical rains, which are now daily expected, and compared with the autumnal rains, may be said to be gentle showers. After these rains have continued a short time, the weather becomes dry, settled and salutary; and the tropical summer or *dry season*, reigns in full glory. The sun, during this space, is always most powerful, and its vivid rays are not mitigated by the same uniformity of breeze that prevails during the other months of the year. Not a cloud is to be perceived; and the nights at this season are transcendently beautiful. The clearness and brilliance of the heavens, the serenity of the air, and the soft tranquillity in which nature reposes, contribute to harmonise the mind, and produce the most calm and delightful sensations.
>
> The moon, too, in these climates, displays far greater radiance than in Europe. The smallest print is legible by her light, and in the moon's absence, her function is not ill supplied by the brightness of the milky-way, and by that glorious planet Venus, which appears here like a little moon, and glitters with so refulgent a beam as to cast a shade from trees, buildings and other objects, making full amends for the short stay and abrupt departure of the crepusculum or twilight.

Even the tropical winter, or wet season, would apparently

hold few terrors for those who had just weathered one of the worst blizzards for years.

At the beginning of November, what are called the *norths*, north winds, commence, and generally continue, with little variation, till the return of the month of March. Whilst these winds last, the mornings and evenings are cold, frequently unpleasantly so; and what in this country is understood by a *wet north*, might perhaps furnish no very imperfect idea of a November day in England; a *dry north*, on the contrary, is healthful, agreeable and invigorating. The north wind having acquired sufficient force, the atmosphere is cleared; and now comes on a succession of serene and pleasant weather, the north-east and northerly winds spreading coolness and delight throughout the whole of the country. If this interval, therefore, from the beginning of December to the end of April, be called winter, it is certainly the finest winter on the globe. To valetudinarians and persons advanced in life, it is the climate of Paradise.

It would be almost springtime when the ship arrived at the Black River, according to the estimate of the Captain, who had made this journey many times. The weather should be kind, not too hot yet for the hard labour of building houses, warm and dry enough to live comfortably in the open while the work went on. But what would the place really be like? From the mass of information that had been disseminated, there were almost as many impressions as there were settlers, and these were endlessly compared during the long days at sea.

One of the cabin passengers, Andrew Picken, the young man who had been appointed to manage the national theatre of Poyais, spoke about what he had learned of the capital city, St Joseph, just a few miles from the Black River settlement, on the western side of the bay. It was a place of broad boulevards and colonnaded buildings in the classical European style, with a splendid, domed cathedral, an opera house as well as the theatre, a royal palace, the headquarters of the Bank of Poyais (whose currency many of the settlers had in their purses) and, of course, the seat of the parliament. Not only that, declared another of the elite group – soon to be an official of the Poyaisian civil service – but St Joseph was also home to the impressive offices of the few merchant adventurers who had already seized the opportunities Poyais offered, and who had built themselves grand riverside mansions on the proceeds.

The rest of the party listened enthralled, looking forward to their arrival in this utopia, and dreaming of the mansions they themselves might eventually build with the wealth they would acquire. That they would become rich seemed beyond doubt. It was not simply the fertility of the soil, the abundance of natural resources, and the kindness of the climate that would work to their advantage, but the minimal cost of native labour, as Captain Strangeways made clear in his observations on the agriculture of Poyais:

The native Indians readily engage themselves to any of the settlers, for a given time, and at a fixed price.

Their wages, in general, are about twenty-five shillings sterling per month; but as they commonly prefer receiving clothing and other articles in lieu of money, the most advantageous way for a settler is to keep a supply of such articles always by him, which if he purchases with ready money, will prove a considerable saving to him, and consequently reduce the price of labourage. It is customary for the settlers to feed their Indian labourers, but this after the first four months, by which time he will have a crop of Indian corn, will amount to almost nothing, as the only articles necessary for him to purchase are rum and ammunition: one Indian in a single day's hunting or fishing, being able to supply the whole family, however numerous, with provisions for a week, consisting of venison, wild hogs, game, turtle, fish, oysters, &c.

Bearing this in mind, the author of the guidebook estimated 'the yearly expence [sic] of each Indian labourer to an *established* settler at £13 *per annum*, and to a *new* settler at £16 *per annum*; to which may be added, the additional sum of £4 for provisions, the first year, which will make in all £20 *per annum*, for the expence of each labourer'.

Some of the settlers, especially those who were artisans, were former soldiers who had served in exotic parts of the world and had been exposed to unfamiliar cultures, but others had never been outside Scotland and were slightly nervous about the prospect of contact with the Poyais natives. Captain Strangeways, though, was reassuring, as those who had a copy of his book could attest.

The Poyers were modest, docile and friendly, quick-witted and keen to learn. Most of them spoke at least a little English, because 'a tradition has long prevailed among them that the *grey-eyed people*, meaning the English, have been particularly appointed to protect them from oppression and bondage'. Indeed, there was good reason to believe that the Poyers 'were at one period better acquainted than at present with many of the arts of civilization', because many of their customs, and the antiquities found in their country, suggested that they might be descendants of the great Aztec people of Mexico, whose highly developed and sophisticated society had been destroyed by the brutal Spanish invaders.

They have repeatedly shewn *an anxious desire* to acquire the arts of Europe, as is manifest by their repeated invitations to the English, to form settlements amongst them, as well as by their former offers to cede a part of their country to Great Britain; thereby shewing that their aversion to Spain does not extend to all the other nations of Europe.

That set many minds at rest, but even if the natives were friendly, what about the other inhabitants of Poyais – the wild beasts, the snakes, the insects? The women in particular were worried about this, the mothers among them fearful for the welfare of their children. The place they were going to was called Poyais, but they had heard the sailors referring to 'the Mosquito Coast', and when they looked at the guidebook, they noted that it was entitled

A Sketch of the Mosquito Shore, Including the Territory of Poyais. That was a name with unpleasantly suggestive connotations.

Not at all, said the better-informed members of the party. The Mosquito Coast was named, not after the insect – which was actually spelt *musqueto* or *moscheto* – but after the cluster of tiny islands and rock formations just offshore, called the *Mosquittos*. Anyway, that was an old name, given by the Spaniards many years ago. Nowadays, the vast area of which Poyais was a part was more properly referred to as Mosquitia, as was marked on the maps they had been given.

While the working men talked of gold mines and of building sawmills to exploit the virgin forests they would find, the new landowners among the group debated the merits of the various crops they might grow. Indian corn was a staple, of course, and it appeared that three harvests a year might be obtained from the rich soil. But the real money would no doubt come from the coffee and cocoa beans and the sugar cane, for which the land and the climate were ideally suited. There had evidently been highly successful plantations during earlier periods of British settlement, and such ventures were likely to do even better now, with the dramatic increase in European demand. Great fortunes were being made in the West Indies, but they were as nothing to what might be achieved in the even more favourable conditions of Poyais. The wholesale price of sugar was twenty-three shillings and fourpence for one hundredweight, which represented a profit to the producer of thirty-five per cent. According to a certain Mr Ellis, who had grown sugar cane in the region for many years, a planter with 150 acres might expect an annual revenue, after all expenses, of at least £1,200 – and the government of Poyais imposed no taxes on income.

Then there was cotton, one of the mainstays of the industrial revolution that was gathering pace back in Britain. The mechanization of the production process during the past thirty years had led to the establishment of vast mills in Derbyshire, Lancashire and western Scotland, and their owners scoured the world for supplies of the raw material they needed to meet the rapidly growing demand for cotton clothing. The cotton plant grew wild in Poyais, one of the 'most valuable gifts of a bountiful Creator, superintending and providing for the necessities of man', as Captain Strangeways put it. That being so, it represented the most promising source of revenue for settlers with limited means. A single acre, properly planted, would yield about 250 lbs of cotton which could be sold to merchants for £6, and one man could easily manage three acres by himself, as well as cultivating enough land to provide food for his family. It was estimated that an 'active, industrious emigrant' arriving in Poyais with £150 in his purse could establish a cotton plantation which, in the first year, would bring him a profit of £100, 'with the certain prospect of every year being able to extend it, and so in proportion to augment his capital and income'.

Even the poorer settlers could, quite literally, sow the seeds of a future commercial empire, because cotton merchants were only too happy to extend loans that would be paid off in cotton at market prices. With such a loan, an investment of only £30 would produce a net income of £40 a year. Reinvest £30 of that income, take out another loan, and the following year you would clear £80. It did not take a mathematician to work out that untold riches would eventually follow. Why, there were plantations in the United States, built on just such modest capital, that were now earning their owners hundreds of thousands of dollars each year.

Day after day, under the grey Atlantic skies, these sorts of discussions went on, the natural anxieties diminished, and the sense of excitement grew. The more people thought about it, the wiser seemed their decision to emigrate. Obviously, Poyais was genuinely a land of opportunity where only idleness could lead to failure. Everyone shared the optimism of Captain Strangeways, expressed in the closing paragraph of his useful little book:

Enough has been said to prove the great encouragement, and manifold advantages, which must be derived from commercial establishments in the Territory of Poyais: and now that the well known political circumstances are removed, which have hitherto retarded the advancement of this fine country, in civilization and in the scale of independent states, there seems no reason whatever to doubt, that, protected by the wise and vigorous administration, sound policy, and comprehensive view of His Highness the Cazique of Poyais, this beautiful country will rapidly advance in prosperity and civilization, and will become, in every point of view, and within a very short period, not the least considerable of those 'radiant realms beyond the Atlantic wave'.

The radiant realms, celebrated in prose by a leading West Indies merchant of the eighteenth century, came rather closer during the early days of March 1823, when the *Kennersley Castle* crossed the Tropic of Capricorn, and the weather began to grow warmer and brighter. Less than a week later, Captain Crouch was guiding the ship through the shallow waters of the Guadeloupe Passage, between the Leeward and the Windward Islands, and into the Caribbean Sea. The passengers crowded to the rails for a view of Antigua, on the starboard side, and Guadeloupe, to port. They had their first close encounter with the tropics on 8 March, when the vessel put into Plymouth harbour, in the little island of Montserrat, to take on fresh water and supplies. Some of the gentlemen went ashore, but most of the colonists remained aboard ship, marvelling at the blueness of the ocean, the sandy beaches, and the deep green foliage of the forests spreading as far as they could see over the volcanic lower slopes of the Souffrière mountains.

Late in the afternoon, they set sail again, their course due west, past Puerto Rico and Santo Domingo. Captain Crouch ordered a watch for any sign of the pirates who were known to infest these waters, confident that they could be driven off by his nine-pound cannon, but the only vessels they saw were harmless traders, and by 14 March the

Kennersley Castle was out of the danger zone, with Jamaica fading into the horizon behind her. Four days later, she had reached the Swan Islands, in what the settlers' maps called the Sea of Poyais, where she turned south for Cape Camarón and the promised land.

They reached it towards the end of the day on 20 March, dropping anchor half a mile or so out to sea from the narrow entrance of the Black River lagoon, the Captain being concerned about the reefs and sandbanks that might lurk unknown to his imperfect charts and endanger such a large ship. He would wait until morning before sending out a lighter whose crew would take soundings and find the channel that, at high tide, would bring them closer to the shore to await the pilot boat from the port. After eight weeks at sea, another day was hardly going to make much difference. For the passengers, their first sight of Poyais confirmed everything they had imagined. It really was the most beautiful place. Sun-dappled wavelets lapped gently along the rocks of the lagoon's protective landspits, the surface of which was thick with strange trees and shrubs. Inland, they could make out sandy beaches, and beyond them the dense forests they had heard about. There, dominating the landscape, was the Sugarloaf mountain, just as in the picture they had seen. Below it, too far away and too low to be in view, must be the little township where they would disembark. The settlers stayed on deck watching this vision until it disappeared in the short tropical twilight. As they sat down to the evening meal, which would almost certainly be their last aboard the ship that had been their lodging for what now seemed like an eternity, they could barely contain their impatience to disembark.

When would they be able to take to the boats and go ashore? Would there be some sort of official welcome for them? Perhaps it would be as well to dress up in whatever finery they could muster, just in case.

RETURN OF THE HERO

W hile the new settlers prepared themselves for their welcome to Poyais, His Highness the Cazique was in London, busily putting the finishing touches to the elaborate financial structure necessary to underpin the economic advancement of his country.

By the spring of 1823, Gregor MacGregor had become firmly established as a celebrity in Britain. He was eulogized in the press, sought after as a guest among the superior levels of society, and enthusiastically supported in the City of London, the world's most influential financial centre, because he was that rare species, a political leader with entrepreneurial imagination and a thorough understanding of the importance of the capital markets. For a man who had arrived, virtually unknown, in London two years earlier as the representative of a faraway country of which no one had ever heard, it was a remarkable achievement.

However, in coming to Britain to promote the development of his adopted country, MacGregor had enjoyed certain advantages that made him a natural candidate for rapid renown. To begin with, he could claim descent from Rob Roy MacGregor, the legendary clan leader who had been recently immortalized in a novel by one of the most popular writers of the age, Sir Walter Scott. Moreover, the name MacGregor acquired particular resonance at about the time of Sir Gregor's appearance in London, since it was announced that the once outlawed clan would receive the privilege of escorting the Honours of Scotland* to greet the new King, George IV, when he arrived in Edinburgh for the first royal visit since the union of Scotland with England in 1707. Remarking on this final rehabilitation of the clan, the newspapers drew attention to the fact that it had been one Gregor MacGregor, a nephew of the great Rob Roy, who had been instrumental in persuading the authorities to lift the 170-year-old proscription in 1774. And who was he? None other than Gregor 'The Beautiful', grandfather of Sir Gregor MacGregor of Poyais.

Nor was this the only connection that worked in the Cazique's favour. It became known that he had been an officer in the British army, serving under Sir Arthur Wellesley – later the Duke of Wellington – in the Peninsular War. His regiment was the 57th Foot, the

---

* The Honours consisted at the time of a crown, sceptre and sword dating from the fifteenth and sixteenth centuries. The Stone of Scone was added in 1996. The Honours are now on public display at Edinburgh Castle.

famous 'Die-Hards' who had fought heroically at the battle of Albuera in 1811, when two-thirds of the First Battalion were killed. Even more notable, though, was MacGregor's subsequent military career on the staff of the late and much lamented General Francisco de Miranda in South America.

General Miranda had been one of the most admired soldiers and champions of liberty in the western world. Born in Venezuela, he had begun his military career in Spain, gone on to fight for the rebels in the American War of Independence, for the Russians led by Catherine the Great, for the revolutionary army of France in the 1790s, and finally for the liberation movement associated with the famous name of Simón Bolívar, who in 1819 created the first independent republic in Spanish-America. With such a record, Miranda's political connections were both extensive and elevated, and he was particularly well remembered in London, where he had lived in magnificent style during his periods of respite from making war.

Among Miranda's English friends and political collaborators were the prime ministers Henry Addington, William Pitt the Younger and Lord Liverpool; the foreign secretaries George Canning and Viscount Castlereagh; and, of course, his fellow-soldier Sir Arthur Wellesley. The general had also been something of a ladies' man – reputedly one of the lovers of Catherine the Great – and had formed intimate relationships with leading London hostesses such as Lady Holland, wife of a prominent Whig politician, and Lady Hester Stanhope, niece of Pitt the

Younger. All of which meant that Sir Gregor MacGregor, who had served as a senior officer under Miranda and gone on to become a brigadier general, had little difficulty in finding his way to the right people when he arrived in London during the late summer of 1821 to promote his great Poyais project.

His association with Miranda produced the first few important introductions in the most influential circles, and it was not long before the people who met MacGregor – and the society reporters on the newspapers – began to remember that they had once read about the exploits of the Scotsman who had gone to fight in Venezuela, which at the time had been part of the Spanish colonial province of New Granada. The press had paid great attention to the liberation struggle, as had the British government, which naturally viewed with interest the prospect of the dissolution of the Spanish empire. The military campaigns of Bolívar and Miranda against the Spanish had been copiously reported, and the mysterious General MacGregor had appeared in some of those dispatches. He had distinguished himself during notable battles at places with appealingly romantic names, such Onoto and Chaguarames, Quebrada-Honda and Alcran. His tactical retreat from Ocumare – during which he led an army through hundreds of miles of jungle infested by overwhelming numbers of Spanish forces – had become a classic tale of derring-do. Then there had been the crushing defeat of the Spaniards at Juncal, in which MacGregor's military skill had earned him the Order of the Liberators, presented by Bolívar himself. With such a record, it seemed only fitting that the General should have found himself elevated to the South American aristocracy, and should be presented to his new acquaintances with the exotic title of His Highness the Cazique of Poyais. A man who had contributed so much to the cause of freedom in the Spanish colonies must be a natural choice as a leader in the emerging new world.

The Cazique certainly impressed all who encountered him as one to whom authority came naturally. Standing about five feet nine inches tall, he had a broad, open face, with a long nose, full lips above a strong chin, and limpid blue eyes. His erect, military bearing carried elegant clothes well on his sturdy but trim frame. When he talked, it was with the energy, enthusiasm and directness of a man who knew his own mind, and his conversation evinced a broad education informed with the wisdom of experience and knowledge of the world. MacGregor was suitably modest about his military adventures, but referred with pride to the honour of knighthood bestowed on him by the King of Spain for his services to the country during the Peninsular War, and of the kindness of the present King of England, when he had been Prince Regent, in permitting him to apply the foreign title and style himself Sir Gregor. That was all in the past, however, and the Cazique was at pains to point out that Poyais was now his country, granted to him by the native king of the Mosquito Coast, along with his title and the Knighthood of the Order of the Green Cross of Poyais. He sometimes wore the insignia of the green cross on a ribbon at his throat.

Such a handsome, charming and obviously brilliant man proved to be a great adornment for the dinner tables and ballrooms of sophisticated London, the more so when his wife – referred to simply as the Princess of Poyais, there being apparently no feminine form of *cazique* – arrived to join him from Ireland, where she had recently given birth to their second child, at the home of her husband's sister, who was married to a doctor. The Princess Josefa was a dark Spanish-American beauty, a cousin of the great Bolívar himself, who displayed all the reserve and hauteur of her class, and her presence could only enhance MacGregor's appeal. Soon, the couple were almost overwhelmed with invitations, and their names were on the lips of everyone who was anyone. There was even an official reception for them, hosted at the Guildhall, the ancient seat of City government, by the Lord Mayor of London, Christopher Magnay.

By the winter of 1821, the MacGregors were also repaying this hospitality, and in grand style, having had the good fortune to be introduced to someone who was prepared to provide them with a temporary home in keeping with their status.

Quite how this came about is something of a mystery, but somehow MacGregor made the acquaintance of Major William John Richardson, a man of considerable wealth and some influence behind the scenes in politics (he would go on to become one of the founder members of the Reform Club in 1832). Richardson lived at Oak Hall, a small country estate at Wanstead in Essex, about eight miles north-east of the City of London, and it was there that the Cazique and the Princess Josefa were invited to establish their official residence during their stay in England.

It is unlikely that Major Richardson would have known General Miranda, though he would certainly have heard of him, and Richardson had no obvious connection with South America. To be sure, the whole of Britain at the time was fascinated by Latin American affairs, but the Major's generous offer to MacGregor was hardly likely to have been prompted by any such general interest. There must have been a more direct and personal reason for Richardson's decision to throw open his home to a complete stranger, however celebrated.

MacGregor did not rely solely on his relationship with Miranda and his reputation to make himself known in London. A large number of former officers in the British army had been persuaded to join the fight to liberate South America from Spain, and many had served with, or met, or at least heard of Gregor MacGregor. One of them was Gustavus Butler Hippisley, the son of an early explorer of South America, and himself a member of the liberation armies for five years. Hippisley would later write an epic poem, part of which celebrated MacGregor's military exploits in Venezuela, and it seems inconceivable that he would not have contacted his now ennobled former comrade-in-arms when the Cazique arrived in London. Evidence that he did so comes from the fact that Hippisley was subsequently to play his own part in the affairs of Poyais, but in 1821 his contribution to MacGregor's cause was probably that it was he who introduced the Cazique to Major Richardson.

That Hippisley and Richardson moved in the same circles is confirmed by the fact that, in 1834, the Major married Hippisley's younger sister, Jane, who had developed into something of a society beauty. Whether the two men actually knew each other in 1821 cannot be definitely established, but the coincidences of the links between them and MacGregor do appear persuasive enough to suggest that Gustavus Butler Hippisley might well have been partly responsible for Major Richardson's invitation to the Cazique.

Oak Hall, of which no trace now remains, was a large and attractive house, if not a particularly distinguished one. Its appeal lay principally in its extensive grounds, especially the magnificent sunken Italian garden that was Richardson's pride and joy. The MacGregors were suitably impressed as their carriage took them through the massive gates and up the long drive to the house. They were delighted, too, by the gracious welcome of their host, the urbane and charming Major, who in turn was captivated by the glamorous couple and their patina of exotic foreign royalty.

Richardson, with his interest in political affairs, was keen to know everything about Poyais, and the reason for the Cazique's visit to Britain. He listened intently as MacGregor explained that he had been created cazique in April 1820 by the Anglophile King George Frederick of the Mosquito Shore and Nation, who had grown up in Jamaica. Along with the title went the 12,500 square miles of land known as the Territory of Poyais, which the Cazique was required to govern in the interests of its native inhabitants and the King.

The new ruler had inherited a democratic system of government, the rudiments of a civil service, and the makings of an army. These he had strengthened through the recruitment of several of his former comrades from the campaigns in South America, but a great deal more needed to be done, and that meant encouraging greater numbers of people to take an interest in the country, both personally and in terms of investment. MacGregor had felt bound to travel to London to attend the coronation of King George IV (which had taken place that July), given that the Poyaisian natives had long been sentimentally attached to the British monarchy, and he intended to use the opportunity afforded by his stay to promote the development of his Territory in whatever way he could.

Perhaps, MacGregor suggested, the Major might care to see a copy of the declaration he had issued before leaving Poyais. It encapsulated the purpose of his visit to Britain.

The printed document was headed 'PROCLAMATION To the Inhabitants of the Territory of Poyais', dated 13 April 1821, issued by Gregor, Cazique of Poyais at his Head Quarters at the Camp of Rio Seco, and endorsed as 'A true copy of the original' by Thomas Strangeways, 'Aid-de-camp and Captain 1st Native Poyer Regiment'. It read:

POYERS!

On the 29th April 1820, the King of the Mosquito Shore and Nation, by a deed, executed at Cape Gracias á Dios, granted to me and my heirs for ever, the Territory of Poyais.

The moment that the situation in Colombia would permit me, I have hastened to assure you of my firm and unalterable determination to come and spend the remainder of my days, I trust, in peace and tranquillity, amongst you.

POYERS! It shall be my constant duty to render you happy, and to exert myself in improving your situation, by every means in my power.

The Territory of Poyais shall be an asylum only for the industrious and honest, none others shall be admitted amongst us; and THOSE, I trust, you will receive with open arms, as brothers and fellow-citizens.

With a view to avoiding a misunderstanding with our Spanish neighbours, which, under *all circumstances*, would be disadvantageous to both parties, I have this day published a MANIFESTO, addressed to the AUTHORITIES and INHABITANTS of the adjoining SPANISH AMERICAN PROVINCES of HONDURAS and NICARAGUA, giving them the most positive assurances, 'that I have no other views *here*, than those which my duty as Chief of this Territory inspires.'

This last paragraph, MacGregor pointed out, was important for the development of Poyais. Anyone seeking to invest or settle in the Territory must be assured that it had no intention of challenging the authority of Spain in its neighbouring provinces, and there was no desire to interfere with the Spanish dominance of trade in the region. Poyais was a naturally rich country which, as a result of both its successful resistance against Spanish incursion and the unwillingness of British governments to assume colonial responsibility for it, had been held back both economically and socially. Its ambitions now were entirely concerned with making progress in and for itself, primarily through closer trading links with the West Indies and, by extension, the United Kingdom.

The document continued:

Animated with the hope of establishing our neutrality upon a safe and solid basis, as well as to enable me to take the most active measures for procuring you religious and moral instructors, the implements of husbandry, and persons to guide and assist you in the cultivation of the valuable productions for which our soil and climate are so well adapted, I have determined upon visiting Europe; and in consequence, have this day appointed the Governor of San Andres, H.E. BRIGADIER GEN-ERAL GEORGE WOODBINE, M.G.C. to act and take upon him the office of my VICE-CAZIQUE during my absence; charging him to pay the most paternal attention to your interests, and with positive orders to observe the most strict neutrality with respect to the adjoining provinces of HONDURAS and NICARAGUA, as the most certain and sure means of encouraging emigrants to come and settle in our country, and of avoiding the expense of maintaining a large military force, at a moment when all our resources are required for carrying into effect the establishments already projected, and in progress; and I confidently trust, that you will shew the said Vice-Cazique that respect and detachment which the citizens of all countries are bound to pay and feel towards those who lawfully command, particularly when they exercise their authority with justice and impartiality.

General Woodbine was a very sound fellow, MacGregor said. They had been in some tight spots together during the years of fighting, and he had always relied on Woodbine's courage and good sense. He had actually led the charge that had won them the famous victory over the Spanish at Porto Bello, in Panama. Under Woodbine, Poyais would be in very good hands during the absence of its Cazique. The letters M.G.C., incidentally, signified that the general was a Member of the Order of the Green Cross, which was named after the symbol on the flag of Poyais.

The proclamation concluded:

POYERS! I now bid you farewell for a while, in the full confidence that the measures I have adopted for your security, defence, government, and future prosperity, will be fully realized; and I trust, that through the kindness of Almighty Providence, I shall be again enabled to return amongst you, and that then it will be my pleasing duty to hail you as affectionate friends, and yours to receive me as your faithful Cazique and Father.

Major Richardson was struck by the simple sincerity of MacGregor's declaration, and by his guest's evidently deep sense of responsibility towards the territory he had been chosen to lead. The two men talked at length about the Cazique's plans for Poyais, and about the rewards that would accrue to people with the vision and spirit to help make them come to fruition. MacGregor, for his part, warmed to the openness and transparent honesty of his host, and hinted that Richardson might himself be in a position to be an important advocate on behalf of Poyais. The Major was gratified that a man such as the Cazique should so readily indicate his trust in him, and, at some stage, offered MacGregor the use of Oak Hall as his base of operations during his stay in Britain, if that would be of convenience to him. MacGregor pronounced himself overwhelmed by Richardson's extraordinary generosity, and willing, in all humility, to take advantage of it. There was a great deal to be done, there were many arrangements to be made, many people to interview, and Oak Hall would provide an ideal setting for his affairs of state. Equally, he would be honoured to have the Major at his side to offer advice and, perhaps, more practical assistance in the great project.

So the Cazique and the Princess – along with their seven-year-old son, Gregorio, and their baby daughter, Josefa Anna Gregoria – took up residence at Wanstead, and Major Richardson threw himself enthusiastically into the complex business of transforming Poyais into a modern state. MacGregor showed him the hand-written land grant he had been given by the Mosquito King, which designated the extent of the Poyais Territory as:

NORTH. – All the Sea Coast comprehended between the 84° 25′ to the 85° 42′ degree of Longitude West from the Meridian of London.

SOUTH. – By a straight line drawn due West from Longitude 84° 42′ to Longitude 85° 42′ West, along the 13th Degree of North Latitude.

EAST. – From the Longitude of 84° 25′ West, by a line drawn due North and South, until it touches the western bank of the Plaintain River in Latitude 15° 37′ North, and then following the western bank of that River to Latitude 15° North, and Longitude 84° 42′ West, and from thence in a straight line, drawn due South, until it touches the 13° of North Latitude.

WEST. – From the mouth of Zacarylyon River, in Longitude 85° 8′ West, and following the eastern bank of the said River, South, to Latitude 15° 28′ North, and then by a line drawn due West until it touches the Rio Grande, or Romaine River, in Latitude 15° 28′ North, and Longitude 85° 42′ West, and then by a straight line, drawn due South, until it intersects the 13° degree of North Latitude, and in Longitude 85° 42′ West from the Meridian of London.

MacGregor produced a copy of an official chart and on it sketched out the rectangular outline of Poyais, stretching south from Cape Camarón, along the basin of the Black River and into the mountains of the interior. It was Chart No. 18 of the Bay of Honduras, produced by Thomas Jefferys, Geographer to His Majesty (George III), in 1775 and published in London in 1782 as part of the collection of maps called *A Compleat Pilot for the West Indies, &c.* The land inside the boundaries, said MacGregor, comprised about eight million acres. It was his intention to divide that land into lots of 540 acres each, and to offer those lots for sale to as many people as wished to settle in Poyais and work the land for the benefit of themselves and the country.

However, in order to reassure potential settlers that they would be well looked after, it would be necessary for him to appoint administrators who would supervise the emigration, accompany the colonists on their voyage, and carry out the essential liaison work with the authorities in Poyais. For this to be achieved, MacGregor felt it important that the Poyaisian government should have some sort of recognized presence in London. He himself was unable, because of his position as Cazique, to act as an ambassador, and in any case, since Poyais was really a principality within the sovereign territory of the Mosquito Shore, it was debatable whether a fully fledged embassy would be considered appropriate. Instead, MacGregor had it in mind to establish a Poyaisian Legation, in order to maintain proper contacts with the British government and to explain the ways of the country to the civil servants he proposed to recruit. The legation would also serve as the authority through which the land would be sold.

Major Richardson, a man who liked things to be arranged in the correct way, thought this an excellent idea. In that case, MacGregor said, might the Major consider taking up the post of chargé d'affaires at the legation? Quite apart from the kindness Richardson had shown in making his home available, the Cazique could not think of a better man for the job, given the fairly extensive knowledge of Poyais he was acquiring, and his considerable social and political standing in London. Naturally, the thing would be accomplished through the usual channels, with proper accreditation to the Court of St James, and as Poyais developed, the position would become increasingly important. It seemed the perfect way to repay Richardson's generosity, allowing him to share fully in the bounty that would come from the managed exploitation of the country's limitless natural resources.

The Major was deeply touched by this display of confidence in him, and grateful for the opportunity to benefit personally from what he could see was both a worthwhile and highly profitable venture. He readily agreed to MacGregor's request, and a ceremony took place at Oak Hall in which he was formally inducted by the Cazique into the Most Illustrious Order of the Green Cross, with the rank of commander, and presented with a major's commission in the Poyais Royal Regiment of Horse Guards. Following this acknowledgement of Richardson's Poyaisian status, a letter of credence was drawn up, as protocol demanded: 'We, Gregor the First, Sovereign Prince of the State of Poyais, to His Most Gracious Majesty George the Fourth . . .' and so on, and presented to the King. In due course, William John Richardson was gazetted as chargé d'affaires at the Legation of the Territory of Poyais in the United Kingdom of Great Britain.

An office for the legation was opened at Dowgate Hill in the heart of the City, midway between the Mansion

House – official residence of the Lord Mayor – and the Monument, commemorating the Great Fire of London. Advertisements in the press quickly produced a staff for the office, and MacGregor and Richardson marked the creation of this Poyaisian outpost with a series of state banquets at Oak Hall, to which were invited government ministers, foreign ambassadors, leading figures from Court, and senior military officers. The seriousness of the Cazique's purpose became apparent to all, as he described the carefully constructed system of government in his country, with its twelve provinces and three legislative assemblies, which ensured that all sections of society were represented. He went on to summarize the history of his country's relations with Britain.

St Joseph, now the capital of Poyais, he explained, had been founded by British settlers during the 1730s, and had grown to flourish as a trading centre, thanks to its position on the Black River lagoon. British communities had also been established at Cape Gracias á Dios, to the west, and Bluefields, to the south, but the rest of the country had remained largely untouched by Europeans, in spite of repeated requests by the native rulers of the Mosquito Coast, who had long been supported by Britain. As a result, while Poyais boasted an elegant capital city on the European model, the interior had been unable to develop at the same pace, and it was this situation that must be addressed. Peaceable and industrious though the natives were, they needed European knowledge, skills and resources in order to achieve the progress they earnestly desired. That was a significant part of the reason for the Mosquito King's appointment of a European to head the government in Poyais, and for his grant of land to the Cazique, on the understanding that it would be made available to settlers.

Of course, it was by no means as potential colonists that the Cazique was addressing his distinguished guests. He merely wished to acquaint them with the situation of his country, in the hope that he could rely on their support in his endeavours to encourage settlement there. It was important to emphasize that Poyais was unlike some other virgin lands, in that settlers there would not have to endure the uncertainties and hardships that so often faced the adventurous in less civilized parts of the world. As he had indicated, his country had a well-established and stable government, and a body of law that was respected by the native population. In addition, the climate of Poyais was not subject to the extremes found in other tropical regions, and the land was more fertile than that of the West Indies, where fortunes had already been made by means of agriculture. Nor should it be forgotten that Spain had benefited immensely from the South American deposits of gold and silver, of which Poyais also had its share. He was confident that his listeners would appreciate the tremendous opportunities offered by his project, and would do everything in their power to help ensure its success.

Away from these splendid banquets, MacGregor confided to Major Richardson that his enthusiasm for the resettlement of Poyais was motivated, at least in part, by a desire to compensate in some way for the failure of an earlier attempt at South American colonization in which a member of his family had been involved. He, like many other Scots, had grown up hearing terrible stories of the Darién Scheme, a disastrous venture of the 1690s that was meant to establish a settlement on the eastern side of the isthmus of Panama. One of his ancestors had been among the 2,800 Scots who had set out from the port of Leith for the colony of New Caledonia, and had been lucky to escape with his life as disease, mismanagement, lack of supplies and attacks by Spanish troops had wiped out two-thirds of the settlers. Nearly a century and a half later, the Darién affair still weighed heavily on the conscience of Scotland, which had invested and lost an estimated half of the entire capital available in the country at the time.

It was to make up for the failure of Darién, MacGregor said, that he proposed to draw perhaps the majority of his Poyais settlers from Scotland. While Major Richardson's legation at Dowgate Hill would be the clearing house for the sale of land, agents would be appointed and sales offices opened in Edinburgh and Glasgow, and probably also in Stirling, to attract the hardy folk of the Highlands. With so much in its favour, the inevitable success of Poyais would obliterate the stain of Darién, many Scots would deservedly benefit, and Gregor MacGregor would have played his part in restoring the honour of Scotland.

During the early months of 1822, Oak Hall became, in the words of a reporter from *The Times*, 'all a-buzz with comings and goings – servants in livery, officers in uniform ...', as MacGregor and Richardson came to grips with the complexities of the Poyais scheme. One of the first tasks was to have a facsimile made of the chart of the Bay of Honduras, with the boundaries of Poyais added to it, and the 540-acre parcels of land that were being offered for sale. Then came the drawing up of land certificates, which would, of course, be legal documents. They were based on the original grant MacGregor had received from the Mosquito King, and entitled the bearer to take possession of a specified number of acres within the geographical limits of the territory, which were outlined in the preamble to the certificates.

The Cazique and his chargé d'affaires spent much time discussing the price at which the land should be sold, finally settling on an introductory offer of two shillings and threepence an acre, which meant that 100 acres could be bought for a little more than £11. That would bring the purchase of land in Poyais within the reach of a large number of people, since the wages of skilled workers in 1822 averaged about £1 10s a week in London, and probably something like £1 a week in the industrial cities of the provinces. Even the less well-paid, earning perhaps half the average wage, could participate, given that a parcel of ten acres, on which they could easily support families, would cost them not much over £1. If Poyais was to prosper in the way MacGregor envisaged, he could not afford to put people off by charging too high a price for his land. And, in order to make absolutely sure that enough people would be available to fulfil his grand design, he decided also to offer government contracts to unskilled workers and domestic servants who, in addition to guaranteed wages, would be given land on which to build houses for themselves.

With these fundamental arrangements in place, it remained for the public to be made aware of the unique opportunities Poyais had to offer. The first step was to invite to Oak Hall newspaper reporters, such as the man from *The Times*, whose probing questions were answered in great detail: 'His Highness was excessively civil; he had just come in from riding in the park ... He called me into his private closet, where he sent for wine and called for Major Richardson to join him. They discoursed seriously for above an hour, and I marvelled to learn of the enlightened conditions in His Highness's dominions.' The resulting informative articles were followed by advertisements that set out the manifold benefits of emigration to Poyais and advised interested parties to visit the legation at Dowgate Hill, where they would be shown the maps and documents relating to the sale of land and where, for a deposit of just twenty-five per cent of the purchase price, they could secure a stake in the new El Dorado.

Meanwhile, doubts were starting to arise in the mind of the Cazique, as he confessed to Major Richardson. He had begun to realize that putting his plan into action was going to prove more expensive than he had expected, and he was becoming concerned about the impact of all this expenditure on the limited resources of a small country such as Poyais. With Dowgate Hill now fully staffed, and the Scottish offices due to open shortly, the financial demands seemed to be growing every day. Then, if the response from the public was anything like it ought to be, there would be the costs of chartering ships to take them across the Atlantic, purchasing supplies to sustain the emigrants while they established themselves, and paying the new government officials who would oversee the whole enterprise. It would be a tragedy if the whole scheme were to fail because of a lack of funds.

Richardson suggested that they talk over the matter with some of his friends in political and financial circles. London was the greatest capital market in the world, and it was becoming common even for governments to raise finance in the City. Meetings were arranged, and a consensus soon emerged. Poyais should underwrite its bold project by means of long-term debt in the form of bonds offering investors repayment at some future date, with a good rate of annual interest guaranteed by the revenues of the government. The bankers were sure there would be no difficulty. What sort of figure did the Cazique have it in mind to raise? In its present mood, the market would snap up as many Poyais bonds as he cared to issue.

MONEY TALKS

There was one very good reason why Sir Gregor MacGregor's advisers confidently predicted that he would be able to raise a substantial loan for his Poyais government on the London capital market: the simple fact that Poyais was in South America.

Britain had looked with envious eyes on Spanish domination of the continent ever since the loss of her own North American colonies, as a result of the revolution of 1776. Spain had jealously guarded the vast stores of gold, silver and natural resources from the South American continent, and had maintained a virtual monopoly on trade with the continent by means of both treaty and force. The British had gained a toehold in the middle of the seventeenth century by establishing a settlement in Belize, a territory measuring just 174 miles by 68 on the east coast of what became known as Central America, between Mexico and Guatemala, but the Spaniards had aggressively defended their sovereignty, and it would not be until 1862 that Britain officially claimed its colony, as British Honduras.

Elsewhere, an unofficial British force had used the excuse of war with Spain between 1806 and 1807 to invade and take possession of Buenos Aires, then the capital of the Viceroyalty of Rio de la Plata. The government in London, though completely unaware of the expedition, had gratefully accepted this *fait accompli*, only to find itself seriously embarrassed a year later, when the troops were forced into a humiliating withdrawal in the face of a popular uprising against the idea of swearing allegiance to yet another monarch.

Other than that, fortune-seeking British merchants had to content themselves with whatever South American pickings they could accumulate from naval blockades of Spanish ports – which had the effect of cutting off supplies to the American provinces – and from the use of neutral third-party ships to export and import goods from the continent. So when, as a consequence of the Napoleonic wars, Spain's grip on South America began to loosen under the pressure of revolution and civil strife, Britain was quick to try to exploit the situation to her commercial advantage, not least to prevent a newly confident United States from seizing the opportunity in what she saw, under President James Monroe, as her natural sphere of influence. Not only did British merchant vessels supply and maintain communications among the various armies of independence, but a disgraced British admiral, Lord Cochrane*, commanded the navies of Chile and Peru, and thousands of former British soldiers emulated Gregor MacGregor and devoted their skills to the fight for freedom.

As a result of all this, South America became a subject of intense interest in Britain. There was much airy talk of the cause of liberty and republicanism, and leaders of the independence movement, such as Miranda, Bolívar and the Colombian Francisco Antonio Zea, were fêted as heroes in London. In truth, however, the fashionable obsession with all things Latin American was motivated less by political considerations than by the prospect of making large amounts of money, as the leading magazine the *Quarterly Review* made clear when it noted that whatever happened – victory for the republicans or the re-imposition of Spanish control – 'South America presents a market for the skill and expertise of our merchants, which we hope will not long be withholden from them.' Even those who actively supported the liberation movements often did so for reasons that were less than altruistic, looking forward to a day when new republics would open their borders to British trade, industry, technology, financial services, arts and even people.

* Thomas Cochrane (1775–1860), later Earl of Dundonald, had been discharged from the Royal Navy in 1814 as a result of false allegations regarding his involvement in a Stock Exchange fraud. He was reinstated in 1832, after brilliant service as an admiral in the navies of Chile, Brazil and Greece, and became a British admiral in 1851.

Throughout the land, not merely in London, the newspapers and magazines were full of news, opinion and optimistic forecasts about the future of South America. On occasion, as much as one whole page out of the customary four in the daily papers might be devoted to details of battles – usually many weeks after they had taken place – and to political events, profiles of the republican leaders and military men, conditions in the various regions, and so on. This blanket coverage served to make celebrities out of General Sir Gregor MacGregor, along with others such as Admiral Lord Cochrane, who went on to repeat his victories in Chile and Peru against the Portuguese in Brazil. It also stimulated an almost feverish demand for information on every aspect of South America: its topography, its flora and fauna, its peoples, and the wonders found within this most mysterious and exciting of places. Colonel Gustavus Hippisley, future father-in-law of the man who would become Poyaisian chargé d'affaires in London, had a notable success in 1819 with his ponderously entitled book *A Narrative of the Expedition to the Rivers Orinoco and Apure, in South America, which Sailed from England in November, 1817.* The German natural scientist Baron Alexander von Humboldt contributed greatly to the circulation of the *Quarterly Review* after 1815, when the magazine began to publish a long series of his observations made during five years of exploration in some of the most inaccessible regions of South America.

In the middle of all this, Poyais could hardly fail to attract intense interest from the media, the public and the financial markets. Being in the part of the world that most exercised the British imagination was reason enough, but its appeal was enhanced by the fact that there was no Spanish colonial legacy attached to it, which meant that, unlike the newly independent republics of the region, Poyais had a stable government that had been allowed to evolve in its own way. Better still, such European influence as there had been in the country had been British, culminating in the appointment of a British subject as the de facto head of state, which guaranteed that any British investment would be both welcomed and protected.

The attraction increased as more became known and the extent of the opportunities offered by Poyais began to emerge. Within this accessible and relatively small space – in addition to all the crops that might be grown there – were contained many of the valuable natural resources trumpeted by the explorers of South America and the enthusiastic press: gold, an astonishing variety of timber, medicinal plants, spices, and the raw materials of industrial processes such as zinc ore, indigo, cochineal, rubber, turpentine, pitch and so on. Equally, since there had been no colonial power supplying Poyais, as a dependency, with manufactured goods, the Poyers represented a completely new and unexploited market for British industry.

For the farmer, the merchant, the industrialist, the banker and even the labourer, Poyais was a genuine land of opportunity. As it was, too, in the opinion of the financiers who were invited to meet the Cazique at Oak Hall, for the investor seeking a secure and rewarding home for his money. It was not just what Poyais itself offered, but what the future held for the whole region. Everyone knew of the long-standing plans to build a canal through the narrow, central part of South America that would join the Atlantic and the Pacific oceans, 'an easy process of human labour and enterprise', *The Times* observed, that would 'change as it were the physical boundaries of the world'. It was simply a question of finding the correct route, and in 1821 that appeared to be via Lake Nicaragua, which lay just below the southern boundary of Poyais. The project, said *The Times*, was 'impossible to contemplate without a mixture of awe and exultation', and, increasingly, impossible to contemplate without the urge to put one's money where one's awe and exultation were.

There was certainly plenty of money available for investment at that particular moment in economic history. By the 1820s, the City of London had, largely as a result of the Napoleonic wars, finally supplanted Amsterdam as the most important financial market in the world. To be sure, Britain had incurred enormous costs in defeating Napoleon, but it had also been the recipient of huge outflows of capital from the European mainland, as a safe haven in uncertain times. One of the reasons for this flood of inward investment was that London had the financial institutions to accommodate it. The Bank of England, founded in 1694 to manage the national debt, now controlled the market in British government securities, as well as taking deposits, making loans and issuing banknotes which were almost universally accepted as guaranteeing the bearer payment in the gold and silver coins that were still the only currency for cash transactions. By virtue of its reputation and its connection to government, the Bank also underpinned something like one thousand commercial retail banks throughout Britain, all of which sought to make profits by investing the money deposited with them.

In addition, there was a further layer of banking for which London had become the main centre, again thanks mainly to the upheavals on the Continent. This was merchant banking, so-called because its practitioners most often traded directly in precious metals and commodities as well as in currencies and financial instruments such as bills of exchange, bonds and securities. For example, the renowned Baring brothers, John and Francis, who were among the first in the field, came from a background in the wool trade, using the profits from that to establish their investment banking business in 1762. It was Barings, along with another merchant bank, Hope and Company – which had transferred its business from Amsterdam after the French invasion of Holland in 1795 – who managed the loan that allowed the American government to purchase Louisiana from Napoleon for $15 million in 1803. One of Barings' rivals, the former cotton dealers Rothschilds, raised loans of more than £100 million to help finance the armies of Britain and her allies during the Napoleonic Wars. London banks like these – among them other famous names such as Kleinwort, Hambro, Warburg, Schröder and Morgan – soon became the chief sources of capital, both their own and other people's, for industry and trade throughout the world, as well as for governments seeking to raise money.

To channel all this available capital in directions where it would be most useful, and most profitable, the City of London had developed sophisticated systems for matching people who had money to invest with those who needed it for their businesses. These arrangements had begun during the reign of Queen Elizabeth I, with the founding of the Royal Exchange, where traders dealt mainly in commodities, but also in government securities, bills of exchange, credit notes and, later, shares in joint stock companies. There was little regulation of such deals and, as industries and markets expanded, during the eighteenth century, the increasing appetite for investing caused traders to spread their operations to the coffee houses of Exchange Alley, notably Jonathan's and Garraway's. In this free-for-all of continuous buying and selling, fraudsters flourished, and the notorious affair of the South Sea Bubble in 1720, when the collapse of a spectacular share-dealing confidence trick ruined many businesses and individuals and provoked a financial crisis that brought down the government, made it obvious that some sort of discipline must be imposed on the securities market.

Various laws were enacted in an attempt to limit speculation and prevent fraud, but it was soon recognized that the best way to regulate the market was for the stockbrokers themselves to adopt a code of conduct that would give investors confidence in the deals they made.

An attempt was made to turn Jonathan's coffee house into some sort of official exchange, when a group of 150 traders agreed to certain rules, and to pay £8 each a year for exclusive use of the place as a dealing room, with everyone outside the circle barred from operating there. The scheme was abandoned after a legal challenge, and even the construction of a building called the Stock Exchange, which opened in 1773, failed to attract enough brokers willing to underwrite an organized market.

Things changed at the turn of the century, when the Stock Exchange reformed itself into the Stock Subscription Room, requiring paid membership and adherence to a strict code of conduct in return for institutional administration and the power to exclude undesirable brokers. Within a year, the Subscription Room could count almost 500 members and had re-established itself as the Stock Exchange in a larger building, and by the end of its first decade it was confining membership to specialist brokers, refusing those who were not prepared to give up their other businesses.

The emergence of this regulated, specialized market in securities, combined with the well-established arrangements for merchant and retail banking, made London a magnet for investors both domestic and foreign. Its success served not only to increase the demand for things in which to invest, but also to encourage the buying and selling, as products themselves, of securities, bonds, loan stocks and other forms of contract. Previously, this internal market in paper had been mostly the preserve of stock jobbers, who traded on their own behalf but, as economic growth spread wealth and individuals found themselves with cash to spare, dealing for its own sake became more popular with the public. Most people were content to stay with safe British government securities – of which there were about a quarter of a million holders in 1815 – but, in the burst of optimism following the defeat of Napoleon and the prospect of lasting peace that emerged from the Congress of Vienna, the confidence of investors soared, and with it their willingness to take risks.

By the early 1820s, the public desire to deal in stocks and shares had developed into something of a mania, as people saw the opportunity to make quick and painless profits by betting on the fluctuations in share prices, or being the first to snap up stock in new companies which could be sold later at a much higher price. It was a craving the new class of professional brokers was only too eager to meet, since its livelihood depended on continuously moving and expanding the market.

So widespread and fevered did the trading become that, in 1821, a critical exposé of what we would now call the financial services industry complained that the Stock Exchange, 'a body growing out of small beginnings in speculation', had now reached 'a height that has given it the command of this nation – its destinies – its ministers of government – its resources – its morals – its private property'. The newspapers, however, always with an eye on changes in the public mood, and keen to exploit them so as to build their circulations, saw value in encouraging the new passion for investment. They began to provide their readers with business news, financial advice, reports and comment from the City, and even share tips. And it was the press, perhaps more than anything else, that stimulated sudden and all-consuming fashions in investment.

At one stage, shares in companies planning or building canals were what everyone wanted to buy, and their prices soared. However, just as Sir Gregor MacGregor was describing the delights of Poyais and the potential for turning them into ready money, it happened that the trend in investment was moving overseas, and especially towards loan issues and bonds from foreign governments.

One reason for this was the very economic growth that had provoked the investment boom. As the British government's revenues increased and its expenditure fell back to the normal levels of peacetime, the Treasury was able dramatically to reduce the national debt, which had trebled to more than £700 million during the course of the European conflict. The diminishing requirement for borrowing meant that the government no longer needed to pay the high rates of interest that had ensured a steady flow of money into its coffers, and in the spring of 1822 it announced that its most popular stocks, known as consols, which paid an annual five per cent interest, were to be transformed into a new issue paying only four per cent. This change affected hundreds of thousands of investors, nearly all of whom declined to convert their holdings and instead withdrew their funds and accumulated interest. In consequence, a little less than £3 million unexpectedly became available in the capital market. But where could it go to achieve the sort of returns to which its owners were accustomed?

Commercial stocks were still too risky for such investors and, in any case, shares in businesses were not very plentiful, consisting mainly of the likes of the venerable East India Company, some insurance firms, water companies and a few property and civil engineering undertakings. There were opportunities in America, and share prices in New York were listed alongside shipping movements in the journal *Lloyd's List*, but although the British did invest heavily across the Atlantic, many preferred to look for the sort of steady returns they had enjoyed with government securities, and those were to be found elsewhere abroad.

It was the merchant bank Barings that first demonstrated the potential for investment in the finances of foreign governments, with a series of bond issues, beginning in 1817, to raise FFr315 million, or about £28 million, for France, which was obliged to pay reparations for the damage caused by the military ambitions of Napoleon. The bonds, denominated in francs, returned five per cent interest a year and were offered at a discount rate of fifty-eight, which meant that, on maturity, FFr100 would be repaid for each FFr58 invested, with five per cent interest payable on the full amount. The issues were a huge success from the point of view of both the French government and the investors, and the subscription was such that, within a couple of years, the bonds were changing hands at FFr68 as some investors made quick profits from others taking a longer-term view. Barings, meanwhile, received a commission of two-and-a-half per cent on the whole amount raised, more than £500,000. That was very good business for the bank, and its rival Rothschilds soon followed suit with a £5 million loan issue for the government of Prussia. Again the interest rate was five per cent, but this loan was different in that it was denominated in sterling, which made it even more appealing in the London market when it was floated at a discount rate of seventy-two.

Apart from high interest rates and attractive discounts, these foreign securities seemed to offer a guaranteed level of return similar to that of British government bonds, for those who were happy to rely on the interest and capital repayment. The Prussian loan, for instance, was founded on the collateral of state revenues and the value of land owned by the royal house. For more adventurous investors, however, they created a new market with the prospect of almost instantaneous returns from speculation on price fluctuations. So when the Bank of England reduced the interest payable on consols, it was to the coffers of foreign governments that the bulk of disaffected investors' £2.8 million went – along with some £7 million more as the fashion for bond buying took hold.

Loans were floated in quick succession for Denmark, Russia, Spain and Austria, all at the prevailing interest rate and substantially discounted. The issues were extremely well subscribed, and trading in the bond certificates was brisk. But by then something much more exciting had appeared in the market. In March 1822, the public received its first opportunity to invest in the place that everyone had been talking about for months, the region whose profits seemed limitless – South America.

It came in the form of a £2 million loan issue on behalf of the government of Colombia, the new republic that Simón Bolívar had created out of elements of the former Spanish province of New Granada, including Venezuela and Ecuador. At a discount of eighty-four for each £100 – with an extra reduction for people who paid the full amount of their investment in a lump sum, rather than instalments – the twenty-year bonds offered interest, payable every six months, at an unheard-of six per cent per annum. In fact that rate was illegal in Britain at the time, which limited interest payments to five per cent, so the issue technically came from Paris, underwritten by a group of British merchants with interests in South America, who had formed themselves into an ad hoc bank for the purpose.

In a prospectus that was not even printed, the promoters told potential purchasers that their repayments would be guaranteed by revenues from the state monopoly in the Colombian tobacco market, by the government's income from gold, silver and salt mines – which 'is considerable when they are in full work which it is expected they shortly will be' – and by duties levied on imports and exports. Of course, the new government had no credit history, but now that it had established itself there was no reason to suppose that Colombia would not prosper in a long period of peace and stability, during which its leaders would be keen to demonstrate their reliability and financial probity. The entire debt of the country was small, not more than £2,500,000, and 'perhaps no nation on Earth can be pointed out so rich in resources', as the prospectus put it.

The Colombian loan was a sensation in the City, and quickly oversubscribed, so that there was feverish trading in the impressive certificates, which *were* printed, and beautifully, in London. Since dealing in foreign government bonds was forbidden under the rules of the Stock Exchange, there were no 'official' trading prices. For the brokers handling the stock in the more open markets at the Royal Exchange or the Rotunda of the Bank of England – and, still, in some coffee houses – it was simply a question of what investors would pay. They were prepared to pay a lot. Within weeks the bonds were changing hands at ninety, rising to ninety-two, then ninety-five, eventually reaching ninety-seven, almost their full paper value. It seemed there were not enough bonds to satisfy all the people who wanted to buy them. That unfortunate situation, however, was quickly alleviated when a new South American loan was floated.

This time, the issue was on behalf of the new government of Chile, sanctioned personally by its Supreme Director, Bernardo O'Higgins, who had driven out the Spanish, created a republic, and then turned his attention to helping neighbouring Peru do the same. Anxious to show their credibility, the Chileans had their prospectus printed. It sought £1 million and offered 10,000 bonds yielding six per cent and offered at a bargain seventy. In addition to the security of a mortgage on Chile's national income, to be held by the Bank of England until the bonds matured in twenty years, a sinking fund would be maintained to ensure repayment at face value. The City could hardly contain itself, and the price of the bearer bonds reached seventy-two and a quarter within hours of their issue. Not long afterwards, they were being bought and sold at eighty-eight and a quarter, a rise of very nearly four per cent on the offer price.

Where Chile led, as in the struggle for liberation, Peru followed, with a director of the Bank of England, no less, among its promoters. The loan was to be £1,200,000, the interest was, naturally, six per cent, and the discount price was seventy-five. The guarantees were almost identical to those of the Chileans, but the larger and richer Peru saw no need to give details of its 'well-known' economic resources, such was its confidence that investors would rally to the cause. It was right. Brokers, jobbers and members of the public were so desperate to lay hands on the bonds that there was a near riot at the Royal Exchange on the day of the offer, as certificates with face values of £100, £200 and £500 were snapped up at 'discount' prices of eighty-eight or ninety.

Of course, there were some people who appeared to be immune to the spreading fever of investment in South America. Commentators in the more thoughtful news-papers pointed out that the continent was a very long way from Britain and, in consequence, little was known about it other than the information that emanated from explorers, the merchants who often acted as unofficial foreign correspondents for the press, and the prospectuses circulated by those who had an interest in promoting investment. What was clear was that South America was in the throes of violent conflict, from which these loan-seeking governments had just emerged – and none of them had as yet been recognized by the British government.

Such thoughts did not trouble the market, though. The loans would secure the future of the new republics, helping them to exploit the natural resources they said they had, and that must be there in order to have attracted the Spaniards in the first place and sustained them all these years. Why would Spain be fighting so hard to retain territory on the other side of the world if it were worthless? Meanwhile, the loan contractors were taking healthy commissions – anything between two per cent and five per cent of the nominal value of the loans – and the brokers and market-makers were doing almost more business than they could accommodate. As for the investors, six per cent was more than they could get anywhere else, and there was the best possible security available to ensure that interest and full redemption values were paid.

The fact that the governments of Colombia, Chile and Peru were not accepted by the British as sovereign states signified nothing but the dilatoriness of politicians. Far more important was the fact that the Stock Exchange had reacted to this amazing opportunity by bestowing its approval on it and deciding to create an 'official' market in overseas government bonds.

So far as Sir Gregor MacGregor and Poyais were concerned, the timing could hardly have been better.

THE SALE OF THE CENTURY

Among the South American countries exciting the bond market in the remarkably bullish year of 1822, Poyais occupied a unique position that brought with it both advantages and disadvantages. It would certainly appeal to investors in the first instance because of its geographical position, and probably the more so because, as the Cazique made clear, there was no question of any past or future conflict with Spain. To reinforce the point, Sir Gregor had his parting proclamation to the Poyer nation printed and distributed widely through his legation and the land offices he had opened in Scotland, as well as on the streets in the form of handbills.

However, the lack of any direct Spanish connection worked against the reputation of Poyais: it meant there was no substantial trading history to assure potential investors that any promised profits would be forthcoming. Neither had as much been written in the newspapers about Poyais as there had been about the now independent provinces which had played leading parts in the struggle against Spain, so that people were less familiar with the name and situation of Poyais. No recent explorer had extolled the wonders of the great, rolling plains, the mountain ranges, and the broad rivers of Poyais. No merchant or adventurer had thought to send reports from St Joseph to *The Times* or the *Morning Chronicle*, because there was nothing particularly interesting to report, in contrast to the dramatic events unfolding in Colombia, Chile and Peru.

However, Poyais did enjoy one distinct advantage over the new republics in having its head of government available for interview in London, and the Cazique made it his first task to ensure that at least as much was known about his country as about any of the others on the continent that were provoking such interest. As well as giving detailed interviews to the press, MacGregor employed his rapidly growing team of assistants to compose informative newspaper advertisements, leaflets and even ballads to be broadcast by the ubiquitous street singers of London, Edinburgh and Glasgow.

Typical of the advertisements was one published in the Glasgow *Sentinel*, over the name of William Ker Thomson, Agent, Poyais Land Office, 26, Nelson Street. After describing precisely where Poyais lay, it went on:

The CLIMATE is remarkably healthy, and agrees admirably with the constitution of Europeans; many of whom, having become much debilitated by a long residence in the West Indies, have been completely restored to health by a removal, for a short period, to the Bay of Honduras. – The SOIL is extremely rich and fertile, bearing *Three Crops* of Indian Corn in a Year; and produces not only all the necessaries of life in profusion, but is also well adapted for the cultivation of all those valuable Commercial Commodities which have rendered the West Indies so important – especially Sugar, Coffee, Cotton, Tobacco, Cocoa, &c. &c.

The copy proceeded to describe the variety of commercially desirable timber native to Poyais, along with a range of sought-after plant species 'plentifully dispersed all over the Country', and native livestock such as 'Horses and Black Cattle . . . also Deer, Wild Hogs, Poultry'. The rivers were full of fish, the seashore replete with 'Turtle, especially the species denominated Hawksbill, which is particularly desirable on account of its shell, so much prized in Europe, under the name of *Tortoise-shell*'. Several of the rivers were navigable for a considerable way into the interior of the country, 'and many of them produce, by washing the sand in fine sieves, native Globules of pure Gold'. In addition, there were 'many very rich Gold Mines in the Country, particularly that of Albrapoyer, which might be wrought to great benefit'.

It was also felt necessary to explain why Poyais, with all these natural resources for the taking, had not been colonized by the Spaniards:

This Territory adjoins the Spanish American Provinces

of Honduras and Nicaragua, from which, however, it is separated by a chain of almost inaccessible Mountains. The Spaniards, in former times, made several unsuccessful attempts to subdue the Native Indians; but since their last defeat, which happened about thirty years ago, they have never shown any disposition to molest them. This Country is indeed so completely defended by Nature, that any hostile attempts against it are impracticable.

All this information, and more, was included in the handbills that MacGregor and his staff distributed in their thousands, accompanied by specially commissioned engravings showing the countryside, the broad avenues and fine buildings of St Joseph, and the many natural harbours along the coast of Poyais.

It was vital to the Cazique's plan that as many people as possible be encouraged to emigrate to Poyais and set up businesses there. Since he was unable to quote the current revenues of his government as security for his loan issue, his intention was to pledge future income from trade, taxes and excise duties as a guarantee of interest payments. There was no risk in this, he explained to the bankers and brokers he consulted. The reason why Poyais did not already have the necessary revenues was merely an historical failure of policy, occasioned by the fear of Spanish reprisals against anyone attempting to break the colonial monopoly of commerce. Now that the region was to be open to free trade – as enshrined in a treaty with Spain – Poyais would very quickly realize her full potential. Moreover, the very limited development in the country thus far meant that, unlike Chile, Colombia and Peru, Poyais had no existing debt to make the first call on its loan capital. The money raised would go directly towards assisting the new settlers to establish productive farms and businesses, which would naturally accelerate the flow of revenue to the government from imports and exports.

It was as much to reassure the market-makers and prospective investors as to add to the numbers of would-be colonists now coming forward that MacGregor published the *Sketch of the Mosquito Shore, including the Territory of Poyais, descriptive of the country; with some information as to its Productions, the Best Mode of Culture, &c,* by his aide-de-camp, Thomas Strangeways. True to his commitment to the interests of Scotland, Sir Gregor arranged for the book to be printed in Leith, and nominated the Edinburgh bookseller, William Blackwood, as the main distributor, but he was careful to ensure that plenty of copies were also available in London, from Cadell's bookshop in the Strand – conveniently close to the City and Westminster.

In a preface, the author noted that, 'being impressed with a thorough conviction of the immense benefit which not only the native tribes of Mosquitia, but the neighbouring countries in general, must derive, from the civilization and improvement of one of the fairest portions of the globe', he had endeavoured to 'attract the attention of enlightened Europeans to the subject, by combining the knowledge of its history, natural productions, the best mode of culture,

&c which he acquired during a portion of his life spent in that part of the world – with the information afforded to him by the few but authentic authors who have written any thing [sic] on the subject'.

He apologized for the fact that the book might seem dull to the general reader, but he was sure that 'those who are likely to be more nearly interested' would appreciate his decision 'to avoid making any statement which might appear doubtful or exaggerated, especially to such of his readers as are unacquainted with the circumstances that have until now retarded the civilization of this hitherto neglected country', and to confine himself 'to such plain and positive facts, as are established beyond the shadow of doubt'. This was not the inspirational work of a von Humboldt or a Colonel Hippisley, but a thoroughly practical guide for 'the industrious planter or farmer' and for hard-headed businessmen who would know a good thing when it was shown to them.

For that purpose, the topography, flora and fauna of Poyais were approached in an intensely utilitarian manner. The *Black River* was 'navigable for small craft till within about twenty miles of its principal source', while *Brewers Lagoon* had 'a wide mouth, with anchorage off the entrance from twelve to eight fathoms water', and the *Rio Grande* had 'considerable depth of water at its mouth'. The harbour of *St John's* was 'somewhat obstructed by a bar, on which there are only five feet water [sic]', but there was a channel 'which, although narrow, would admit a vessel drawing *twenty-five* feet', and there was room in the harbour for fifteen ships of war and 'for one hundred sail of transports besides'. Fortifications sufficient to 'keep off, effectually, a great and numerous enemy' could easily be built at *Bluefields Bluff* 'for stone is found near it in abundance, and the oyster shells would afford all the lime necessary'. Similarly, when discussing the great variety of trees to be found in Poyais, Captain Strangeways tended to concentrate on the commercial rather than the botanical:

> The mahogany tree is seldom found in clusters, or groups, but single and often much dispersed; there are two seasons of the year for cutting it; the first commencing shortly after Christmas, the other about the middle of the year. The tree is commonly cut about twelve feet from the ground. The workmen raise a scaffolding four or five feet high for the axe-man employed in levelling it ... The body of the tree, from the dimensions of the wood it furnishes, is deemed the most valuable ... The price of mahogany on the Mosquito Shore, is only £12 Jamaica currency per thousand feet. At Balize [sic] it sells from sixteen to thirty pounds. This difference of price arises from the cheapness of labour in the Mosquito territory, and its greater abundance ...
>
> The CALABASH TREE ... is generally irregular, and the branches crooked and spreading; the wood is very tough and flexible, which renders it very fit for the coach-makers purposes, where it is observed to answer better than any other sort of timber hitherto known. The shell of the fruit is so thin and close, that it serves to boil water, as well as an earthen pot. The thicker parts are frequently used for button

moulds, and it also makes a light and convenient drinking cup.

Sometimes, the Captain's practical bent led him to devote considerable space to technical discussions of plant husbandry, and the methods of obtaining marketable products. Thus the aloe plant is:

> Pulled up by the roots, and carefully cleansed from the earth, or other impurities. It is then sliced, and cut in pieces, into small hand-baskets or nets. These nets or baskets are put into large iron boilers or cauldrons, with water, and boiled for ten minutes, when they are taken out, and fresh parcels supplied, till the liquor is strong and black. At this period, the liquor is thrown through a strainer into a deep vat, narrow at the bottom, where it is left to cool, and to deposit its feculent parts. Next day the clear liquor is drawn off by a cock, and again committed to the large iron vessel. At first it is boiled briskly, but towards the end the evaporation is slow, and requires constant stirring to prevent burning. When it becomes of the consistence of honey, it is poured into gourds, or calabashes, for sale, and hardens by age.

Towards the end of the book, the author's enthusiasm for useful information led him to give exhaustive financial estimates. In more than twenty pages given over to the purchase, construction and management of a 640-acre sugar plantation, Strangeways concluded that a planter producing both sugar and rum could expect profits of between £655 and £1,200 a year.

The initial costs were computed as:

Lands	200 0 0
Buildings	1500 0 0
Stock	196 0 0
Total in Sterling money	£1896 0 0

As for the returns, Strangeways noted:

The produce of such a plantation has been stated at 100 hogsheads of sugar of 16 cwt. and 65 puncheons of rum, of 110 gallons, which may be worth on the spot, for internal consumption, as follows:

100 Hogsheads of sugar at £17 per hogshead	£1700 0 0
65 Puncheons of rum, at £12 per puncheon	780 0 0
Gross Returns	£2480 0 0

From this sum, however, the annual disbursements are to be deducted, viz.

Labour and Sundry Charges

Wages of 125 Labourers, at £13 *per annum*, for each	£1625 0 0
Annual supply of mules and steers	50 0 0
Millwrights, coppersmiths, plumbers, and smiths bills annually	50 0 0
A variety of small supplies and sundries, supposed	100 0 0
	£1825 0 0

This sum deducted from the gross returns, leaves an annual profit of £655 per annum, from a capital of £1896, which is nearly 35 *per cent*.

However, the Captain continued:

The most profitable plan for a planter in this country, would be to sell his sugar and rum to his neighbours and the retail dealers, and to keep a store in the town, with a clerk for their disposal: in this way he would readily get 3s 6d per gallon for his rum, and £1 3s 4d per cwt. for his sugar; this is even below the present prices . . . By this mode, the planter would obtain, after deducting the sum of £92 18s 4d for the hire of a store and the wages of a clerk, a clear income of £1200 sterling per annum, free of all taxes whatsoever.

There were similar calculations for the operation of a cotton plantation, with the addition of an extremely tempting forecast of profits of millions of dollars – based on figures from North America – for anyone enterprising enough to establish a cotton mill on the spot. Then Strangeways offered specimen accounts for a modest indigo plantation, producing powder for the dyeing industry, and for coffee, cocoa and tobacco plantations. 'In this country', the author observed, 'the Indians raise tobacco of a very mild and excellent quality; and there is no doubt, if attention were paid in selecting the seeds and soil, that a quality equal to the Havanna might be raised.' Finally, the guidebook provided carefully calculated prospective balance sheets for farmers growing maize, otherwise known as Indian corn, and rice, along with detailed instructions for their cultivation in the soil and climate of Poyais.

Rarely, if ever, can potential settlers in virgin lands have been supplied with such comprehensive information, and this certainly had its effect. By July 1822, so many people had come forward to buy land in Poyais that the newspaper advertisements were pointing out that:

> The present price of the lands registered for sale in this Territory is two shillings and threepence per acre, but will shortly be advanced to two shillings and sixpence per acre, and a further advance will take place soon thereafter. Purchasers may, however, secure to themselves Grants at the price of the day by making a deposit of 25 per cent, on the amount of their intended purchase previously to the next advance, and the remainder of the purchase money within such a period as may be agreed upon.

Before long, as the word spread, and early purchasers also persuaded their friends to join them in their great adventure, land in Poyais was selling at up to four shillings an acre. The response was everything that Sir Gregor MacGregor had hoped for, and it led to a summer of furious activity at Oak Hall, Wanstead, as the Cazique and Major Richardson were swept along by the swelling tide of emigrants. There were ships to be chartered, passages to be booked, merchants to be found to provision the voyages, initial supplies for the settlers to be ordered and assembled. Arrangements had to be made without undue delay, since the colonists were selling their homes and goods, and giving up their incomes, so as to be ready for their departure. Time spent in temporary accommodation, and without earning money, ate into the capital they intended to invest in Poyais.

Fortunately, one suitable vessel was immediately available, and, from the Cazique's point of view, an eminently reliable one. It was called the *Honduras Packet*, registered in London, and its captain and crew were very experienced in South American waters where, of course, MacGregor had first encountered them. In fact, it seemed he had used the ship himself on occasion during his military adventures, and some of the members of its crew had been present when MacGregor had received his grant of land from the King of the Mosquito Nation at Cape Gracias á Dios in 1820. So the *Honduras Packet* was engaged for the inaugural voyage to Poyais, scheduled to sail from the Port of London in September 1822 with a party of seventy emigrants and all they would need to establish themselves in the new colony. Five London merchants were awarded the contracts to supply the colonists with everything from foodstuffs, tools and rum to muskets, powder and cannon.

Organizing the settlers, however, was only part of the task that the Cazique had undertaken. The new colony required leaders with the authority to direct its development, to maintain the rule of law, and to protect the interests of the Poyaisian government. Indeed, the government itself was in need of some expansion in order to accommodate the influx of people and commerce that would result from its leader's hugely successful efforts in Britain. MacGregor

found himself conducting interviews almost daily throughout the summer as prospective officials presented themselves
at Oak Hall, some responding to advertisements placed in
the London newspapers, others encouraged, and recommended to the Cazique, by families anxious to secure
worthwhile positions and prosperous futures for younger
sons. Even one of the bankers MacGregor had met in the
City, a man named Mauger, offered his services to the
Poyaisian government, and was gratified to receive the post
of Manager of the Bank of Poyais, where his expertise was
clearly going to be in demand as the economy of the country
both supported and benefited from what seemed certain to
be successive waves of immigration.

For the important position of leader of the first expedition, and the Cazique's personal representative in the
colony, it was natural that Sir Gregor should turn to a
man with a military background, like himself. A former
British army officer named Hector Hall was commissioned
as a lieutenant-colonel in the 2nd Native Regiment of Foot
and, since his official duties would require his presence in
the capital, he was also created Lieutenant Governor of
the Town and District of St Joseph, 'acting in the name
and on behalf of His Highness Gregor', and President of
the Ordinary Council, which placed him at the centre of
national politics. Lest his army and civil salaries should
prove insufficient to maintain his exalted status, Hall
was granted an estate of 12,800 acres carrying with it
the title of Baron Tinto – *Rio Tinto* being the Spanish
name for the Black River. All this was a measure of the

great responsibilities that were being entrusted to him by the Cazique.

To support him, Hall could count upon a small group of young men whose families had purchased commissions for them in the Poyaisian army, just as they might have done in England had it not been for the fact that the period of peace and stability ushered in by the Congress of Vienna in 1815, after the final fall of Napoleon, had led to military reductions in Europe that promised little glory or promotion for a professional soldier. There were also doctors, who saw ministering to the settlers as a precursor to what would undoubtedly be thriving medical practices in the new country, and clerks for the civil service – and the Cazique had been thoughtful enough to recruit a few servants for the governmental and professional classes.

By the end of August 1822, all the official positions had been filled, all the supplies had been delivered to dockside warehouses, and the farmers and workmen who would break the first ground in Poyais had all divested themselves of the encumbrances of their old existence and assembled in London to embark on their new lives. On 10 September, the Cazique travelled from Wanstead to the Port of London to witness the first act of the realization of his dream. He personally wished God speed and good luck to each of the settlers, and consigned to the care of Mr Mauger a chest containing 5,000 banknotes denominated in Poyais dollars, which had recently arrived from the official printer to the Bank of Scotland – and now the Bank of Poyais – in Edinburgh. Then he returned a salute to Lieutenant-Colonel Hall as the last members of the party were rowed out to their ship. The *Honduras Packet* made sail and weighed anchor, the Poyaisian flag fluttering at her masthead as she slowly disappeared eastwards along the Thames and towards the open sea. The colonization of Poyais had begun.

For Sir Gregor MacGregor, however, there was still a great deal of work ahead. His agents in Scotland had been doing very good business, and hundreds of people who had bought land, or simply signed up to work for the Poyaisian government, were now waiting to hear when they, too, would be able to depart. The Cazique was expected in Edinburgh to meet his settlers and to make sure that the arrangements for their voyage and arrival proceeded as smoothly as those for the emigrants who had sailed from London. More immediately, however, he had to complete the formalities for the issue of the first Poyaisian loan in the London money market.

After much consideration, MacGregor had chosen as underwriters of the loan the highly respectable City banking firm of Sir John Perring, Shaw, Barber & Co., with offices in Cornhill, close to the Bank of England and the Royal Exchange. Perring's could not be compared to Barings, Rothschilds or Schröders, but Sir John was a City man of long standing and impeccable contacts, having held office as Lord Mayor twenty years earlier, before succeeding to a baronetcy. Equally, there was no comparison between the Poyais issue and the loans floated by Colombia, Chile and Peru: where those countries were seeking to raise millions of pounds, MacGregor's requirement was £200,000, a relatively modest amount intended primarily to finance the creation of the new settlements. It would not have been worth the while of the bigger merchant banks to take on what, in their terms, was a trifling amount, but for Sir John Perring, the loan offered an opportunity to develop his business in a market that was beginning to look very different from the one he had first entered, as the demand for capital overrode the demand for cash.

To be sure, South American loans were very new, and there was no means of judging what risks might be associated with them, but fashion has always been an important factor in financial markets, and no company likes to see competitors taking too much of a lead in the next boom. In any case, Sir John had been deeply impressed by MacGregor's record and the seriousness of his purpose, and by the prospects for Poyais that had been laid before him – not to mention the five per cent commission the Cazique was able to offer both his banker and the contractor for the loan, a broker named John Lowe.

The scrip, or provisional certificates, for the Poyais loan was offered for sale on Wednesday 23 October 1822, in the amounts of £100, £200 and £500. The discounted purchase price was eighty, and a deposit of fifteen per cent secured the certificate, with the remainder due in two instalments on 17 January and 14 February 1823. The bonds were to mature in thirty years, and the annual interest rate was, of course, six per cent, payable from 24 October 1822 and secured on 'all the revenues of the Government of Poyais', together with receipts from the sales of land then in progress. As a guarantee of probity, MacGregor had registered his own land grant from the Mosquito King at the High Court of Chancery in London, where it had been officially 'inrolled' by the Deputy Clerk, a Mr Ensom, on 14 October.

With his loan safely launched, the Cazique was free to make his way to Edinburgh to supervise the next stage of his great scheme. As had been his hope and expectation, Scots had embraced the idea of emigration to Poyais with even more enthusiasm than had been seen in England. From the reports of his agents, it appeared there would soon be enough settlers to fill half a dozen ships, so no time could be lost in getting the exodus under way. Again, MacGregor preferred to entrust his new citizens to people he knew, and he turned to his old acquaintance Captain Henry Crouch, of the *Kennersley Castle*, which had lately docked in Leith after a voyage to the West Indies and South America. As a merchantman, the vessel was not well suited for the transport of large numbers of passengers, but Crouch readily agreed to MacGregor's proposal to refit her with both cabins and bunk space to accommodate the emigrants. On arrival in Poyais, the new timber would be stripped out and given to the settlers for use in the houses they would build for themselves.

The refit would obviously take some time, so MacGregor rented a house in Edinburgh and set to work enthusing the colonists about the prospects that awaited them in his country. He also recruited artisans to help the land-owning settlers, on contract to the Poyaisian government at wages equivalent to £20 for the first year and £25 for the second, with free passage and supplies and a generous advance on account to maintain them until their real work began. The new world of their dreams suddenly became a very real world as the men accepted the Cazique's dollar notes, with the coat of arms, the crest of the Bank of Poyais, and the promise that 'On demand or Three Months after Sight in the option of the Government of Poyais, One Hard Dollar will be paid to the bearer at the Bank Office' in St Joseph. The people who had bought land, and who had planned to take their savings with them in coin, were also delighted to exchange their gold for the legal currency of Poyais. The dollar notes represented the first evidence of the fortunes they could expect to make.

As MacGregor waited for the departure of the *Kennersley Castle,* however, rather disturbing news reached him from London. The financial market was beginning to worry about the money it had invested in South America after the Colombian government had cast doubt on the validity of its loan issue, suggesting that its representative, Francisco Antonio Zea, might have exceeded his authority in raising such a large sum. At the end of November, the unease turned to something approaching panic when Zea died without the matter having been resolved.

The contagion of uncertainty spread to holders of Chilean and Peruvian bonds. Warnings began to appear in the press addressed to 'those who are afflicted with the passion for foreign stocks'. They ought to ask themselves 'why they should abandon the certainty of the British funds to dabble in others, the value of which, as it appears, so entirely depends upon the unaccredited Chargé d'Affaires of an unacknowledged Republic'.

There was, of course, no suggestion that Poyais might be in the same situation. Not only was its loan a small one, but it had also been authorized directly by the head of state, and he was in Britain. Yet MacGregor's bonds were inevitably affected as the market in South American securities went into reverse, the feverish buying of recent months replaced by equally hectic selling.

By the middle of December, the exchange price of Colombian bonds fell from ninety-seven to sixty-nine as investors tried desperately to pass on their holdings to increasingly reluctant buyers. The Poyais bond, which had not been seized upon as avidly as the other issues, and consequently had never traded above its discount price, collapsed to sixty-seven. This was disappointing indeed. Large amounts of scrip remained to be sold, and even if buyers could now be found for it, the amount of cash remitted to the government would be considerably smaller than the sum expected. Still more pressing was the worry that, since most people who had actually acquired the scrip had naturally opted for payment on the instalment plan, the prevailing climate might dissuade them from meeting their subsequent commitments as they tried to sell their holdings instead.

That, in fact, was precisely the situation MacGregor found when he returned to London after the eventual departure of the *Kennersley Castle*. Many of the payments due on 17 January were not made, as nervous investors sought to limit their losses, while the selling price of the scrip continued to fall steadily. Sir John Perring and the broker John Lowe kept their nerve, trading among themselves and their colleagues in an effort to maintain the market they had created, but their efforts were frustrated by persistent political difficulties in the new South American republics, compounded by the decision of France to invade Spain in order to restore the authority of the Bourbon King Ferdinand VII – which many saw as the precursor of serious Spanish attempts to re-conquer the lost Latin American colonies.

Faith in the ability of South American countries to redeem their loans, or even to pay the promised interest, all but evaporated. Many banks and brokers lost heavily, having sold short or bought bonds for later delivery. Some individual investors with significant exposure in the market went bankrupt. Newspaper commentators revived memories of the infamous South Sea Bubble, almost exactly a century earlier. Accusations of fraud began to be made, and City lawyers sharpened their quills.

For the Cazique of Poyais, it was all intensely irritating. The prospects for his insignificant little loan had been seriously damaged by developments over which he had no control and which, in any event, did not affect his country. With the first party of immigrants already in Poyais, with a second group now on its way, and with further shiploads in preparation, he should have been celebrating the success of his scheme, and banking a steady stream of cash from the sale of his bonds. Instead, he was obliged, through no fault of his own, to seek ways of restructuring the loan and restoring the public confidence he had previously worked so hard to encourage.

Still, at least the sales of land had gone well. Unlike the bonds, they were unlikely to be affected by the anxieties attached to other South American countries – and there remained plenty of acres to sell. The loan business was something of a setback, but it was not serious enough to dent the confidence of Gregor MacGregor.

THE BLACK LAGOON

Captain Henry Crouch had waited in vain for the appearance of a pilot cutter from the port of Black River. On the day after the arrival of the *Kennersley Castle* off the coast of Poyais, the captain had dispatched a boat to determine the depth of the channel into the harbour. The boat crew had reported not a single ship – or even a small skiff – at mooring, which seemed curious for what had been described as the principal port of the country. Indeed, the sailors had seen no sign of life at all on shore, and neither had they been able to identify the location of the settlement that seemed so obvious in the engraving contained in the guidebook. But the lagoon appeared to be much wider in reality than in the artist's depiction, and it was possible that the town was hidden from view by a low bluff close to the mouth of the river.

As the ship made her way into the outer part of the

lagoon, Crouch scanned the shoreline through his telescope, but even when he was as close as the depth of water would allow, he could discern no buildings or anything else that suggested habitation and population. The Captain gave the order to drop anchor for the night, and told his restive passengers that they would be taken ashore in the morning, when no doubt they would find the town and could organize the unloading of their supplies. It was odd, though, he reflected, that nobody on land should have noticed the approach of a vessel as substantial as the *Kennersley Castle*, which could surely be seen for miles in such clear weather.

The ship was astir early on the morning of Saturday 22 March. After breakfast, women and children crowded the rails to watch as the first party of men who would set foot on the soil of Poyais scrambled down rope ladders into boats and were rowed away across the tranquil waters of the lagoon, towards the two spits of land that formed part of the bar of the river. Mounting excitement was mixed with vague anxiety as the passengers left behind waited for the boats to return with news of what had been found on the increasingly mysterious shore. But nothing could have prepared them for the reports that came back.

Among the first to land was James Hastie, a sawyer who had given up a good job with an Edinburgh timber merchant to accept a contract from the government of Poyais, and who had brought his wife and three children with him. As Hastie was later to report, he found himself standing on damp, sandy ground thick with low trees and brush, the undergrowth so dense and tangled that passage would have to be cut through it. The low-lying shore and the impenetrable scrub meant that Hastie could make out nothing of the surrounding countryside, save for a long, pine-covered ridge some miles off, and the more distant, bare slopes of the Sugarloaf hill. Of any road into the interior or any sort of town – still less a bustling port – there was absolutely no vestige.

For Hastie and his companions, the sense of disappointment was acute. As their boats were rowed back to the ship to collect more men, they stood at the edge of the swamp and stared at each other in disbelief, struggling to come to terms with the loneliness and desolation of their surroundings. Then, suddenly, on the far side of the stretch of water that still separated them from the river mouth, they saw human figures emerging from the undergrowth, at first standing still and shading their eyes against the sun, then gesticulating and waving. The figures were close enough to be seen not to be natives, and to be wearing European clothes. Hastie and the rest of the landing party broke into joyful laughter and hugged each other. They were not alone after all – those people over there must have come from the town, which was perhaps further away than they had expected. They called after the returning boats, trying to tell the crews that there was habitation where they had landed, but the rowers were too far away to hear. The group decided not to wait for the next party to arrive, but struck out round the rim of the inner lagoon to meet their new neighbours.

By the time Hastie and the others reached the welcoming party, the boats were delivering more arrivals from the ship. Their crews, having seen what was happening ashore, had navigated their way over the bar of the river and were landing their passengers close to its mouth. With new people also coming from the settlement, there was soon quite a crowd on the beach, all talking at the same time, anxious to introduce themselves and hear each other's stories. What the new colonists heard, however, soon extinguished their sense of excitement.

It seemed that there was, indeed, no town at Black River. The people ashore were only the members of the original party of settlers who had sailed from London the previous September aboard the *Honduras Packet*, and their settlement was no more than a collection of tents and bamboo huts they had built themselves. One of their leaders briefly summarized the circumstances of their arrival.

Like the *Kennersley Castle*, their ship anchored at the entrance to the lagoon and waited for a boat to approach from the shore. The Captain even fired a cannon to attract the attention of the authorities they had expected to find at the port of Black River. When there was no response, and it began to seem likely that the port was not where they had assumed it to be, the settlers' first conclusion was that they had made landfall at the wrong place, perhaps because of a mistake in the map they had been given. In fact, when they paid close attention to the official charts of the area, they discovered an error of thirty-five minutes in the longitudes noted on the Poyais map, meaning that the boundaries of the country were further west than they appeared to be. Nevertheless, from the charts and the topography, as well as from the sightings the Captain took, there was no doubt that the *Honduras Packet* was anchored off what could only be the mouth of the Black River.

Having thus established that they were precisely where they should be, the settlers next supposed that the town must be situated at some little distance upriver, so the decision to disembark was taken. Once ashore, however, they found no more trace of human life or habitation than had been visible from the ship. While some of the party began the laborious process of unloading their supplies, others set off to follow the course of the river until they came upon the town. After hours of hacking their way through the tangled undergrowth, they returned to report that they had seen no buildings, no roads, not even a track. This naturally aroused a certain amount of consternation, but the man in charge of the expedition, Lieutenant-Colonel Hector Hall, insisted that they make the best of the situation. There had clearly been some mistake, and the conditions were not as they were meant to have been, but these were matters that could be settled once they did make contact with the Poyaisian authorities. In the meantime, the party was well supplied and could shelter, feed and maintain itself where it was, until such time as transfer to a proper settlement could be arranged.

The Colonel was, of course, the personal representative of Gregor MacGregor and, with his encouragement, the unloading of the *Honduras Packet* continued in a reasonably optimistic atmosphere. Hall wrote a letter explaining the settlers' circumstances and seeking guidance, which would be delivered to the Cazique when the ship returned to London, so that the Poyaisian government would be alerted even if the colonists themselves had not managed to make their presence known during the eight weeks or so the voyage would take.

So what, the newcomers wanted to know, had happened? The people from the *Honduras Packet* were evidently no better off than they had been on the day they had landed. How was it that no help had reached them?

In fact, came the reply, they were in a considerably worse condition. After some weeks of unloading, and with supplies of food, drink and medicines still in the ship's hold, a fierce storm blew up, and the Captain sent a message ashore saying that he would have to run for shelter. The vessel sailed away, and that was the last they saw of her. Since then, they had been entirely on their own, apart from the local natives – some of whom were friendly, some distinctly antagonistic – and two mysterious American men who, for whatever reason, had made their home a couple of years earlier on higher ground a mile or two upriver.

But surely, said one of the new arrivals, they could have gone for help to the capital, St Joseph, which could not be too far away. The suggestion provoked bitter smiles. Various expeditions had set out to try to locate St Joseph, using the map of the territory brought from England, but the city had never been discovered. Some of the friendlier natives had heard of a place with that name, but when they had guided the settlers to where they thought it was, the much-vaunted capital had proved to be nothing but the rubble of a fort and the foundations of a collection of wooden huts, a small settlement obviously abandoned many years before.

Among the immigrants from the *Kennersley Castle*, shock and disappointment began to turn to anger. One of the cabin passengers demanded to speak to Colonel Hall, only to be told that the governor was absent. He was travelling overland to Cape Gracias á Dios, some 150 miles to the south-east, in the hope of finding the *Honduras Packet* in the large harbour there. Rumours had reached the settlers, through their contacts with the natives, that rum, coffee and medicines from the ship were being sold at the ramshackle village on the cape which was all that remained of a former British colony. The Colonel also hoped to obtain help from the King of the Mosquito Nation, whose headquarters were at the cape and who had, of course, been responsible for the land grant that had brought the settlers to Poyais.

The bewildered newcomers tried to discuss among themselves what they should do – or at least the cabin passengers did. The rest were mostly labourers, accustomed to having their lives controlled by other people, and they had in any case received advances on the wages agreed with the Cazique, so they tended merely to listen to their superiors and await whatever instructions might be forthcoming.

In truth, however, there was little choice for anyone. The contract with Captain Crouch had been for a one-way passage, and a return journey would be costly. And what was there to return to? The independent settlers had sold their land and property, and had even exchanged what cash they had for Poyais dollars. If they did go home, they would be obliged to rely on family and friends while they set about rebuilding their lives from nothing, and in the shadow of an embarrassing failure. It did not really bear thinking about. Moreover, they were, for the most part, hardy and stubborn Scots who were not in the habit of giving up at the first setback, and who had, at all events, paid good money for land that was now rightfully theirs and that they intended to claim.

So the decision was taken to make themselves as comfortable as possible where they were, and subsequently to explore the country further until they found the elements of civilized life they had been led to expect. They could not believe that Prince Gregor had deliberately deceived them – the distressing circumstances of their arrival in Poyais must have something to do with failures on the part of the Cazique's advisers, or the people he had entrusted with organizing his project. After all, it appeared that the Captain of the *Honduras Packet* had proved to be less than reliable, and it was recalled that it had not been MacGregor himself, but his agents in Scotland and some of the passengers, who had extolled the attractions of St Joseph. But those were matters that could be taken up with Colonel Hall when he returned, and a full report sent back with the *Kennersley*

Castle, her Captain having always shown the utmost concern for the welfare of his passengers.

For the present, the settlers could feel secure in the knowledge that they had a good twelve months' supply of provisions and were equipped with all the tools necessary to clear land for planting and to build shelters for themselves – the materials for construction were to be found in profusion all round them. If they were now required to be rather more pioneering in spirit than they had expected, they could at least take comfort from the fact that everything necessary had been provided for them.

In this mood of optimism and determination, a request was relayed to Captain Crouch to begin the unloading of the supplies, sending the tents first. The original settlers took their new neighbours to their encampment, where they found a group of Poyer natives willing to help transport the goods from the ship in return for old clothes and household articles. James Hastie, the Edinburgh sawyer, was surprised to see that, after four months, the settlers had still made little attempt to provide themselves with proper shelter – many of them were still in tents, and those with greater ambition had constructed nothing better than bamboo huts thatched with reeds. Hastie and his friend Malcolm McDougal resolved to do better, and began to scout for timber and pieces of land that might easily be cleared for wooden huts.

Not all their fellow passengers, though, were so inclined to start work. Discovering that there were no stocks of rum, tea, or coffee – which the merchants who had provisioned the *Kennersley Castle* had omitted, believing that the supplies sent out with the earlier party would be sufficient – some of the men refused to do anything, and wandered off into the woods, where they simply lay down and went to sleep. They did not return until evening, when they marched mutinously through the settlement carrying a black flag they had made.

There were difficulties, too, with the bringing ashore of the supplies. Some of the boats were too heavily laden and shipped water as they forced a passage over the bar of the river, which resulted in the ruination of a portion of the stores of flour and rice on which the settlers depended. That caused more grumbling among some of the men who, having taken no part in the operation, blamed their leaders for carelessness and mismanagement. Many of the labourers were 'from the very first, both lazy and regardless' as James Hastie observed in his *Narrative of a Voyage in the Ship* Kennersley Castle *From Leith Roads to Poyais*. Hastie hoped that some discipline would be imposed when Colonel Hall returned.

Discipline was not something that Hastie and his friend Malcolm McDougal lacked. Both former soldiers, they were used to shifting for themselves in unfavourable conditions, and they wasted no time in getting down to work. Having cleared the ground where what they assumed would be their temporary accommodation was to be built, they spent their first night in tents, then, the following day, assembled a team of men to dig a cellar for the storage of the provisions and to build a wooden shelter over it. That done, they immediately turned their attention to the construction of their living quarters, cutting bamboo, felling small trees and collecting reeds for the roofs. Hastie, who had his wife and children to accommodate, chose to build his hut round a huge old mahogany tree, and within a week or so had his family settled in reasonable comfort.

Though questions remained about the dramatic disparity between what the settlers had been told they would find in Poyais and what had actually greeted them on their arrival, most had resigned themselves to creating their own colony from the virgin land upon which fate had unexpectedly deposited them. It was certainly true that the countryside could provide almost everything they needed. The woods were teeming with game, from ducks and quail to turkeys and small wild pigs, and there was an abundance of fish in the river and the lagoon. The natives brought bananas, plantains and other exotic fruits and vegetables for the colonists to sample, and although it was disconcerting that the tribesmen would not accept Poyais dollars in payment – claiming they had never seen them before and did not know what they were – at least the recipients had the opportunity to identify what was edible and could seek out for themselves the natural provisions that were freely available.

With the foodstuffs they had brought with them, there was no reason why anyone should starve, while the general health of the party could be maintained by the two doctors among them, and the supply of medicines in the store. In such a mild climate, and surrounded by such natural resources, there was nothing to prevent the settlement from thriving, even if its establishment was going to be rather more difficult and take longer than anyone had imagined.

As James Hastie soon discovered, however, there were many among the colonists who either would not or could not come to terms with the challenges that faced them.

Some were elderly and lacked both the physical capacity and the will to build their new lives literally from the ground up. It was not that they had come unprepared for hard work, but they had expected to find at least some sort of accommodation waiting for them, even if they lacked the comforts they had left behind. And they had been told that they would be able to hire labour easily and cheaply to help them work the land they had bought, and produce the crops that would sustain them. In the absence of those things, they were at a loss, ill-equipped to fend for themselves and unable to rely on their fellow passengers, whose first thoughts were naturally for their own survival.

There were others, particularly the more gentlemanly settlers, who had never done a day's hard, physical work in their lives, and had not envisaged doing so when they came to Poyais as government officials, army officers, land surveyors, doctors, bankers and the like. What shocked the old soldier Hastie was that 'our officers', as he referred to them, not only refused to buckle down and help themselves, but also declined to take a lead in guiding the rest of the party towards creating a proper colony, as their social status might have indicated they should.

Instead, finding that the roles the Cazique had assigned to them did not apply, these gentlemen seemed to spend their time merely amusing themselves in fairly aimless fashion. They went out into the woods shooting, and always came back with game, but showed little inclination to hunt systematically, and so to provide a regular supply of fresh meat. Their one attempt at organization ended in disaster, when they took a large fishing net unloaded from the *Kennersley Castle* and, as Hastie reported, 'contrived to get it torn to pieces upon the stumps and roots of float-wood in the river, instead of hauling at a clear place or sandy beach'.

What was most worrying, however, was the combination of a mood of despondency among some of the original settlers, and the signs of a rebellious spirit in a group of the newcomers. The silent protest at the lack of rum, tea and coffee fizzled out after a few days, but the men who had engaged in it still showed no appetite for work, and a new dispute was provoked when already disaffected members of the *Kennersley Castle* party accused those from the *Honduras Packet* of taking more than their fair share of the rations that had now been combined in the newly built storehouse.

'Great discontent began to exist', recalled James Hastie, 'but we comforted ourselves as well as we could, in the hope, that when Governor Hall arrived, he would keep some order and regularity, and that he would either bring back the *Honduras Packet*, or some of the supplies which she had carried off.'

Colonel Hall, however, had little to offer when he eventually returned from Cape Gracias á Dios, about two weeks after the second party of colonists had landed at Black River. He had failed to find the *Honduras Packet* or to obtain any assistance from the Mosquito King, and he brought with him only two puncheons of rum, which, according to Hastie, 'was scarcely a mouthful for us, although some spirit was absolutely necessary to correct the quality of the water, which we got out of the sand'. Nor had any word from the Cazique come by ship from England. MacGregor had not even contacted the Mosquito King, who had been unaware that the settlers had arrived, or indeed that they were coming, and therefore did not regard them as any responsibility of his. It appeared that the settlers could not expect assistance from either the King or – since the *Kennersley Castle* had sailed before Colonel Hall's return – from the Cazique, at least not in the near future. They had no choice but to rely on their own resources.

The Colonel welcomed the new arrivals, but pointed out that their presence constituted something of a problem for the settlement. With the rainy season due to begin in a few weeks, there was not enough proper shelter for more than 200 people, and that could lead to serious consequences for their safety and health. The makeshift huts would not withstand the weather, and must be replaced by more substantial dwellings.

Hall made no attempt to take charge of the construction,

to set a schedule of work, or even to divide the labourers into work parties, so it was left to Hastie, McDougal and a few other men to scour the locality for suitable timber. They finally settled on a pine forest on a ridge some six miles upriver from the camp, where they found hundreds of splendid trees standing up to ninety feet tall and with circumferences of up to two feet. Once cut, the trees could easily be floated downstream, but reaching the ridge from the settlement was a slow and exhausting trek because of the thickness of the undergrowth, so the first task was to build boats, rafts and canoes to transport the workers. Hastie and McDougal then dug large saw-pits so that the trees could be cut into manageable lengths, and the work of felling began.

The operation was not a success. The pines were cut down easily enough, but when they were rolled into the river, they sank immediately because of the weight of the large amount of resin they contained. The solution was to bleed the trees before they were cut, but for that to be successful, it really had to be done a full season before felling, which meant the timber would not be available in time to build huts before the onset of the rains. The settlers would have to manage with the basic shelters they had. Hastie, McDougal and some of the other men began the task of tapping the pines of their resin so that they could be used in the future, but they failed to collect the sap, which would have provided valuable pitch for sealing roofs. That was an omission they would regret when the rains came.

'It seemed to be the will of Providence', James Hastie

reflected later, 'that every circumstance should combine for our destruction.'

Hastie took seriously Colonel Hall's strictures about lack of shelter for the rainy season and, since it was now obvious that the settlers would not have enough timber ready to build proper houses in time, he and McDougal suggested to the governor that the party should move to higher ground, where they might be better protected against the weather. They could, for instance, move up to the pine forest, and continue to prepare the trees for later felling or, because there would be no need to float them downstream, even cut them down as they were and use them to build at least solid wooden huts. Those who had worked in the forest had also noticed that it was alive with game, so Hastie also proposed that men who knew how to shoot should be given muskets and ammunition for their own use and try their luck at organized hunting, to augment the settlers' food supply. Hastie said he and his friend were willing to be the first to move, and would build huts near their saw-pits.

'This, however,' Hastie recalled, 'the colonel, whatever might be his motives, positively refused to allow; and although many old soldiers amongst us were fully aware of the necessity and importance of order, yet as the governor did not seem inclined to divide the men into sections or working parties, but appeared to be more taken up with journeys to the cape (for what reason we could not understand), and as the other managers did not attempt any measure of this kind, it was vain for us to speak.'

The Colonel had already announced that he intended

to pay another visit to Cape Gracias á Dios, though he did not see fit to share with his fellow colonists the purpose he had in mind. His lack of candour served to increase the spread of confusion and deep discontent among the settlers, particularly after some of the labourers contracted to the Poyaisian government asked the governor for their wages. They had received advances of a month's pay from the Cazique, but now that month was up. Since so much seemed to have gone wrong, the knowledge that they were at least to be paid as promised would reassure them even if, in their present circumstances, they were unable to spend the money – it could be saved against the day when all the difficulties had been resolved and a permanent colony had been established. Colonel Hall said he was sorry, but all he had to give were promissory notes against future payment. Confusion turned to suspicion in the minds of some of the settlers. They knew of the existence of the cash box the *Honduras Packet* had carried from London, and could not understand why the governor refused to distribute any of the money. Was there a connection with these trips to the cape?

It was not surprising that the departure of Colonel Hall should leave the colonists 'still in a very discontented state', as James Hastie put it, but hardly had he set off when their state began to deteriorate even further. Diseases such as malaria and yellow fever broke out, as the effects of drinking the brackish water, without spirit to purify it, wrought further damage to constitutions already weakened by a lack of fresh food, inadequate shelter, and the depredations of the insects that infested the foetid swamp in which the settlers had built their encampment. Men who were already demoralized rapidly sank into utter despair through sickness and, wrote Hastie, 'in spite of every exhortation, some would not exert themselves to get their huts made water-tight; so that, now when the rains did begin to come on through the night, the improvident were at times obliged to get up and sit with their blankets about them, or to run to the tents for shelter.'

Even among those who still had the will to survive, and who could continue to sustain themselves with the hope of perhaps eventually prospering, dissatisfaction with the attitude and behaviour of Colonel Hall and the 'officers' became the overwhelming feeling. It was clear to all that the colonists had been betrayed, and the likelihood was that the Colonel, as the man in charge of the party, was responsible. He had refused to take a lead in arranging for the establishment of a proper settlement; he had insisted that the settlers stay where they had landed, instead of seeking out better places inland; he had allowed the *Honduras Packet* to sail away leaving her former passengers to an uncertain future and possibly an unknown fate; he had failed to take advantage of the resources that were evident all about them in order to ensure the well-being of the people over whom he had control – and now all he seemed able to do was run away, at every opportunity, to the comparative safety of Cape Gracias á Dios.

What the despairing settlers did not understand, however, because the governor did not have the heart to tell them, was that his journeys to the cape were the only means he could think of to obtain help. He hoped to find a large ship in the harbour there whose captain he could persuade to sail round the coast, take aboard the unfortunate colonists, and carry them to safety, perhaps at the British outpost of Belize, 500 miles to the north-west.

Cape Gracias á Dios was the only place where ships of sufficient size might make port, and even if none were to be seen, the village on the cape was the home of the only government there appeared to be in the Territory, and therefore the only other possible source of aid for the settlers. That was at least part of the Colonel's reason for retaining the Poyais dollars in his cash box. His first trip had proved fruitless, and he was trying again so soon because he realized that time, and the endurance of the settlers, were running out, and that if they were not rescued within a reasonably short time, many of them – if not all – would probably die.

The colonists were also ignorant of the fact that Colonel Hall had declined to organize any attempt at the construction of a permanent settlement because, after the failure to find a town at Black River, or a city at St Joseph, he knew it would not be viable. He had rejected the idea that the settlers should establish themselves on a more favourable site further inland because he believed that staying where they were represented their only chance of rescue. He had been as shocked as everyone else at the sudden departure of the *Honduras Packet*, and he had been disappointed, on his return from Cape Gracias á Dios, to discover that the *Kennersley Castle* had also been allowed to sail away, though it was questionable whether she could have carried the entire party if the decision had been taken to abandon the settlement.

But the most frightening thing of which the settlers were unaware was that, long before the arrival of the *Kennersley Castle*, Colonel Hall had reached what by then had seemed to him the inescapable conclusion that he and everyone else who had set sail on this expedition must be the victims of a clever and callous fraud, and that the responsibility for that fraud could only lie with the man who called himself the Cazique of Poyais.

PART TWO

THE SOLDIER'S TALE

HIGHLAND JOURNEY

The suspicion that had formed in the mind of Lieutenant-Colonel Hector Hall, marooned with his colonists amid the desolate swamps of the Mosquito Coast, was entirely correct. It was not simply that there was no port at Black River and no elegant capital city at St Joseph, but there were no substantial settlements at all, there was no Poyaisian government, or civil service, or army. In fact, there was no such country as Poyais.

There was, evidently, a king of sorts in the region, and it was also a fact that His Majesty George Frederic Augustus II had put his name to a piece of paper granting a large tract of land to General Sir Gregor MacGregor. But the rest of the story that had convinced hundreds of people to stake their fortunes and their futures on emigrating to Poyais, and still more to invest their savings in financing the emigration, was a complete fiction.

Far from lending itself to easy cultivation, the land acquired by MacGregor was rugged wilderness, and even if the supreme efforts required to grow coffee, sugar and cotton were to be successful, there was no population to buy them and little prospect of export, since the infrastructure to make trade possible did not exist. If there were gold mines, the country would have to be explored in order to find them, something at which even the determined Spaniards had balked.

The whole Poyais project outlined by MacGregor and his associates was a lie, a gigantic fraud.

Nor was MacGregor himself quite the eminence he pretended to be. He did hold the rank of general in the Venezuelan army of liberation, and he certainly had some notable military achievements to his name – though not as many as he claimed, and they were rather outweighed by equally memorable military disasters. As for the rest of his story, it was largely invented.

His title of Cazique he had conferred upon himself: how could it be otherwise, since there was no Poyais, no government of which he could be head, and no authority to award such an honour? Equally bogus were his 'knighthood' and the British army record he professed to have, while his direct line of MacGregor descent was from the side of the family whose claim to the chieftainship had been disproved when the proscription of the clan had finally been set aside.

However, he was a bold and imaginative confidence trickster, and he had been practising for many years before attempting what was intended to be his greatest coup.

There was nothing in Gregor MacGregor's background to suggest the strange and ultimately criminal path he was to take. He was born on Christmas Eve 1786 in the old MacGregor house of Glengyle, at the northern end of Loch Katrine, Stirlingshire, in the middle of the wild, beautiful, mountainous region known as The Trossachs, north-east of Loch Lomond. His parents were Daniel MacGregor, a sea captain with the East India Company, and Anne Austin, a doctor's daughter. The heroic Rob Roy had been a MacGregor of Glengyle, where the farm and lands had been developed by his father, but by the time of Gregor's birth, the family had been relegated, in terms of their status in the clan, in spite of their descent from some of its chiefs.

In 1775, after an investigation by Lord Lyon* and a petition from more than 800 MacGregors, the chieftainship, and the baronetcy that went with it, had been officially awarded to John Murray of Lanrick, descendant of an earlier chieftain, who had been forced to change his name during the years of proscription. Nevertheless, the MacGregors of Glengyle still commanded respect, as descendants of Rob Roy, and were undoubtedly worthy of it. Young Gregor's grandfather – also Gregor, but known as *Boidach* ('the Beautiful'), and using the surname Drummond – had served with distinction in the British

---

* The Lord Lyon King of Arms, originally the Court official responsible for identifying the true heir to the throne of Scotland, later became – and still is – the authority charged with determining claims to Scottish coats of arms.

army before retiring to become the Laird of Inverardine, Breadalbane, and taking a prominent part in the campaign to restore the legal status of the clan. The family was also related to the earls of Breadalbane, and had many other connections to the Scottish aristocracy.

Of young Gregor's home life and education, nothing is recorded, though it is known that he had at least one sister. Presumably his father was often absent on the business of the East India Company, so it is likely that Gregor was mostly raised by his mother, probably with the help of other female relations, and that might have led to his being somewhat indulged. Certainly his later behaviour suggests someone who was treated as a special person, and accustomed to getting his own way. His grandfather would no doubt also have influenced him, though Inverardine is some way north of young Gregor's birthplace, through wild country, and the amount of time the two spent together might have been limited.

He would probably have grown up speaking Gaelic and is most likely, from the age of about five-and-a-half, to have attended a school that taught him English, mathematics, book-keeping, probably geography and possibly Latin. His subsequent career suggests that he might also have learned French, along with geometry and land-surveying, all of which were taught in some late-eighteenth-century Scottish schools. There were parochial schools all over Stirlingshire at that period, but Gregor is more likely to have attended a private grammar school, partly because of the position of his family, who would have been among the better-off members of the community, and partly because the parochial schools were increasingly influenced by the Presbyterian Church, whereas the MacGregors were by tradition staunch Roman Catholics (which was one of the reasons for their proscription in 1604).

It was usual for Scots children at that time to leave school at the age of fifteen, and Gregor was no exception, since we find him at the age of sixteen, in the spring of 1803, joining the British army, the youngest age at which he could do so. The intervening year he would later claim to have spent at the University of Edinburgh, Scotland's leading academic institution, but the truth of this has never been established because, of course, he did not take a degree. Certainly his mother appears to have had Edinburgh connections, and the family would have been well able to afford the university's annual fee of about £30. Equally, Gregor does appear to have been well educated, though his boast in adult life that he had a library of more than 1,500 books seems fanciful, as was so much else of what he said about himself.

His decision to join the army might well have had something to do with the military background of his grandfather. Gregor's family would doubtless have had the wherewithal to buy him a commission as an ensign, which would have cost about £450, and the contacts to find him a vacancy in an infantry regiment, the 57th Foot. Old Gregor might well have been acquainted with the venerable Scottish commander of the regiment, General Campbell of Strachur, which would have eased his grandson's passage, and the young ensign was also a nephew of another renowned Scottish soldier, Lieutenant-General Robertson of Lawers.

The men of the 57th Foot were a refractory bunch who had earned themselves the nickname of 'Steelbacks' because of the number of floggings they underwent to maintain discipline – and skin something like steel was required to survive sentences of perhaps 900 lashes. The commander of the first battalion once described his troops as 'fighting villains', and a regimental inspection produced the following comment by the inspecting general: 'From the description of the men of which it is composed it will perhaps never arrive at what would be called a fine regiment, but it is a very serviceable one.' No doubt the officers were rather better behaved – but not that much better, as events were to show.

Aside from the possibility of family influence, Gregor was welcomed into the regiment because, in 1803, it was expanding under the pressure of renewed fears of a French invasion of Britain, after the collapse of the peace treaty signed with Napoleon at Amiens the previous year and the resumption of hostilities. The 57th was based at Ashford, in Kent, when Gregor joined, and he spent his early months being drilled by a veteran sergeant until he knew every move described in the *1792 Regulations*, which formed the basis of army training until the middle of the nineteenth century. He was also required to study the new *General Orders and Observations on the Movements and Field-Exercise of the Infantry*, which reflected the most up-to-date military thinking in the early years of the new century, together with the Mutiny Act and the Articles of War, and military text books such as *Manual and Platoon Exercises* and *Regulations for the Exercise of Riflemen and Light Infantry*.

More importantly, from the point of view of his later activities, Gregor was schooled in the art and science of administration, which in the army of those days required meticulous attention to detail, the ability to collect, absorb and communicate vast amounts of information, and inexhaustible patience. These were attributes that would be extremely useful to the man who would go on to invent an entire country, together with a sophisticated system of administration for it, and succeed in persuading large numbers of people to accept it as real.

MacGregor obviously showed a great deal of promise as a soldier, for by the spring of 1804 – when the 1st battalion of the 57th, in which Gregor had served for a year, was posted to the charming Channel Island of Guernsey in the face of the growing threat from France – he had achieved the rank of lieutenant without having to purchase it, a process that would normally have taken up to three years. No doubt the shortage of officers in a rapidly expanding military force had a part to play in his rapid promotion, but his superiors would certainly have noted his quick brain and supreme self-confidence, which would have been sources of both admiration and reassurance among the soldiers he was called upon to lead.

Gregor's new status, and the light responsibilities of garrison duty in Guernsey, allowed him to take full advantage of the social opportunities that were among the attractions of military life to young gentlemen. The infantry officer's uniform, with its scarlet coat, gold braid, splendid embroidery and metallic thread, acted as a magnet to the opposite sex. As the wickedly observant Jane Austen put it, a gentleman became 'completely charming' when decked out in 'full regimentals', and MacGregor's good looks and haughty, dashing manner made him especially attractive to young women, not to mention their mothers, who would have been anxious to secure suitable husbands for their daughters. There was no shortage of social invitations for the young lieutenant.

It might well have been during this period in the Channel Islands that Gregor met his future wife, for by the end of the year, the 57th had sailed closer to the developing war in the Iberian Peninsula, taking up station on the island of Gibraltar. Alternatively, she could have been introduced to MacGregor while he was still in England, by her brother, who was an ensign in the 49th Regiment of Foot.

Her name was Maria Bowater, and her social credentials were impeccable. Her father, who was dead by this time, had been an admiral with a grace and favour residence at the royal palace of Hampton Court, and her uncle was a lieutenant-general. Other family connections included a member of parliament, another general, and the leading botanist Aylmer Bourke Lambert, Vice-President of the Linnæan Society and Fellow of the Royal Society. The young woman also commanded a considerable dowry, as a contemporary pointed out: 'Miss Bowater brought her husband the moiety of the Dock Yard at Woolwich, besides a considerable sum of money in the funds.' She was an excellent catch for an eighteen-year-old infantry lieutenant whose own social status – and, it must be said, developing delusions of grandeur – were not matched by any accompanying fortune.

The couple were married in some splendour at St Margaret's Church, Westminster, in June 1805, and took up residence in the London home of Maria's aunt, Mrs Lambert – though the bridegroom, of course, was soon recalled to duty in Gibraltar, this being the year when decisive action by and against Napoleon was expected. It may be assumed that Maria's family was less than happy with her new husband's relatively lowly rank because, just two months after the wedding, Gregor paid about £900 to purchase a captaincy in his regiment, rather than waiting the seven years or so it would have taken to achieve the command of a company in the ordinary way.

Malicious gossip suggested that, through his marriage, he had 'obtained an accession of interest and pecuniary means, sufficient to insure a certain, and extremely rapid, promotion', but MacGregor always maintained that the purchase money had been lodged before the marriage 'from his own funds'. That might well have been true, representing a successful attempt by MacGregor to prove that his prospects were sufficient to make him worthy of the hand of such an elevated young woman.

Thereafter, the young Captain's progress should have

been assured. Using his new-found wealth, MacGregor could have bought himself the rank of regimental major – which could take anything between six and seventeen years on the basis of promotion – and then, with war a certainty, could have either counted on distinguishing himself sufficiently to move up to lieutenant-colonel or else paid again for the highest purchasable rank in the army. There appeared to be no reason why, in due course, he should not become a general, as his wife's uncle had and her brother subsequently would.

By this time, however, certain traits in the young man's character were beginning to turn him into his own worst enemy. One of his later military comrades, if that is the right term for a man who disliked him intensely, observed: 'MacGregor was spoiled by prosperity, and his versatility and haughtiness of disposition soon overturned his flattering prospects.'

For example, upon his elevation to captain, he began to display something of an obsession with 'extreme affectation of dress and fashion; and an overpowering fondness for the nicest distinctions of rank, and the imposing spectacle of honorary badges and tangible tokens of merit'. That sort of attitude did not endear him to his brother officers, especially when 'he permitted neither private nor non-commissioned officer to appear out of quarters unless dressed to the extreme of their ability, and accompanied by a handsome walking cane; and they had particular orders never to associate with the Battalion men, unless of a superior grade to themselves'. Subordinates, and no doubt more senior officers, muttered that Captain MacGregor seemed to care more about appearances than about doing his job as company commander.

Meanwhile, the 57th Foot remained in Gibraltar, training hard to create a reliable fighting force as Napoleon made himself the Emperor of not only France but the whole of western and central Europe. How much time MacGregor and his new wife were able to spend together is unknown, but it is likely that he returned periodically to England and Maria might well have travelled to Gibraltar, and might even have established a home there, because it was normal for women of all classes, from officers' wives to whores, to live on or near British military bases, wherever they were in the world. The voyage to the southern tip of Spain would have been hardly more risky than in peacetime, since Nelson had virtually destroyed French naval power at the battle of Trafalgar, in October 1805, leaving Britain in complete command of the seas off the western coasts of Europe, and the route to the Iberian Peninsula was the main one for British trade with the Continent.

By 1807, the 57th had become, in the words of the inspecting General, 'a very serviceable regiment', but it was not called to join the British expeditionary force sent to counter the French invasions of Portugal and Spain during the winter of 1807 and the spring of 1808 – a venture which ended with the celebrated Battle of Corunna and the evacuation of the 14,000 remaining British troops. Not until the summer of 1809 did Gregor MacGregor's famous Peninsular War record begin, when his regiment was shipped to Portugal as reinforcements for the soon-to-be Duke of Wellington's second, and ultimately successful, attempt to drive out the French.

MacGregor was to make much of his association with the 'Die-Hards', who heroically fought their way into history at the Battle of Albuera. The impression he gave was completely unjustified, but the sequence of events that leads to the truth is not easy to follow accurately.

What is beyond doubt is that the 57th Foot landed at Lisbon on 15 July 1809, almost three months after the beginning of the campaign. From the capital, the troops were transported by boat along the river Tagus to Vellada, whence they marched eastwards to Castel Branco, not far from the Spanish border. Almost as soon as the unit had arrived, however, the British-Portuguese force of which it was to form a part, commanded by Marshal Beresford, retreated westwards for fear of being encircled in a determined push by the French, and the 57th found itself on the march again, south to Elvas and what would become the front line as Napoleon's troops approached Badajoz, just across the frontier in Spain. It was September when the 57th settled itself at Elvas to await a possible French assault, but within a few weeks of having done so, Captain MacGregor was no longer with the regiment. He had been given the temporary rank of major and seconded to the 8th Line Battalion of the Portuguese army. This is where a degree of confusion arises.

According to the later published account of one of MacGregor's detractors, Colonel Michael Rafter, 'he served, for a short time, with his regiment, where a misunderstanding with a superior officer, originally of a trivial nature, became at length so serious, that he was obliged to request permission to sell out, which was granted accordingly; and, on 24 May 1810, he retired from the British service, receiving £1,350, the purchase money of his Ensigncy and company'.

There is no record of this 'misunderstanding', but the emerging character of MacGregor makes it possible to imagine what the background might have been. The Captain, Rafter says, was 'much addicted to the pleasures of the table, and was frequently intemperate to excess ... smoking (a general concomitant to drinking) he was also excessively fond of, and was scarcely ever seen without a segar [sic] in his mouth'. These vices, along with MacGregor's increasing arrogance and overweening concern with the niceties of appearance, would have made for some interesting exchanges in the officers' mess, and might well have brought forth an unflattering response from the senior officer with whom the dispute arose. At the age of twenty-three, MacGregor had neither the wisdom to see that he was attempting to punch above his weight, nor the common sense to realize that it was a fight he could never win. And it seems he learned nothing from the exchange, because Rafter continues:

The cause which had obliged MacGregor to sell out, was not of a nature to prevent him entering the Portuguese service, in which he immediately obtained a majority;

119

but he did not retain it long. Circumstances occurred, of a similar description to those which had taken place in the 57th Regiment, and which resulted more from the wildness of unreflecting youth, than the viciousness of depraved manhood: they were however such as to merit the severe reprehension of Marshal Beresford, by whose orders it was intimated to Major MacGregor that his further services in the Portuguese army were [to be] dispensed with.

The story appears rather differently, though, in military records. MacGregor is listed as having served as a major in the Portuguese army from October 1809 until April 1810, and as having then received £1,350 for his commission on 24 May.

The truth, never easy to establish in the case of MacGregor, must lie somewhere between the two accounts. What probably happened was that, following the mysterious row with a senior officer in the mess at Elvas, MacGregor was swiftly removed from the regiment and placed in a Portuguese battalion also under the overall command of Beresford – with a paper promotion to keep him happy. It may have been that he protested at what he saw as unjust treatment, reflecting badly on his competence and his honour, or perhaps his 'haughtiness of disposition' was too much for the battalion commander and his officers to bear, and a request was sent to Beresford to remove him. That might account for the month between his apparent departure from the Portuguese lines and the date on which his resignation from the British army is recorded: MacGregor and his commanding officer might have been negotiating the terms of his exit.

At all events, Captain Gregor MacGregor was not with the 57th Regiment of Foot when the French attacked from Badajoz and the 'Die-Hards' earned their glory at Albuera. That battle did not take place until 16 May 1811, by which time MacGregor had been back in Britain for the best part of a year, and was well established in the initial phase of his career as a fantasist, deceiver and confidence trickster. His exploits in the Peninsular War, upon which his reputation would later rely heavily, consisted merely of a lot of marching and a petty personal dispute in which he would obviously not back down, and which he so far aggravated as to bring his official military life – brief and fairly undistinguished as it was – to an end.

Some recollections of MacGregor suggest that he and his wife remained in Portugal after his resignation from the army, but there is no evidence for that, and it may have been a smokescreen created by MacGregor himself to cover a lacuna in his life story. What he would have done there in the middle of the war is hard to imagine, and Colonel Rafter confidently asserts that the couple went home almost immediately. The Bowater family cannot have been overjoyed at this premature return, or the sudden disappearance of MacGregor's prospects, and that might explain why the couple next appeared in Edinburgh, living in a house that Gregor's mother rented there, rather than settling back with the Lambert family in London.

'Liberated from the fetters of a military life', as Rafter

puts it, 'MacGregor now appeared to enjoy his freedom with little foresight and less reflection.' He would have seen no need for either, since he had Maria's fortune to support him in the indulgence of his devotion to appearance and status. Rafter goes on:

> Having honoured the city of Edinburgh with his residence for some time, he there assumed the title of Colonel, decorated his heels with gilt spurs and his breast with the badge of a Portuguese order of Knighthood: his lady was – (soi disant) – a foreign Comtesse, his footmen were dressed in a very whimsical livery, and the pannels of his chariot were highly emblazoned, and shone in all the 'blushing honours' of a Coronet!

Up to this point in his life, Gregor had followed the time-honoured military practice of buying rank, but in civilian life, his elevation cost him not a penny, save for what he spent on the accoutrements of the exalted status he simply awarded to himself. It was the future Prince of Poyais in the making, but these were early days, and he still had techniques to learn in order to convince others of his importance. Colonel Rafter describes the unsuccessful efforts of the aspiring confidence trickster:

> Thus provided with a 'nom de guerre', and equipped for conquest, MacGregor paraded the most fashionable streets of the Caledonian metropolis, attended chymical, and other lectures at the University, and gave occasional parties at his mother's lodgings in Princes Street; practising all those delicate stratagems, to obtain notoriety, which have been in use since the burning of the Temple of

Ephesus*; but unfortunately without effect. – The people of the good city of Dun Edin are rather slow of belief, and somewhat sceptical in all which does not regard their own personal merit, and MacGregor, notwithstanding his very able manoeuvres, was (in vulgar phrase) smoked by the wary Burghers, who, in the significant, though unceremonious, idiom of their language, bestowed upon him the denomination of *Intak*, or Adventurer.

His failure to create the required impression must have been intensely galling for a man of Gregor MacGregor's delicate sensibilities. He obviously explained his failure to be taken seriously by the fact that Scotland was a close-knit society – in which one's background was usually widely known and any display of unwarranted airs and graces tended to be greeted with earthy Celtic ribaldry – because his response was to remove himself to the wider social opportunities of England, where there was more appreciation of the exotic and greater respect for appearances. Certainly the English set great store by background, but MacGregor may have thought they would be more likely to accept his story so long as he gave the right signals and followed an appropriate way of life. MacGregor chose his new location with care, settling on the Isle of Wight, where the aristocracy mingled happily with the merely rich in a newly fashionable social whirl.

* This would have been a story familiar to Rafter's classically educated readers. On 21 July in 356 BC, the Temple of Artemis at Ephesus, one of the Seven Wonders of the Ancient World, was burned to the ground by a young man called Herostratus, for no other reason than that he wished his name to become immortal.

'Our hero', Colonel Rafter wrote,

repaired to the Isle of Wight, where, during a summer which he spent at Ryde, with his wife and sister (a beautiful and amiable woman), he affected a degree of style and fashion much beyond his means. He there represented himself as heir to a Highland Baronet, and to a castle, with an estate, in the Highlands: his gay disposition, handsome figure and good address, procured him ready admission to all circles, and the assemblies of Ryde were considered devoid of their principal attraction, unless graced by the presence, and succeeded by the petits soupers, of the lively Scotchman.

Emboldened by this triumph, MacGregor left Ryde at the end of the summer season of 1811 and attempted to repeat and even build upon his success in the more challenging and less forgiving currents of London society. In view of the level of competition he would encounter, he raised himself a further notch by styling himself Sir Gregor MacGregor, Bart., claiming to have succeeded to his Highland estate on the death of his guardian, Sir John MacGregor Murray, and to the chieftainship of the clan MacGregor. Of course, none of this was true, any more than were his intimations of kinship with the Dukes of Northumberland, Athol, Gordon and Montrose; the Marquis of Londonderry, and a selection of earls and barons. How long 'Sir' Gregor MacGregor would have been able to sustain his deception is a matter for speculation, but it was never put to the test – at least, not for a decade.

In December 1811, Maria MacGregor died, and with her went any hope her husband harboured of re-establishing his credibility with the well-connected Bowater family and so improving his financial future. Having spent almost all his wife's money to give the impression of status and wealth, he realized, as Colonel Rafter reported, 'that a continuance of his expensive mode of living would, at no very distant period, totally consume his income', so 'he resolved to employ his faculties in the formation of some plan which might tend to retrieve his broken fortunes'.

His choices were limited. He could have sought out another heiress to marry, but an engagement to a suitable candidate would not have passed without notice, and the Bowaters would have had something to say about it which might have ruined the chances of a marriage ever taking place. He might have returned to the Highlands and farmed some of his ancestral lands, but that would have been completely unacceptable to his romantic and delusional nature. Given his capacity for deceit, he could presumably have launched himself into a life of crime, perhaps of a financial kind, but thus far his lying had been related to social rather than any criminal ambition. His only marketable skills were military, yet any return to the British army was, of course, out of the question.

A foreign army, though: now that was an entirely different matter. London was alive with talk of the revolution against the Spanish in South America; the celebrated General Miranda, lionized in the highest social and political circles of the capital, had recently sailed for his native

Caracas with a party of idealistic adventurers and had taken command of the revolutionary army of Venezuela and its associated provinces. MacGregor began to imagine a dazzling prospect for himself. Why should he not become a figure like Miranda, welcome at every dinner table and grand ball, with women falling at his feet, his exploits turned into the stuff of legend?

He had, in fact, come into an inheritance, though unfortunately not on anything like the scale of the one about which he had boasted in his assault on English society. His grandfather and father were both dead, so the bulk of Gregor the Beautiful's small estate at Inverardine had come his way. This MacGregor sold and, with whatever else he could convert into cash, he gathered the resources to travel to South America and establish himself there in a manner that would both satisfy his pretensions and bring him to the notice of the people who might help him to fulfil his dreams.

At that time, there was no established direct shipping route between Britain and Spanish America, so MacGregor sailed to the island of Jamaica, where, it seems, he was tempted to change his plan and settle in Kingston, among the almost unbelievably wealthy merchants and planters. But, in the words of Colonel Rafter's account, 'having no introductory letters to that place, he was not received into society'.

In Kingston, according to Rafter, and indeed throughout all Jamaica, the term 'gentleman' was proverbially reproachful, and an idler was regarded as 'a leper who, to prevent social infection, should be hunted from society. MacGregor therefore knowing nobody, living well, and having no visible means of support, became an object of considerable jealousy and suspicion'.

Without the means, and probably the will, to pay his way into the mercantile aristocracy of what was, at the time, a vital part of the British economy, there was nothing for it but to pursue his original intention and seek future fame and fortune among the revolutionists of Venezuela. In the early spring of 1812, Gregor MacGregor left the comfortable surroundings of Kingston and made his way across the Caribbean to Trinidad, where he was finally able to find a ship that would take him to Caracas, arriving there in April.

Characteristically, it was not exactly as himself that he set about attracting the attention of the emerging republican hierarchy. He was no longer the Scottish baronet, but a fraudulent Sir Gregor he remained, this time as a Knight of the Portuguese Order of Christ.

THE REVOLUTIONIST

In some respects, 'Sir' Gregor MacGregor could hardly have chosen a worse time to offer his services to the republican movement in Venezuela. Much of the country was beginning to perceive itself as suffering a harsh judgement from heaven, after two devastating earthquakes, the first in 1811 and the second – with its epicentre near Caracas – on 28 March 1812, just a week or two before MacGregor's appearance in the capital. More than 30,000 people were dead, and the damage to buildings was so extensive that some of it would still be unrepaired thirty years later.

Priests thundered from their pulpits that it was the punishment of God, imposed on a people who had mocked Him by rejecting their legitimate and divinely blessed ruler, the King of Spain. The message was beginning to he heard, notwithstanding the fact that most of the priests had been appointed by the Spanish church, and might therefore be somewhat biased, and that the current King of Spain, Joseph Bonaparte, had been anointed not by God but by the Emperor Napoleon, whose brother he was. Opposition to the Venezuelan republic, declared on 5 July 1811, was beginning to spread among a fearful and deeply religious population, and even some of the leaders of the Republican party were considering negotiations with the commander of the Royalist armies that still occupied large swathes of the country. For MacGregor the would-be fighter for liberty, the future appeared rather limited.

On the other hand, this confused situation did present opportunities to a Scotsman on the make. The founders of the Venezuelan Republic were divided as to whether they should, in the light of growing popular sentiment, try to reach an accommodation with the Royalists, or whether they should fight for the independence they had claimed, in the hope that victories would bring the people with them. The 'hawks', as it were, recalled the success of their military operations against royalist forces in Caracas and the city of Valencia, west of the capital, and took heart from the occupation by the revolutionary army of several important fortresses along the coast. They also believed they could count on the support of Britain in a continuing struggle against the Spaniards, since the British government had long declared itself in favour of South American independence.

So far as MacGregor was concerned, this more aggressive faction seemed to offer the best hope of honour and glory. Leaving aside any idealistic attachment he might have felt towards the revolution, he had little to gain in practical terms from the restoration of the old regime. The Venezuelan patriots, for their part, welcomed with enthusiasm a man who was not only British but who had also been an officer in the famous 'Die-Hards' of Albuera and had – so he said – turned an indifferent Portuguese regiment into an effective fighting force. It was natural that the two should gravitate towards each other.

Quite what MacGregor hoped to achieve from the association is not immediately obvious. Altruism does not seem to have been among his distinguishing features. Colonel Michael Rafter, who was one of MacGregor's fiercest critics, commented: 'MacGregor, possessing an ardent and romantic disposition, the temporary impulses of which he mistook for the noblest sentiments of philanthropy, and the most exalted love of Freedom, was seduced ... by the golden dreams of transatlantic adventure, which displayed to his dazzled imagination a long perspective of glory and of riches.'

Still, it seems strange that a man noted for his self-indulgence, not to say selfishness, should be prepared to expose himself to mortal risk for the sake of a cause in which he had no direct interest. Of course, he was not alone: during the years of the conflicts in South America, thousands of English, Irish and Scottish volunteers rallied to the revolutionary cause for a variety of reasons, idealistic and otherwise. Yet, given MacGregor's embryonic career as an impostor, following his inglorious departure from the British army, it is hard to believe that there was no ulterior motive for his sudden excess of libertarian zeal.

There is, however, a possible – indeed, probable – explanation, and it relates to the man who had apparently inspired MacGregor to head for South America in the first place: General Sebastián Francisco de Miranda.

The General was everything that MacGregor was not, as well as some things the Scottish pretender actually was. Miranda was a genuine man of action, an accomplished soldier, a politician, an intellectual, an idealist, a bon viveur, and an international celebrity. He was also a dedicated hedonist, an almost professional amorist and, according to a diplomat in St Petersburg, 'imprudent and violent in disposition, and with a surprising rudeness of manner which he displays on all occasions'. To a very much younger man with an 'ardent and romantic disposition', Francisco de Miranda was, as we now say, something of a role model. Gregor MacGregor recognized the arrogance, the desire to live well, the self-belief and the urge to fame that were in his own nature. Unfortunately, MacGregor lacked Miranda's 'rare genius' – as the diplomat quoted above characterized it – but that did not prevent him from trying to emulate his hero, using such talents as were available to him.

In the aftermath of the Caracas earthquake, Miranda, whose sixty-second birthday had fallen on the very day of the disaster, had become the virtual dictator of the Venezuelan Republic. The Federal Congress, which had sprung out of the Declaration of Independence in 1811, turned to its ablest soldier in panic when the priestly campaign to convince the people that they should return to the fold of the Spanish monarchy encouraged royal troops to occupy the western town of Barquisimeto and begin a two-pronged advance towards the capital. The Congress declared martial law, called to arms every able-bodied citizen, introduced harsh penalties for traitors espousing the Royalist cause, and appointed Miranda Commander-in-Chief and Head of State. The General was instructed, on 2 April 1812, to take 'all measures necessary in order to preserve the territory invaded by the enemies of [Venezuelan] liberty'.

Miranda's first task was to instil order and discipline into the Republican army, a ragtag force composed mainly of cowboys, peasants and freebooters who showed more interest in the spoils of war than in its prosecution. Its former Commander-in-Chief had resigned: some said that he knew he was unequal to the challenge, others that he had no faith in the fighting ability of the men under his command and foresaw that they would crumble before the Royalists. Miranda understood the problems he had inherited, but in dealing with them, his genius seems to have deserted him. Instead of awakening the fighting spirit of his men by emphasizing the glory of their cause and the great prizes they could win, he concentrated on trying to turn them into something like the professional armies with which he had been associated in the past.

'He became obsessed with the idea of prolonged, meticulous military drill,' one of Miranda's biographers has written. For this, of course, he needed experienced and competent leadership, so it must have seemed like a blessing when the veteran British officer Sir Gregor MacGregor presented himself at headquarters and applied for a command – 'flattered', says Colonel Rafter, 'at the idea of commencing his South American career under the auspices of so celebrated and enterprising a man'.

MacGregor's boldness in going straight to the Commander-in-Chief – not to mention the gloss with which he no doubt varnished his military background – was rewarded with the rank of colonel, though, curiously, in view of his infantry experience, he was placed in charge of a cavalry battalion. He had little time to become acquainted with his new command before being called upon to prove himself in battle. By the end of April, the Royalist forces advancing towards the capital had moved on from Barquisimeto to San Carlos without much difficulty, and on 3 May they captured the strategically important city of Valencia. Here the Spanish Commander, Domingo de Monteverde, halted to await reinforcements, concerned that his troops might be encircled by the Republicans, who held the territory on each of his flanks. This was the breathing space Miranda needed, and he collected the bulk of his army in the heavily fortified town of Maracay, from where the Spaniards would have to dislodge it if they were to march on Caracas.

For the next few weeks, the war settled into a series of skirmishes with indeterminate results. Colonel MacGregor stirred Republican spirits when he led his cavalry into the rout of a royal force near Cerro Gordo, between Maracay and Valencia, but it was something of a peripheral action and could not be developed into a general offensive by Miranda's troops. MacGregor's next action, at Los Guayos, near the shores of Lake Valencia, was rather less successful, with Colonel Rafter reporting that 'his cavalry suffered terribly'. But the Scotsman 'conducted himself in such a manner as to excite the admiration of Miranda and his officers, and he was generally considered, not only by the South Americans, but also by the French and German adventurers in Miranda's army, as a man of a daring and excessive courage'.

It seemed that MacGregor had really found his vocation, a cause that appealed to his imagination and a part in it that satisfied both his restless nature and his ambition. He had characteristically relied on deception in order to ingratiate himself with Miranda and the other Republican leaders, but in achieving the position he coveted, he was obliged to expose the admirable, and real qualities that normally lay hidden behind his fantasies. Had he been able to remain close to the inspiring and generous Miranda, and if the Republican movement had triumphed at that period, MacGregor's future might have been every bit as glorious as he had hoped. The times were against him, however: he had embraced the struggle for independence at the precise moment when it was about to suffer the first of its many reverses.

Like most revolutionaries, the Venezuelan Republicans

were riddled with political dissent and factional jealousies. Even the unimpeachable Miranda was not universally supported. Among many of the conservative and class-conscious members of the native Venezuelan establishment, he was regarded with suspicion, and often something like disdain. For one thing, he was not a Venezuelan by blood, his wealthy family having originally come to Caracas from the Canary Islands and, secondly, he had spent most of his life abroad, which made him appear to some as a 'foreign' opportunist exploiting the Venezuelan revolution to fulfil his own dreams of power. This inward-looking Republican elite had no interest in Miranda's pan-American vision of liberty, and it became even more alienated when, as the Spanish Commander Monteverde hesitated at Valencia, the titular leader of the Republic appeared to be spending most of his time trying to persuade foreigners – mainly the British and the North Americans – to help save the fledgling state in its hour of crisis.

Miranda himself was under no illusion. 'I am selected for responsibility,' he had said bitterly, 'in order that there may be someone to officiate at the funeral services of Venezuela, but I cannot deny to my country my help in the calamitous conditions produced by factors both human and material.' Yet the very realization that the cause was probably hopeless, at least without substantial aid from overseas, seemed to rob him of the will to win.

At the time when MacGregor's exploits and Miranda's insistence on discipline and training were beginning to raise the morale of the Republican army – in spite of the soldiers' aversion to the constant drilling – the General himself was spending his days doing little more than reading dispatches in the luxurious villa of the Marquis de Casa León at La Trinidad, a few miles east of Maracay. He even moved his military headquarters eastwards, to La Victoria, which served further to diminish the confidence of Republican supporters and offer comfort to the Royalists. There were riots in parts of what remained of 'free' Venezuela, and two of Miranda's trusted staff officers resigned their commissions.

How involved Gregor MacGregor was in his hero's plans, such as they were, is impossible to establish, but the military prowess he had displayed with the cavalry resulted in his promotion to the rank of Brigadier-General, and it is likely that, as a senior officer, he spent time in the company of Miranda at the villa Casa León. He would certainly have appreciated the splendid table kept by the Marquis, and the meticulous attention lavished on the guests by the legion of servants. No doubt there were also many discussions relating to military strategy, but they must have produced little of use. The Commander-in-Chief was reluctant to take the only step that might have saved the day, which would have been to throw his whole force of four thousand men against the hesitant Spaniards, whose lines of supply were severely stretched. He was to pay dearly for his uncharacteristic caution.

Throughout the month of June, the 'phoney war' continued. Monteverde's Royalist troops took control of two more towns along the front line, but this was mainly as a result of unprincipled opportunism among the local Republican leadership, rather than any tactical manoeuvre on the part of Monteverde. The blow that would crush the first South American Republic came on 5 July, as Miranda entertained MacGregor and his other staff officers to a banquet at La Victoria in celebration of the anniversary of the Declaration of Independence.

In the middle of this somewhat surreal event, a courier burst through the door with the news that, four days earlier, Spanish troops from the Royalist base at Coro, north-west of Caracas, had gained control of the strategically vital Republican stronghold of Puerto Cabello. This, together with the capital and La Guaira, on the other side of Caracas, formed the triangle that was to have been Miranda's last line of defence while he waited for reinforcements to arrive from overseas. The fortress of San Felipe, on an island overlooking Puerto Cabello, was also one of the Republicans' main supply depots.

'Venezuela has been pierced to the heart,' cried Miranda when he heard the news. 'Yesterday, Monteverde had neither powder, nor lead, nor muskets. Today he can count upon four hundred quintals [4,000 kg] of powder, lead in abundance, and three thousand guns.'

The news was all the more shocking because Puerto Cabello had been under the command of Lieutenant-Colonel Simón Bolívar, the Venezuelan aristocrat who, more than anyone else among the republican-minded elite, had inspired and worked for the Declaration of Independence. How could a man such as Bolívar have allowed this disaster to happen? It had perhaps been a mistake on Miranda's part, some of the battle-hardened officers thought, to entrust such an important command to an inexperienced twenty-eight-year-old. Later, there would be accusations of incompetence and dereliction of duty against Bolívar from formerly loyal men among whom he had made enemies, but on that fateful night at La Victoria, nobody knew that the Colonel had slipped away from Puerto Cabello with a few other officers, leaving the garrison without leadership. In any case, the overwhelming consideration was what should be done in the light of the catastrophe.

Miranda summoned the leading members of the Republican government to a council of war the following day. The mood was grim. As the Commander-in-Chief pointed out, Monteverde had acquired not only the supplies he needed to continue his push towards Caracas, but also 1,200 extra troops who had been prisoners of war at Puerto Cabello. Furthermore, the loss of the port meant that it would be well nigh impossible for foreign aid or troops to reach the Republicans.

There was only one course of action left open to them and the General recommended it: they must seek an armistice with the Spaniards on the best terms they could obtain. The British government had sent envoys to the West Indies with orders to mediate between the two sides, and perhaps they could ensure that there would be no reprisals against the Republicans. The government ministers unanimously agreed that arrangements should be made for an honourable surrender. It would be no more than a temporary setback, Miranda said. They could take what gold remained in the treasury and withdraw to the island of Curaçao, in the Netherlands Antilles, to rebuild the independence movement. The meeting decided to appoint two emissaries to go to Monteverde's head-quarters at Valencia and negotiate the armistice. Miranda, meanwhile, called his officers together and explained his plan for a strategic withdrawal – 'to retire in order to surge forward again'.

Neither the retirement, however, nor the surge forward when it came, would be under the control of Francisco de Miranda. Perhaps his powers were fading with age, or it might have been that the prospect of the imminent collapse of his dream so depressed him that he was no longer capable of clear thinking. Whatever the reason, he fatally misjudged both his enemy and the men closest to him.

To begin with, Domingo de Monteverde was not the sort of honourable soldier Miranda had faced in his pre-vious wars. A jumped-up naval officer – to whom the Venezuelans referred contemptuously as 'the Midshipman' – Monteverde was out to make the most of this unforeseen opportunity to gain glory, wealth and power. Far from obeying orders from the Spanish Parliament, the Cortes, to treat the beaten Republicans with fairness and generosity, he would say and do anything to make his triumph rapid and complete, and to establish himself as undisputed ruler of Venezuela in the name of the Spanish crown. He had no intention of standing by any agreement he might make with Miranda, and he was also determined not to let the Republican leadership escape.

The emissaries selected by Miranda were no match for the shrewd and ruthless Spaniard. They naively described to him the parlous state of the Republican army and the disaffection of many formerly loyal supporters of independence. Thus armed with the knowledge that he need not fear a serious fight, Monteverde peremptorily refused either to allow the British mediation on which Miranda had been relying, or to guarantee the safety of the Republican troops and leadership.

The unbending attitude of the Spaniard prompted Miranda to make his second serious misjudgement, in appointing his host, the Marquis de Casa León, to take charge of the negotiations. Casa León, anxious to preserve his magnificent estates, had already engaged in secret contacts with Spanish agents, and he was more than ready to reach an agreement that would at least secure his own position. It never occurred to the idealistic Miranda that, in such a situation, self-interest was likely to come first in the order of priorities.

What really sealed Miranda's fate, though, was his misunderstanding of the man who had so badly let him down at Puerto Cabello, Simón Bolívar. Although he had been one of the chief proponents of the Venezuelan revolution, Bolívar was capricious in his support of the drive towards independence despite the fact that he had helped to set it in motion. Many years later, the former Chief of Staff of the man who, by then, had become known as The

Liberator, reported that Bolívar had taken no part in the developments that led to the initial break with Spain on 19 April 1810:

At the beginning of 1810, the principal leaders of the intended revolution were desirous to see Bolívar among them; and his cousin J. Felix Ribas offered to sound [him out] and gain him over ... Ribas had an interview with Bolívar, who treated the attempt as a foolish and impracticable one ... The resolution of the 19th of April, therefore, was made without Bolívar's participation ... When the Patriotic Junta assembled at Caracas, its members, among whom Bolívar had various friends, were anxious to see him taking an active part in their new government; and proposals were made to him to choose a civil or a military office ... He declined every office under the pretext of the state of his health.

Eventually – the writer, General Ducoudray Holstein, continues – Bolívar was prevailed upon to undertake a mission to London with his friend Luis López Mendez: 'The two deputies could obtain nothing [from the British government] but leave to export some arms, at a great price ... Bolívar, much disgusted, after a short stay, left London and came with these arms to the [Spanish] Main* ... Shortly after, he retired again and declined all military service.'

* Strictly speaking, the term Spanish Main refers to the South American mainland bounded by the Caribbean Sea, from the mouth of the Orinoco river in Venezuela to the Yucatan Channel between Mexico and Cuba. It is often applied loosely to the whole of the Caribbean region.

What he did do, however, on 3 June 1811, was make an impassioned speech in favour of Venezuelan independence, which helped to rouse popular support for the Republic declared just a month later. Again, Bolívar eschewed office, but the growing influence of General Miranda as Head of State appears to have changed his mind, and he agreed to take command of the garrison at Puerto Cabello in September 1811, with the rank of Lieutenant-Colonel. It was a command that would end ingloriously, as we have seen.

There has been much dispute among historians about what really happened at Puerto Cabello in July 1812, and whether Bolívar was to blame. His modern legend has provoked revisionism on both sides, and much evidence has been produced in the effort to prove that he was either a genius, or something of a psychopathic villain whose fame really rests on the shoulders of others. These questions are germane to the story of Gregor MacGregor, since Bolívar was to exert considerable influence over his career.

One thing that is certain is the humiliation Bolívar felt over the loss of Puerto Cabello, the event which, more than any other, brought down the Republic. Having escaped in, as some thought, cowardly fashion, he was unable to face the Commander-in-Chief and fled to his estate at San Mateo, in the Aragua valley, south-west of Caracas. From there, he wrote to Miranda:

General, my soul is crushed to such an extent that I do not feel able to command a single infantryman; my presumption led me to think that my desire for

achievement and my ardent love of country would supply
the talents which I obviously lack to fulfil a command . . .
I did my duty, General, and if a single soldier had
remained at my side, I would have given battle to the
enemy; if my troops abandoned me, that was not my
fault. There was nothing I could do to retain them or
to engage them to protect our fatherland, the country,
alas!, which suffered loss in my hands.

The later part of this letter is somewhat disingenuous,
according to Bolívar's subsequent Chief of Staff. General
Ducoudray Holstein, pointing out that Bolívar might have
faced court martial and a firing squad, writes that, after
the fortress at San Felipe was seized by Republican traitors
who released Spanish prisoners of war and turned the
fort's heavy guns on the town, 'Bolívar secretly left his
post, embarked precipitately with eight of his officers
and withdrew in the night without the knowledge of his
garrison.'

Bolívar told Miranda that he had attempted to mount
an attack against the fortress, but had suffered deser-
tions and treacherous conduct and watched the sea-borne
reinforcements he had summoned forced back by bad
weather. Ducoudray Holstein, on the other hand, says
that 'the garrison at Porto [Puerto] Cabello, waiting in
vain for orders, saw, at day break, that the commander
had departed, and judging that all was lost, retired in
good order, leaving the place to its fate'.

Whatever the precise truth, Bolívar's hasty departure
is less likely to have been motivated by cowardice than by

a deep-rooted sense of his own destiny and a realization that, for the moment at least, the cause in which he believed so passionately was lost. The man who saw himself as the South American Napoleon – to the extent that he would even stand in the famous pose of the French Emperor, with his right hand tucked inside his tunic – would not have been prepared to risk his life in a venture he could see was hopeless. In his mind, he owed it to his country to survive, whatever the cost, so that he could one day build on firmer foundations the independence he had, as a young man, vowed to bring to Venezuela and the rest of South America.

Miranda, who had simply commented, 'That helps us to know human nature', when he had seen Bolívar's report of the events at Puerto Cabello, did not read the personality of the young Colonel correctly, or understand the overwhelming strength of the vision that would drive him to commit acts of which he, and others, might properly be ashamed.

That Bolívar himself felt shame over what he believed he had been forced to do at Puerto Cabello seems clear from his letters to his Commander-in-Chief, and, unfortunately for Miranda, that sense was compounded by the knowledge that the consequence of his failure was to be surrender. He was somehow able to absolve himself of blame, writing that, 'although I am free from guilt, I am an unfortunate wretch', but a nagging feeling of inadequacy to the great task he had set himself – 'My head, my heart are good for nothing' – was selfishly turned into condemnation of Miranda for 'cowardice and treason' in offering an armistice to the hated Spaniards. That appears to have been the only way in which the complex psychology of Bolívar could come to terms with the collapse of the Republic, even though he had already seen that it was inevitable. Interestingly, it was a trait that would show itself in Gregor MacGregor: when things went wrong, someone else was always to blame.

The armistice negotiated by the Marquis de Casa León, largely for his own benefit, was signed at Bolívar's now abandoned estate at San Mateo on 24 July 1812. It provided for 'the application to all the inhabitants of Venezuela of the sum total of statutes ordained by the Spanish Cortes', but also for 'the absolute immunity of persons and property throughout the territory'. Almost immediately, however, Domingo de Monterverde let loose his army to kill, burn and pillage its way to Caracas. Miranda himself led a party of lancers in a desperate and successful counter-attack on 29 July, but the overall position was untenable so, among a tide of refugees, Miranda, Bolívar, MacGregor and the other staff officers left La Victoria for the capital. Finding Caracas in utter confusion, with Royalist mobs roaming the streets and even Republican supporters fighting each other, they went on to the nearby port of La Guaira, where Miranda had arranged for a British brig, the *Sapphire*, to be waiting to carry the remnants of the leadership to Curaçao if the need arose. But Miranda himself was never to make his escape.

In the early hours of 31 July, while the Commander-in-Chief slept, Simón Bolívar and a small group of other

145

officers held an impromptu 'court martial' at the home of the Commandant of La Guaira, Manuel de las Casas, and concluded that Miranda was guilty of treason. By Bolívar's own admission, he was so enraged that he wanted personally to carry out a sentence of death at once, but in the event Miranda was arrested and locked up in the fortress of San Carlos in the town. When asked to surrender his sword, the General refused to hand it to Bolívar, giving it instead to a sergeant of the guard. It was an act that illustrated the contempt he felt for his accusers.

Bolívar would later claim that, with Miranda out of the way, it was his intention to assume command of the remaining Republican forces and launch a counter-attack against the approaching Monteverde. He was prevented from doing so, he said, by the treachery of the Commandant of La Guaira. It is true that, as Miranda was being marched to prison, de la Casas received an order from Monteverde to close the town and prevent anyone from leaving by sea. Anxious to curry favour with the new master, the Commandant immediately carried out the order. But even allowing for that treacherous act, it is hard to see how Bolívar could have mustered any sort of credible force for an to attack or even for the defence of La Guaira. The town was thronged with refugees, and such troops as there were had more interest in saving themselves than in facing the overwhelming number of their enemies.

Bolívar's assertion was probably intended to cover up the fact that, by arresting Miranda, he effectively handed him over to the Spaniards, to spend the rest of his days in chains and to die miserably in a dungeon at Cadíz in 1816 – Monteverde having reported to the Spanish government that he had been grateful for the 'interesting services' of both de la Casas and Bolívar.

Of course, whatever was in Bolívar's mind, doing favours for Spain was not part of it, and he also found himself trapped by the treachery of de la Casas. He was not imprisoned, however, possibly because of his recent 'interesting service', and he subsequently appealed to a friend of his family, an influential Spanish merchant, to intercede with Monteverde on his behalf for permission to leave the now restored royal province of Venezuela. For reasons of his own, Monteverde provided him with a passport – an unwise decision, as it was to prove – and Bolívar sailed for Curaçao, ironically enough from Puerto Cabello. Among those waiting on the Dutch island to greet him was General Gregor MacGregor.

In the chaos of those desperate last days at La Guaira, Captain Henry Haynes of the brig *Sapphire* had come ashore to plead with his friend Miranda to board the ship and make his escape. The General had resisted the temptation, believing that, as Commander-in-Chief, he must first ensure the safety of his officers and men. Gregor MacGregor had no such responsibility, and as Miranda was arrested and the town was sealed, he was among a handful of Republican officers who dashed aboard the *Sapphire* and waited there under the protection of the British flag until the ship was able to sail.

During the short voyage to Curaçao, MacGregor would

have had time to reflect on what he had learned during his introduction to the life of the revolutionary soldier. It was very different from the British army. You trusted no one, not even your closest associates, unless there was a definite community of interest. The chain of command could change as suddenly and dramatically as the fortunes of war. The loyalty of foot-soldiers was a variable commodity, often dependent upon fear, or the prospect of booty. But there were distinct benefits in this type of war for those of a shrewd and enterprising turn of mind.

It was common knowledge among the officers that aboard the *Sapphire* were twenty-two thousand gold pesos rescued from the Republican treasury by General Miranda, and two large trunks containing church silver that were labelled with the name of Colonel Simón Bolívar. Being a soldier of fortune could obviously mean exactly what it said.

MILITARY MANOEUVRES

The imprisonment of Francisco de Miranda had deprived Gregor MacGregor of his mentor and chief protector, which might have left him somewhat exposed in the dangerous territory of Venezuelan revolutionary politics. Fortunately for him, however, he had established the best possible public connection with the man who now emerged as leader of the independence movement, Simón Bolívar. This had not been achieved by any deliberate strategy on MacGregor's part, and, ironically, it had come about through the intervention of General Miranda.

It must have been during the periods of enforced idleness that marked the 'phoney war', after the Royalists' capture of Valencia, that MacGregor became acquainted with a beautiful young woman whose aristocratic lineage was evident in her name, Doña Josefa Antonia Andrea Aristeguieta y Lovera. How they met is not known, but with Miranda's army securely quartered at Maracay, and Monteverde's advance paused to await reinforcements and supplies, there was plenty of time for the Republican officers to take their ease in the still pleasant social life of Caracas, where Josefa's family were among the leading citizens.

As not only a protégé of Miranda but also, at least by his own account, a Portuguese knight and a Scottish chieftain, MacGregor would have been an object of fascination in the drawing rooms of the capital – particularly, because of his charm and good looks, to impressionable young ladies. He found the daughters of the Venezuelan aristocracy equally attractive, none more so than Doña Josefa, to whom he soon began to pay court. Given the prominence of the family, MacGregor could hardly have failed to learn that Josefa's mother was the aunt of Simón Bolívar, though it would probably be unfair to suggest that such knowledge might have influenced him, since at that time Bolívar – though greatly respected in patriotic circles – was no more than a colonel serving under Miranda. What the Scotsman did fail to understand, however, were the implications, in a deeply religious and strictly regulated society, of his developing intimacy with a well-bred, highly respectable and unmarried woman.

Josefa herself appears to have done nothing to discourage MacGregor's attentions, and the evidence of her later behaviour suggests that she had fallen deeply in love with the dashing officer. But it was not long before word reached her mother, Doña Josefa Maria, that the young woman's virtue had become the subject of intense speculation on account of her being seen so regularly in MacGregor's company. After all, one knew what soldiers were like, even if they were officers who could style themselves 'Sir'. Horrified, Doña Josefa Maria went straight to General Miranda and demanded that he act to protect her daughter's honour. According to the account of Colonel Rafter, Miranda lost no time in 'acquainting MacGregor with the circumstance', and 'recommended him strongly to marry her'. To which MacGregor replied, 'with all that apathy for which he is remarkable, "With all my heart; I have no objection".'

Other records suggest that the marriage was the result of rather more than a mere recommendation. It was solemnized on 10 June 1812 by the Vicar General of the Army of the Republic, who is described as 'following the orders of General Miranda', and the ceremony took place at the home in Maracay of one of Simón Bolívar's closest friends. All that seems to have been missing was the shotgun. Nevertheless, the bond between Gregor and Josefa proved to be genuine and strong, as the vicissitudes of their life together will demonstrate. They would have three children, and the marriage was to survive – as happily as MacGregor's adventures would allow – for almost exactly twenty-six years, until Josefa's death.

The beginning of the MacGregors' married life, however, was distinctly inauspicious, leaving aside any element of compulsion that might have been involved in the marriage ceremony itself. They had been man and wife barely four weeks when disaster overtook the Venezuelan Republic, and the end of another month saw them fleeing into exile in Curaçao and facing an uncertain future. Life in the Dutch colony was pleasant enough, but Doña Josefa does not appear to have been accompanied by any substantial dowry – perhaps reflecting the circumstances in which the marriage took place – and MacGregor's own resources, without his general's pay or any prospect of plunder, were now severely limited.

The eventual arrival of Simón Bolívar in Curaçao offered some hope of action, especially now that MacGregor was part of the family, but, although Bolívar had effectively made himself leader of the Independence movement, his recent experiences had convinced him that the next attempt to free Venezuela from Spain must be much better planned and organized. Simply to regroup his forces and launch a new assault would be to court another disaster. So, as the man who would later become Bolívar's Chief of Staff, General Ducoudray Holstein, put it in his memoirs, 'he passed some time devoting himself to gambling and other amusements', in Curaçao, drawing on what the General described as 'a large amount of gold' that Bolívar and his cousin had smuggled out of Venezuela.

Such idleness, attractive though it might have been, did not suit MacGregor's situation, and Bolívar seemed disinclined to pay much attention to him in spite of the family connection. MacGregor soon resolved to leave the Venezuelans to their own devices while he resumed his search for fame and fortune elsewhere.

The obvious choice was the former Spanish province of New Granada, bordering Venezuela, which had previously been a semi-autonomous part of it. New Granada had now also declared its independence and had formed itself into a series of small republics governed by military juntas. One of the heroes of the liberation struggle in the province was General Antonio Narino who, like Francisco de Miranda, had been granted dictatorial powers in an effort to establish one large, unified republic in what would later become Colombia. In the autumn of 1812, Narino was involved not only in preparing to repel Spanish forces seeking to regain the province but also in a series of local wars with neighbouring dictators who were resisting unification. He would clearly be grateful for the services of a former British officer and valued member of General Miranda's military staff. MacGregor decided to go directly to Narino and apply for a commission, as he had done on his arrival in Venezuela.

Before he could do so, however, he had to make arrangements for the well-being of his new wife. Simón Bolívar was too preoccupied with his own affairs to take any interest, so MacGregor travelled with Josefa to the British island of Jamaica, where he spun a hard-luck story about having lost all his valuable possessions in the flight from Caracas – including a library of 1,500 books worth 20,000 pesos – and found lodgings for his wife, no doubt promising to pay handsomely for the accommodation on his return.

From Jamaica he sailed to Cartagena, on the northern coast of New Granada, then made his way south

153

through the mountains to Tunja, where General Narino's government had established itself. The mere mention of Miranda's name in connection with his own was enough to obtain a commission for MacGregor, and he found himself in command of the military district of Socorro, close to the Venezuelan border.

Colonel Rafter reports that MacGregor, 'by the introduction of the European system of tactics, considerably improved the discipline of the troops committed to his charge', who numbered about 1,200. But he was not universally popular in the district.

The soldiers' commanding officer, Colonel Santander – who was later to become President of Colombia – complained that MacGregor had the air of a dictator himself, and that 'my posting has come down to listening, remaining silent, and doing what I am told'.

An official in the district capital of Cúcuta was utterly scathing about MacGregor in a letter to a friend, which, roughly translated, said: 'I am sick and tired of this bluffer, or Quixote, or the devil knows what. This man can hardly serve us in New Granada without heaping ten thousand embarrassments upon us.' It was to prove an extremely perceptive judgement.

It is likely that MacGregor's wife came to join him at some stage during the year or so he spent in Socorro. There is no documentary evidence to support that proposition but, as we shall see, the claims he would later make in relation to his service in New Granada suggest that Josefa must have been there too. Certainly, MacGregor would have had plenty of time to enjoy the company of his wife, since there was little or no fighting in the vicinity of his command. The war was being fought at the other end of the country, where General Narino was heavily engaged in driving Spanish forces from the city of Popayan. As luck would have it, MacGregor's impatience had robbed him of a better opportunity for glory. Bolívar had also sailed to Cartagena, where he had gathered a force of Venezuelan exiles and, with help from local troops, had invaded his country and captured Caracas.

How 'Sir' Gregor would have enjoyed taking part in the triumphal entry of Bolívar into the Venezuelan capital on 4 August 1813, as described by Ducoudray Holstein. 'The friends of liberty,' recalled the General,

who had suffered so severely, surrounded him from every corner of the country, and welcomed his arrival with many signs of joy and festivity. The enthusiasm was universal, reaching every class and sex of the inhabitants of Caracas. The fair sex came to crown their liberator. They spread the ground with many flowers, branches of laurel and olive, on his passage through the streets of the capital. The shouts of thousands were mingled with the noise of artillery, bells, and music, and the crowd was immense.

But while Bolívar was having himself declared dictator in Caracas, MacGregor had to content himself with much less extensive – even if, as some saw it, equally dictatorial – powers in a small part of New Granada. For both men,

155

though, this was to be a relatively brief interlude. In the case of Bolívar, his failure both to mount a decisive military operation against the remaining Spanish forces, and to unite the rest of Venezuela behind him, led to the collapse of his rule within a year and the recapture of Caracas by the Royalists. MacGregor, meanwhile, was merely a spectator as Narino's army was routed by the Spaniards in the summer of 1814 and the Commander-in-Chief surrendered himself to his enemies in order to allow his troops to escape as best they might. So it was that both Bolívar and MacGregor found themselves retreating again to the same place, this time the tiny Republic of Cartagena.

Once more, there appears to have been little personal contact between the two men. MacGregor, according to Colonel Rafter, 'retired to a life of indolent obscurity at Cartagena', while Bolívar was named Generalissimo of the self-styled Congress of New Granada, with which he soon quarrelled on account of his high-handed manner and the suspicion of some in Congress that he intended to use the army he commanded to reconquer Venezuela, rather than to defend New Granada against the Spaniards. By March 1815, there was open warfare between troops loyal to Bolívar – mostly Venezuelans – and the forces of Cartagena, but the arrival off the coast of a powerful Spanish invasion fleet brought the internecine hostilities to an end in May, on the understanding that Bolívar would relinquish his command to a Cartagenan general. Bolívar left to seek refuge in Jamaica, but he did so with a flourish, issuing a proclamation that read, in part:

Granadans and Venezuelans! – I am torn away from you, who have been my companions in so many disasters and battles, to go and live in inactivity, and not to die for my country! Judge of my sorrows and of the greatness of my sacrifice, which I make of my heart, my fortune, and my glory, in renouncing the honour of leading you to victory. The welfare of the army requires it imperatively. I have not hesitated . . . your and my welfare, that of our brethren, of my friends, in fine, that of all, depends on the welfare of the republic. Farewell, farewell!

The document was couched in a remarkable literary style – 'captivating', Ducoudray Holstein satirically called it – and Gregor MacGregor read it with interest. The impression it made on him would be confirmed a few years later, when the Cazique of Poyais adopted a similar florid tone in addressing his people. Francisco de Miranda had provided MacGregor with a template for his military career, but his model of political leadership was to be Simón Bolívar.

For the moment, however, MacGregor remained in Cartagena, and it was there that the making of his legend really began. On 5 August, with the Spaniards occupying an offshore island and poised to assault the city, martial law was declared and every male aged between fifteen and forty-five was ordered to report for military duty. While the 250 or so foreign merchants in the city formed themselves into a defence corps, MacGregor was given command of a native regiment and ordered to destroy crops, roads and villages in the countryside surrounding Cartagena, so as to deprive the expected invaders of food, shelter and easy mobility.

Two weeks later, the Spaniards landed with a force of 6,000 men, but the modern fortifications of the city and the determination of its 5,000 defenders repulsed every attack, with heavy casualties among the best of the Spanish troops. There then began one of the most celebrated sieges in South American history, as the Spaniards settled down literally to starve Cartagena into submission.

During the early part of the siege, the citizens were able to survive on food supplies smuggled in by sea from Jamaica and Santo Domingo, but when the Spaniards increased the number of their warships patrolling the harbour, and placed artillery batteries on either side of it, attempts to penetrate the blockade became too dangerous. The Cartagenans turned to slaughtering their horses and mules for meat, which was strictly rationed. At the same time, many half-starved women and children were sent out of the city to appeal to the Spanish general, Pablo Morillo, for food to save their lives. Morillo fed the refugees, but threatened to send them back if Cartagena did not surrender. Still the city held out: an attempt by its commander to negotiate with the Spaniards was discovered, and the man was thrown into prison.

By November, however, starvation and disease had reduced the number of men able to continue defending Cartagena to just a few hundred, and the fall of the city became accepted as inevitable. The only question was whether to surrender, and face almost certain death, or to use the dozen gunboats the defenders possessed in a desperate attempt to break through the Spanish fleet and escape. After much discussion, the latter course was chosen, and Gregor MacGregor – who had played an honourable, though not conspicuous, part in the siege – was named as one of three officers charged with organizing the exodus.

The heavy guns of the city were put out of action, and the remaining supplies of ammunition rendered unusable, then, on the night of 5 December, MacGregor and his colleagues shepherded all those who could walk or crawl aboard the gunboats, leaving behind the sick and wounded, and some sixty volunteers who barricaded themselves inside a fortress determined to fight to the death. The little boats sailed out into the great bay of Cartagena, blasted their way through the line of vessels guarding the entrance and, avoiding the Spanish frigates patrolling offshore, made for Jamaica without the loss of a single boat.

MacGregor was delighted to find himself welcomed as a hero among the British community of Jamaica, and enthralled many a dinner party there with heavily embellished accounts of his part in the siege of Cartagena. Some of those listening received the impression that MacGregor had taken personal charge of the defence of the city, with one of them recorded as leaping to his feet and proposing an enthusiastic toast to the 'Hannibal of modern Carthage'.

One of the claims MacGregor made was that he had lost two children during the terrible siege of Cartagena. That was almost certainly a lie, probably designed further to dramatize MacGregor's sacrifices in the cause of liberty.

All the available evidence suggests that Josefa did not bear a child until 1817, though that admittedly leaves an unusually long time between the marriage and the first-born, and the fact that she produced two other children indicates that there were no particular difficulties with conception. It would, of course, have been possible for Josefa to produce two children between the summer of 1812 and the winter of 1815, but only if she had left the safe haven of Jamaica and joined her husband in New Granada. If such were the case, it may be that she became pregnant during that period and suffered miscarriages, so that her husband was guilty of hyperbole rather than outright lying. Whatever the truth of the matter, his assertion does strongly imply that Josefa *was* with him during his service in New Granada, sharing both his triumphs and his privations, as she was to do uncomplainingly at various times during the rest of her life.

Given MacGregor's reception in Jamaica, it is highly probable that he and Josefa were offered hospitality among the merchant class that had once shunned him but, in view of the suspicion of idleness mentioned by Colonel Rafter in connection with the Scotsman's first visit, there would have been limits to the islanders' generosity, even for such an heroic figure.

As a soldier of fortune, MacGregor had so far been rather unlucky in the fortune department, so he would not have had the funds to live as he would have wished. At the same time, he very much enjoyed being a military celebrity, and the lust for glory combined with the pecuniary imperative to send him in search of new battles to fight. He had heard much talk of Bolívar during the desperate final weeks of the siege at Cartagena, with many of the exhausted defenders expressing the wish that the Venezuelan had taken charge of the Republic instead of the local general who had subsequently attempted to betray them. MacGregor had noted that Bolívar was gradually coming to be seen as both a man of honour and as the best hope for the independence of the Spanish American provinces. When he heard that Bolívar was raising a new liberation army in the neighbouring island of Santo Domingo, or what is now the Dominican Republic, he left Jamaica – taking Josefa with him – in order to place his military skills at the disposal of his wife's cousin.

This time, Bolívar was more responsive, partly because his betrayal of Miranda was now far enough removed for him to have overcome any suspicion of lingering rancour among the old general's former staff officers, and also because MacGregor had, by all accounts, proved his worth at Cartagena. When MacGregor approached him in Santo Domingo, pointing out that he had been a brigadier general in the army of the Venezuelan Republic, Bolívar was happy to restore him to the rank he had been given by Miranda. Whether the family connection added any weight to MacGregor's case is impossible to tell: Bolívar was not renowned as a sentimental man.

By April 1816, the new expeditionary force was assembled, thanks largely to the financial support of a wealthy naval man from Curaçao who had served in Cartagena, and on

30 April it sailed in a substantial fleet of schooners from Aux Cayes, in Haiti, now called Les Cayes. The destination was Margarita, an island twenty-four miles off the coast of Venezuela, east of Caracas, where a popular uprising had forced the Spanish army to abandon the main town, La Asunción, and take refuge in a fortress elsewhere. This was to be the springboard for Bolívar's new invasion of his country: he would sweep through the north-east, gathering support as he went, before turning his attention to the capital.

The islanders greeted Bolívar as their liberator, but he declined to clear the remaining Spaniards out of Margarita and instead pressed on with his plan to invade the mainland, disembarking his troops at Carúpano, at the western end of the spit of land that reaches out towards Trinidad. The town was protected by a fort, and Bolívar dispatched two forces to capture it, one led by General Manuel Piar, supported by MacGregor, and the other commanded by General Santiago Mariño.

The official report of the ensuing battle, issued by Bolívar's staff, made no reference to MacGregor, reporting that the army 'landed under the immediate command of the supreme chief, in four divisions, and the divisions of General Piar took, after great resistance and heavy fire, the strong fort of Santa Rosa, by storm. The division of General Mariño distinguished itself by its bravery and coolness.'

It may have been politics that prevented any mention of MacGregor, since Bolívar's expedition had been dogged by rivalries and factionalism since its departure from Aux

Cayes, and the 'supreme chief' was at pains to ensure that his petulant staff officers all received the fair share of credit. On the other hand, it is likely that MacGregor took no part in the action, since General Ducoudray Holstein, who by that time had become Bolívar's Chief of Staff, dismissed the storming of Santa Rosa as pure fiction and was furious that the bulletin should have been issued under his name. He later wrote:

> General Bolívar ordered a detachment of about seventy-five men to take possession of the village and the little fort of Santa Rosa, which lies upon a hill, and commands the harbour. No enemy was found in it, but twenty-five half naked and badly armed men; and these retired after having twice discharged a twenty-four-pounder, the only piece of ordnance then in the fort. Not a man was killed, wounded or taken ... The fact is that General Piar, with his twenty-five men, jumped over a low wall of this *strong* fort, and found it empty; the Spaniards had fled as soon as Piar approached and could not have been taken or killed, being already more than four musket shots distant from him.

It was with some surprise, therefore, that Ducoudray Holstein read the official account of the battle, or what he called a 'pompous bulletin, signed with my name'. He asked Bolívar why his name appeared at the end of such 'a ridiculous satire upon our forces, which did not exceed 800 men, but from which seventy-five divided into *four divisions* were more than sufficient to drive twenty-five enemies from Santa Rosa'. Bolivar laughed, and offered the excuse that the printer had been anxious to finish the bulletin before midnight, and that since attempts to contact Ducoudray Holstein had failed, the Supreme Commander had given the order to print the bulletin under the name of the General, who was, after all, his Chief of Staff.

This piece of deception, however, was universally accepted as the historical record of the battle of Santa Rosa, and was even embellished by overseas newspapermen who had no means of verifying its accuracy and who knew their readers were keen to see the Spanish oppressors soundly beaten. Ducoudray Holstein noted, some months later, a report in a North American newspaper referring to the 'famous and glorious victory' at Santa Rosa and numbering Bolívar's army at '7,000 men strong in infantry and 3,000 in cavalry'.

Here was another lesson that Gregor MacGregor would find useful in the future: tell people what they wanted to believe, and the chances were that they would do so without question, especially when the story they were being told was outside their everyday experience, not easily subject to verification, and delivered with some sort of official imprimatur. Furthermore, a good story was likely to become even better in the re-telling, as those who had heard it first sought to impress their own audiences. The Cazique of Poyais would prove to be even more adept than Simón Bolívar at persuading people that the illusions he created for them were really true. Bolívar, like Francisco de Miranda before him, unwittingly played a part in shaping the man who would be responsible for one of the most meticulously created confidence tricks of all time.

In the early summer of 1816, though, MacGregor's interests lay with the large amounts of booty the victorious Republicans found in Carúpano, and which was quickly divided amongst them and loaded aboard their ships – the greatest share naturally going to the senior officers. The Scotsman probably did less well in terms of plunder than those who were close to Bolívar, or those whom the Supreme Commander felt it necessary to placate, for it is certainly true that MacGregor's role in the progress of the expedition continued to be a minor one in comparison to the likes of Piar and Mariño and even some more junior officers. That is, until things began to go wrong.

Bolívar stayed at Carúpano just long enough to double the size of his army with local recruits then, as the Spanish forces began to counter-attack, he put to sea again, heading westwards to the heavily fortified port Ocumare, on the other side of Caracas and about fifteen miles from the scene of his inglorious first command, Puerto Cabello. Republican sentiment was very strong in Ocumare, and Bolívar knew that if he could secure it, he would attract many more willing soldiers and would soon be in a position to march on the capital.

The sight of the fourteen ships of Bolívar's fleet was enough to unnerve the Spanish garrison at Ocumare, which abandoned the place without even firing the heavy guns that defended its harbour. Again, the citizens welcomed

Bolívar as the liberator, and within a few days he could command a force of almost 3,000 men. At first, he used them well. By the second week of July, the Republican troops had driven the Spaniards out of many of the main towns in the region, including Miranda's former stronghold of Maracay, and were preparing to advance eastwards to Barcelona and Cumaná for the purpose of surrounding Caracas. While all this was going on, MacGregor merely kicked his heels at the little town of Choroni, near Ocumare, where he had been assigned the task of recruiting native tribesmen to the cause.

The Spaniards had retreated to the city of Valencia, where – as they had done years before when facing Miranda – they regrouped and waited for supplies and reinforcements. On 10 July, with a strong and well-equipped force, they attacked the vanguard of the Republican army and drove it back towards the sea. Bolívar set out from Ocumare with fresh troops, but before he could reach his main force, it was routed in a bloody, four-hour battle at La Cabrera. Realizing that he was vastly outnumbered, and that he could not hope to hold Ocumare, Bolívar determined at least to save his ships and attempted to sail the short distance along the coast to Choroní. He knew that there MacGregor had gathered some 1,500 men, which meant that the Republicans might be able to make a stand.

When he arrived, however, after a delay of several days caused by unfavourable winds, he found that MacGregor and his troops, alerted by survivors from La Cabrera, had already evacuated the place. They were retreating towards

El General Mac Gregor.

▲The Cazique: an engraving by S.W. Reynolds of General Sir Gregor MacGregor, at the height of his fame in London, from a painting by J.S. Rochard.

◀The Princess of Poyais: Josefa MacGregor, whose exotic beauty caused something of a sensation when she arrived with her husband in London, painted by Charles Lees in 1821.

◄ The Napoleon of South America: Simón Bolívar was perhaps the greatest of the revolutionary leaders who won independence from Spain, but his ruthlessness, autocratic manner and savage punishment of dissenters turned many of his contemporaries against him, and he died a lonely and disappointed man.

▶ The legendary General Francisco de Miranda, the Venezuelan commander-in-chief from whom MacGregor received his first commission in the revolutionary army. MacGregor greatly admired Miranda, and dreamed of achieving similar heroic status.

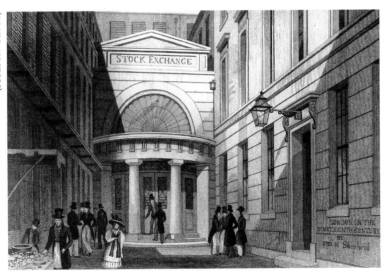

▲ Jane Augusta Richardson, wife of the man who was at one time the Poyaisian chargé d'affaires in London, and sister of Gustavus Butler Hippisley, who helped MacGregor with the Poyais fraud in Paris, and spent many months there in jail with him.

▲ The newly established London Stock Exchange drove the investment mania of the 1820s that allowed MacGregor to float his £200,000 Poyais loan.

PROCLAMATION,

To the Inhabitants of the Territory of Poyais.

POYERS!

On the 29th April 1820, the King of the Mosquito Nation, by a deed, executed at Cape Gracias a Dios, granted to me and my heirs for ever, the Territory of Poyais.

The moment that the situation of affairs in Colombia would permit me, I have hastened to assure you of my firm and unalterable determination to come and spend the remainder of my days, I trust, in peace and tranquillity, amongst you.

POYERS! It shall be my constant study to render you happy, and to exert myself in improving your situation, by every means in my power.

The Territory of Poyais shall be an asylum only for the industrious and honest,—none others shall be admitted amongst us; and THOSE, I trust, you will receive with open arms, as brothers and fellow-citizens.

With a view of avoiding a misunderstanding with our Spanish neighbours, which, under *all circumstances*, would be disadvantageous to both parties, I have this day published a MANIFESTO, addressed to the AUTHORITIES and INHABITANTS of the adjoining SPANISH AMERICAN PROVINCES of HONDURAS and NICARAGUA, giving them the most positive assurances, " that I have no other views *here*, than those which my duty as Chief of this Territory inspires."

Animated with the hope of establishing our neutrality upon a safe and solid basis, as well as to enable me to take the most active measures for procuring you religious and moral instructors, the implements of husbandry, and persons to guide and assist you in the cultivation of the valuable productions for which our soil and climate are so well adapted, I have determined upon visiting Europe; and in consequence, have this day appointed the Governor of San Andres, H. E. BRIGADIER GENERAL GEORGE WOODBINE, M. G. C. to act and take upon him the office of my VICE-CAZIQUE during my absence; charging him to pay the most paternal attention to your interests, and with positive orders to observe the most strict neutrality with respect to the adjoining provinces of HONDURAS and NICARAGUA, as the most certain and sure means of encouraging emigrants to come and settle in our country, and of avoiding the expense of maintaining a large military force, at a moment when all our resources are required for carrying into effect the establishments already projected, and in progress; and I confidently trust, that you will shew to the said Vice-Cazique that respect and attachment which the citizens of all countries are bound to pay and feel towards those who lawfully command, particularly when they exercise their authority with justice and impartiality.

POYERS! I now bid you farewell for a while, in the full confidence that the measures I have adopted for your security, defence, government, and future prosperity, will be fully realized; and I trust, that through the kindness of Almighty Providence, I shall be again enabled to return amongst you, and that then it will be my pleasing duty to hail you as affectionate friends, and yours to receive me as your faithful Cazique and Father.

Given at Head Quarters, in the Camp of Rio Seco, this 13th day of April 1821.

By H. H. Command,
G. DRUMMOND,
Secretary.

GREGOR, CAZIQUE OF POYAIS.

A TRUE COPY OF THE ORIGINAL.
THOMAS STRANGEWAYS, *Aid-de-camp*,
and Captain 1st Native Poyer Regiment.

▲ Documentary evidence: the official version of the proclamation MacGregor claimed to have delivered to the people of Poyais to explain his visit to Britain. Printed some time after the Cazique's arrival in London, it was used to convince people that Poyais was a real place.

POYAISIAN LAND GRANT

NESCIS VINCI

400 Acres

Class C. No. 169¼	**Classe C.** No. 169¼
Grant of 400 Acres.	**Concession de 400 Acres.**

Copy of the Original Grant from the King of the Mosquito Shore and Nation, to His Excellency General Sir Gregor Mac Gregor.

(TRADUCTION.)

Copie de l'Acte de Concession en Original du part du Roi de la Côte et de la Nation de Mosquito, en faveur de Son Excellence le Général Sir Gregor Mac Gregor.

Grant of 400 Acres.

Concession de 400 Acres.

Entered Vol. , Fol.

Enregistré Tom. , Fol.

London April 28, 1834.

▲ One of the impressive certificates sold by MacGregor, entitling the holder to take possession of an unspecified tract of land in a non-existent country. The earliest certificates were hand-written, but that did not stop people scrambling to buy them.

SKETCH

OF THE

MOSQUITO SHORE,

INCLUDING THE

TERRITORY OF POYAIS,

DESCRIPTIVE OF THE COUNTRY;

WITH SOME INFORMATION AS TO

ITS PRODUCTIONS, THE BEST MODE OF CULTURE, &c.

Chiefly intended for the Use of Settlers.

BY THOMAS STRANGEWAYS, K. G. C.

CAPTAIN 1st NATIVE POYER REGIMENT, AND AID-DE-CAMP TO HIS
HIGHNESS GREGOR, CAZIQUE OF POYAIS.

EDINBURGH:

SOLD BY WILLIAM BLACKWOOD, EDINBURGH;
AND T. CADDELL, STRAND, LONDON.

1822.

▲ Guide to nowhere: the title page of MacGregor's guide book, published in 1822. The text went into great detail about the supposed delights and commercial possibilities of Poyais, cribbed from an out-of-date official report and books about other places.

▲ Tropical paradise: an engraving that purports to show the port of Black River, Poyais, taken from the guide book. The picture, and almost everything else that appeared in the book – including, it seems, the name of the author, Captain Thomas Strangeways – were completely spurious.

▲ MacGregor in jail: a satirical view of the Cazique during his incarceration at Tothill Fields prison in Westminster, after his arrest for debt in 1827. He was released after only a week, but it marked the beginning of the end of his career as a confidence trickster.

Barcelona, in the hope of joining up with Piar and Mariño, who were having some success against the Spaniards.

'The conduct of this retreat, by MacGregor', Colonel Michael Rafter later reported, 'has gained him a degree of celebrity, which even all his subsequent errors have not obliterated from the memory of the South Americans.'

It was certainly an ambitious and perilous undertaking, a march covering hundreds of miles across wild mountain ranges and trackless plains, through dense jungle and treacherous swamps, without mules or carts to carry food and ammunition, and with two Spanish armies in pursuit.

As Rafter rather breathlessly described it:

[This] little band of heroes firmly adhered to one another, though suffering the extremes of fatigue and privation; unable, frequently, from the approach of the enemy, to cook the provisions they had killed, their quarters unexpectedly beat up when endeavouring to snatch a moment's repose, so necessary after their fatigues, and necessitated uninterruptedly their route, enveloped in the darkness of night, or sinking under the torrid fervours of meridian day; plunging into morasses, forcing their way through the almost impervious brushwood and tangled gigantic grass, and drenched with torrents of rain, which, at this season, and in this climate, frequently falls with all the fury of the bursting waterspout.

From the very first day, there were constant skirmishes with the Spanish forces, and some pitched battles, in which the retreating Republicans maintained the upper hand, though at a heavy cost in both casualties and precious ammunition. The wounded could not be carried, because the party had only a handful of horses, so they either crawled away into the undergrowth to await death or simply stayed where they fell for the Spaniards to dispatch them more quickly.

On the evening of 27 July, the ninth day of the march, MacGregor found his route blocked by a large Spanish force sent to intercept him at the town of Chaguaramas, south of Caracas and roughly a third of the distance between Choroni and Barcelona. These were elite troops, and their Commander was anxious to achieve what his colleagues had so far failed to do. In spite of the failing light, he ordered an attack. MacGregor's men were tired and hungry, but their desperate situation meant they had nothing to lose, so after firing one volley at the attackers, they rushed forward in a full-blooded charge which so alarmed the Spaniards that they fled into the town. As darkness fell, MacGregor withdrew his fighters into surrounding woods, where they caught and killed two bullocks and enjoyed the best meal they had had since leaving Choroni.

Unwilling to resume his march with the Spaniards so close, MacGregor attacked Chaguaramas the following day, surrounded the town and demanded the surrender of the Royalists, promising that their lives would be spared in return for all their arms and ammunition. The Spanish commander refused, so MacGregor laid siege to the place throughout the day, though he realized that, without cannon, he would never take it. That night, he withdrew his forces again and, after allowing them a few hours' rest, set off once more towards Barcelona. The Spaniards, fearing a new assault, remained where they were in the town, and did not leave in pursuit until after reinforcements had arrived on 30 July, thus giving MacGregor a head start of almost two days.

It was 10 August before the Spanish troops caught up with the Republicans. MacGregor decided to give battle on a site protected by a marsh and a stream near a place called Quebrada Honda. He still had about 1,200 men, though most of them were native warriors who fought with bows and arrows and knew nothing of European military tactics. The Spanish numbers were about the same, but they included 500 dragoons, while the infantrymen were well armed and highly disciplined. MacGregor, however, had displayed genuine military skill in choosing his battlefield: the Spanish infantry were driven back by volleys of Indian arrows as they attempted to cross the rivulet, while the cavalry became bogged down in the marsh and took no further part in the action, except when they fought on foot. The battle raged for almost three hours, until the decisive action came from an unexpected source – Josefa MacGregor.

Josefa had disembarked with her husband in the relatively quiet surroundings of Choroni, and so had been obliged to endure all the hardships of the retreat, riding one of the few horses the party possessed. Reports of her conduct on the march excited the admiration of Colonel

Rafter, who observed that 'with a degree of strength which surpassed her sex, and a courage worthy of an ancient Amazon, [she] rode in the midst of her countrymen and cheered their drooping spirits, or, brandishing her lance, she headed and huzzaed them on to victory.' Towards the close of that afternoon at Quebrada Honda, Josefa 'forgot the softness and timidity of her sex' and, at her husband's side, led the little army in a desperate charge that inflicted heavy losses on the Spaniards and put them to flight.

Rafter wrote,

> During this most trying retreat it is difficult to say which is most worthy of admiration, the able conduct of the Commander-in-Chief, the patient endurance and determined bravery of the Creoles, the fidelity and firm adherence of the Indians ... or the generous and exalted self-devotion of General MacGregor's lady, who, careless of the privations she was suffering, and disdaining the dangers which surrounded her, performed, for her husband and her country, actions which, in more generous ages, would have rendered her name immortal.

After Quebrada Honda, there were no more attacks from the Spaniards, and MacGregor was able to make contact with elements of what was now the main Republican army, which protected his party for the remainder of its journey to Barcelona, where it arrived on 20 August 1816, thirty-four days after setting out from Choroni.

Upon entering the city, MacGregor, flushed with glory, issued a proclamation which, in the extravagance of its language and the grandiloquence of its tone, might have been worthy of Simón Bolívar himself. It recounted, in dramatic fashion, the details of the great retreat from Ocumare, and MacGregor's victories over the Spaniards, and concluded by exhorting the people of Barcelona to offer their support for the great republican dream of Venezuelans symbolized by Simón Bolívar. The mystified citizens, lacking both the means and the will to oppose the Republican army, shrugged their shoulders and went about their business. As for MacGregor, his moment of triumph and his reign as the de facto military governor of Barcelona were short-lived. Not long after his arrival, Generals Piar and Mariño appeared in the city, fresh from their own successful operations against the forces of the Spanish crown and, since they were senior to MacGregor, they immediately assumed command.

'This', wrote Michael Rafter, 'was the zenith of MacGregor's celebrity, and, from this period, his fortune and his fame declined, with a rapidity induced by misconduct and incapacity; and which involved in its fatal vortex, a number of gallant spirits whose actions would have shed lustre on a better cause; but whose names, unfortunately, share the obloquy and reproach which will rest, to all eternity, on the memory of their Chieftain.'

And that was even before Gregor MacGregor had appointed himself Cazique of Poyais.

REBEL WITHOUT A CAUSE

Simón Bolívar was in Aux Cayes, having left Venezuela by sea back in July, when he discovered that MacGregor had withdrawn from the area of Ocumare and that, consequently, there was nothing to stop the approaching Spaniards. The absence of the Commander-in-Chief left General Piar in charge of the now unified Republican army, and he lost no time in establishing his authority – 'a circumstance', wrote Colonel Rafter, 'which gave considerable umbrage to MacGregor, who, perhaps attaching too much importance to his own services, conceived that priority of rank should yield to his extraordinary merits'.

It was Piar who decided, at the end of September 1816, to give battle to a Royalist army that had regrouped and reinforced itself after its disastrous pursuit of MacGregor. It was also Piar who, after the Spaniards had been soundly beaten in the valley of Juncal, some three miles from

Barcelona, rejected MacGregor's recommendation that the Republicans should use their victory to march on Caracas, before the Royalists could recover from their thrashing.

This was too much for the Scotsman, who correctly inferred that Piar was not prepared to tolerate a potential rival. He decided to leave the commander to his own devices and to tout his military prowess elsewhere. In the early days of the expedition, he had formed a great respect for the Republican leader of Margarita, General Juan Bautista Arismendi who, he felt sure, would value his abilities, so, at the beginning of October, he made his farewells to his loyal soldiers and, with Josefa, sailed for Margarita.

Had MacGregor displayed more patience and less pique, however, the course of his career might have been very different. Shortly after his departure from Barcelona, a letter arrived from Bolívar recognizing the remarkable feat of his march from Choroni:

> The retreat which you had the honour to conduct is in my opinion superior to the conquest of an empire ... You will be ranked alongside the illustrious Xenophons and Moreaus for having ensured the survival of the country. You have done even more, saving the remainder of our troops and liberating the people wherever you halted in the course of your retreat ... Please accept my congratulations for the prodigious services you have rendered my country.

Two months later, when Bolívar himself arrived in Barcelona to find that MacGregor had resigned from the army and gone to Margarita, he tried again to show his appreciation, and to encourage MacGregor back into his service with a promotion:

TO THE WORTHY MAJOR-GENERAL GREGOR MACGREGOR

I have the satisfaction of informing you of my arrival here on the last day of the old year, with part of the immense resources I have obtained for the purpose of definitively saving the republic.

One of my first steps in establishing our position must be to reward your notable services by promoting you to the rank of Major-General and by conferring upon you the Order of Liberators ... and to express to you my greatest thanks in the name of the Mother Country ...

It only remains for you to return to our country in order to continue its defence and to offer further proof of its resolution to complete this glorious enterprise in the love of absolute freedom and independence.

Again, it was too late. When Bolívar's letter reached Margarita, MacGregor had already left the island for the United States, where he would attempt to recruit soldiers for a Republican invasion of Spanish Florida. It would be more than two years before he could read the warm praise heaped upon him by the Commander-in-Chief, and by that time his ambitions extended far beyond the desire for recognition and promotion in Bolívar's army.

The Florida expedition was to add a new dimension to MacGregor's life as a soldier of fortune. He was encouraged in it by General Arismendi, who pointed out that if he could seize and hold one of the ports of Florida, he could provide an excellent base for Republican operations in South America, in which MacGregor would obviously have a pivotal position. Still smarting from Piar's arrogant behaviour (for which the General was soon to pay dearly, executed for treason on Bolívar's orders), MacGregor was excited by the idea of making himself governor of part of Florida, a position similar to that of Arismendi in Margarita. The only obstacle lay in raising funds to finance the undertaking, but Arismendi persuaded him that he would have no difficulty in finding both money and volunteers in the United States where, since Mexico had effectively severed its links with Madrid, public feeling was rising against the remaining Spanish presence on the mainland of North America.

Accordingly, just as Simón Bolívar was leaving Haiti to return to Venezuela, MacGregor was travelling in the opposite direction for the purpose of recruiting to his own cause some of the kindred spirits he had encountered during his stay on the island after the fall of Cartagena. In Haiti, he enrolled what he described as a 'hand-picked band' of 105 adventurers of different nationalities, but when it came to the actual departure for the United States, they suddenly melted away, and MacGregor was obliged to sail for Philadelphia with only Josefa for company.

The facts of what happened next are, as so often in the story of Gregor MacGregor, not easy to disentangle. He claimed that he had received a commission from the government of the United States, together with a considerable sum of money, to take possession of Florida on behalf of the Republican movement of New Granada, with the tacit agreement of the Spanish government. He had, he said, attended daily meetings in March 1817 with the American Secretary of State and the Spanish Ambassador in Washington, and they had agreed that he should take a small force to occupy Amelia Island, off the east coast of Florida, which he would subsequently hand over to the Americans. Spain would not attempt any military intervention, so long as MacGregor was seen to be acting in the interests of New Granada: it was willing to cede Amelia to the Americans, but could not do so directly for political reasons – mainly that any display of willingness to give up its American possessions would serve to spread and encourage revolution throughout the South American provinces.

That MacGregor was in Washington in March 1817 is beyond doubt, for in the archives of the State Department is a mandate authorizing him to take possession not merely of Amelia Island but of 'East and West Florida'. The paper, dated 31 March, is not, however, signed by the American Secretary, only by representatives of the Spanish American Republican movements – Lino de Clemente for Venezuela, Pedro Gual for New Granada, Martín Thompson for Rio de la Plata (Buenos Aires) and Luis Aury on behalf of Mexico.

No doubt some State Department official had been involved in the creation of the mandate, but in March 1817 the Secretary of State himself was actually abroad.

The post had been held temporarily by James Monroe, but he had relinquished it on 3 March after his election as President, naming his friend and ally John Quincy Adams as the new Secretary of State. Adams, though, was the American Minister in London, and did not physically move to the State Department until September 1817. Equally, it is unlikely that there was any involvement on the part of the Spanish Ambassador, Don Luis de Onis, who also appears not to have been in Washington during the time MacGregor was there.

The suggestion that MacGregor had the support of the American government is contradicted by the fact that, some years later, when Lino de Clemente presented himself in Washington as the official representative of the then Republican government of Venezuela, the Americans refused to deal with him on the ground that he had been involved in the illegal occupation of Amelia Island. Neither is there substance in the idea that Spain was willing to cede the island to America since, as we shall see, Spanish forces did their best to recapture it.

MacGregor's story was another of his fictions, concocted partly to enhance his status but mostly for the purpose of raising money to finance the venture and to reassure those who might join his 'army' that they would not have much fighting to do. Like his original recruits in Haiti, few men would have committed themselves wholeheartedly if they had known that the Amelia expedition was no more than a speculative and risky enterprise promoted by the unofficial representatives of self-declared South American governments that might at any time be overthrown by vengeful Spanish armies.

MacGregor, however, had no difficulty in convincing a great many people of the legitimacy of his cause, as he visited first New York, then the south-eastern states of South Carolina and Georgia in search of money and manpower. Styling himself 'Brigadier General of all the forces, both naval and military, destined to effect the independence of the Floridas', he rapidly assembled an army of several hundred men, some of them genuine Latin American patriots, but mostly refugees from the now disbanded armies of Europe who had come to seek their fortunes in the United States. As for finance, he was able to amass a large sum in two months simply by selling off some of the land he was supposedly about to liberate. MacGregor issued what he called 'scripts', which, on payment of $1,000 each, promised the bearers either 2,000 acres of fertile Florida land, or their money back with interest.

As Colonel Rafter observed, 'The world is at all times the dupe of some bubble or other, and, although it is scarcely credible, yet it is a certain fact that MacGregor obtained, by this means, $160,000 from the speculative inhabitants of Charleston [South Carolina], Georgia and New York.'

There was a much greater 'bubble' to come. In its audacity and its success, the sale of land in Florida was to be both a model and a dress rehearsal for the Poyais scheme.

Thus enabled to equip his fighting force, MacGregor

sailed from Charleston on 25 June 1817 to begin the invasion of Florida. In just one ship, and with about sixty men, he clearly had no expectation of a serious battle – not because of any Spanish promise of cession, but because his chosen landfall, Amelia Island, was a lawless place in which the Spanish writ hardly ran at all. For years, it had been a haven for buccaneers, criminals, fugitive slaves, gamblers and prostitutes, presided over by a garrison of no more than forty or fifty, commanded by a junior officer, in the main town, Fernandina. MacGregor had every reason to assume that this was going to be conquest the easy way, and so it proved – though the self-proclaimed liberator of the Floridas made the most of the opportunity, as Colonel Rafter reported:

> The order was given to land at one o'clock on the 29th of June; but the heat was so excessive that it was generally supposed MacGregor would not advance till evening. With a degree of firmness and promptitude, however, which unfortunately he has never displayed since, he put himself at the head of his little force and, with a boarding pike in his hand, and exclaiming, 'I shall sleep either in hell or Amelia tonight', he led the attack.

This, together with the fear that there must be a large force in support, was enough for the little garrison to throw down its arms, and the twenty-six square miles of Amelia Island fell to the invaders without a shot being fired.

Taking his cue from Simón Bolívar, MacGregor was magnanimous in victory, assuring the garrison that they had nothing to fear from him and offering to transport both the troops and their possessions either to St Augustine, on the mainland, or to Cuba, where their regiment was based. To the citizens of Amelia, he announced that their lives and property were safe, and that, if they did not wish to remain under the banner of independence, they had six months in which to dispose of their property and leave the island. His next Bolívarian gesture was, of course, to issue a flowery proclamation, 'couched', according to Colonel Rafter, 'in such ridiculous terms of bombast and turgid verbosity as have seldom been equalled, and certainly will never be surpassed'.

The text of this proclamation appears not to have survived, but Rafter must have seen it, or at least received a first-hand account of it, for he wrote:

In this curious document, after extolling the bravery of his troops, which he ascribes to the noble zeal for the happiness of mankind, that influences the sons of freedom when fighting in a great and glorious cause, against a government which has trampled on all the natural and essential rights which descend from God to man; he thanks them, in the name of the governments which he has the honour to represent, and expresses his hopes that, impelled by the same noble principles, having effected the emancipation of the Floridas from tyranny and oppression, he may be happy enough to lead them to the continent of South America to gather fresh laurels in freedom's cause.

He promises them that their names will be transmitted to the latest posterity, as the first who formed a solid basis for the emancipation of those delightful and fruitful regions now groaning under the hand of Spanish despotism; and confidently addresses them, in a brilliant strain of prophetic eloquence, *The children of South America will resound your names in their songs; your deeds will be handed down to succeeding generations, and will cover yourselves and your latest posterity with a never-fading wreath of glory*.

As if this were not enough to place MacGregor alongside the Bolívar who appeared to have rejected him, he ordered that each member of his little force should wear a shield of honour upon his left arm. The round shields, about four inches in diameter, were made of red cloth and were embroidered – in gold for the officers and yellow for the ordinary soldiers – with oak and laurel leaves and an inscription reading: 'Vencedores de Amelia, 29 de Junio de 1817. 7 y 1'. The last two figures referred to the seventh year of independence for Venezuela, and the first year of independence for Amelia. This was the mark of a man who had been the target of resentment and ridicule in his British regiment for his obsessive attention to the tiniest details of uniform and insignia. It was an obsession he could now indulge without restraint, and it would prove to be an extremely useful one in the future.

With his military ambitions satisfied, at least for the moment, MacGregor took it upon himself to set the seal on the independence of Amelia by establishing a government, with himself at its head, naturally. The main purpose of this administration appears to have been to raise money, for one of the first acts of Citizen MacGregor, as he now called himself, was to establish what he described as an admiralty court that would officially value the booty brought back to the island by its resident privateers and pirates. For this service, the court would demand a fee of sixteen-and-a-half per cent of the gross value of the treasure, plus administration costs.

Whether any of the island's maritime entrepreneurs ever took advantage of the offer is not recorded, but to encourage them further in their brutal trade, MacGregor issued so-called letters of marque, which were effectively government licences for buccaneers that helped to protect them in the event of their capture. Again, it is not known whether any of Amelia's motley crews took the trouble to buy the licences, though it seems unlikely, since they had been managing perfectly well without them.

Finally, to underpin this economic activity, MacGregor placed a contract with a printer in Fernandina to produce Amelia Island banknotes, denominated in dollars and cents and signed simply *MacGregor*. These were used mainly to pay his soldiers, much to their discontent.

What the liberator of the Floridas did not seem to be much interested in, however, was actually liberating the mainland. MacGregor appeared to have forgotten the $160,000 worth of bonds he had issued promising land in Florida or money back with interest. In the opinion of Colonel Rafter:

Elated with the facility of his conquest ... and satisfied

that he had merely to express his wish to produce order from confusion ... he yielded to the natural indolence of his disposition ... and gave himself up to those intemperate and unusual enjoyments which seemed to be so necessary to his existence, and the absence of which was the sole punishment capable of making an impression on his apathetic mind.

At first, his excuse for inaction was that he did not have enough men. This was justified to some extent: in open contradiction of MacGregor's claim to have the tacit approval of the United States government, the Americans prevented the departure of the main body of his troops, and threw many of them into prison, so that the largest army he could muster on Amelia Island numbered no more than 200. Still, they would have been sufficient to have mounted an assault on St Augustine or Pensacola, with their small and ill-equipped garrisons, and many of MacGregor's more idealistic recruits – along with those who were simply greedy for the spoils of war – exerted pressure on their commander to pursue the glorious cause of freedom with which he had sought to inspire them.

All MacGregor would agree to was the dispatch of a small force towards St Augustine, its mission being to reconnoitre the Spanish positions and to attract recruits from the area. On 28 July, an open boat armed with one small cannon carried eighteen men across the narrow channel separating Amelia from the mainland. They landed at a little place called Clarke's Mills, where they immediately began to ransack houses in search of booty, infuriating the local residents, who summoned a Spanish force from St Augustine. In the ensuing fight, fifteen of MacGregor's men were killed or mortally wounded, the remaining three taken prisoner. The disaster was enough to blunt the General's appetite for conquest, and to alert the Spaniards, who lost no time in reinforcing their garrisons close to Amelia and in beginning to lay plans for the recapture of the island. So much for MacGregor's assertion about the complicity of the Spanish government in his venture.

With no prospect of further action, and paid first in worthless Amelia dollars and later not at all, the army of independent Amelia Island became increasingly mutinous. When the second-in-command resigned and returned to the United States, and news reached Fernandina that the Spaniards were massing on the mainland for an attack, MacGregor and his wife quietly gathered what possessions and money they had and boarded the schooner *Venus* in Fernandina harbour. On 8 September, as the first Spanish troops landed on the island, the ship sailed for the Bahamas, arriving at Nassau two weeks later.

There, on 9 November 1817, Josefa MacGregor gave birth to a son, who was named Gregorio, while her husband busied himself with the production of a commemorative medallion bearing a representation of the flag of the Floridas and inscriptions reading: 'Amalia Veni Vidi Vici', and 'Duce Mac Gregorio Libertas Floridarium'*.

---

* 'Amelia, I Came, I Saw, I Conquered' and 'Liberty for the Floridas under the leadership of MacGregor'.

Amelia Island and the rest of the Floridas were left to their fate, which turned out to be an interesting one from the point of view of MacGregor's involvement. The occupying force he had abandoned easily beat off two Spanish attacks then, at the end of September, it was considerably reinforced by the arrival in Amelia of 300 men led by Luis Aury, the Mexican representative who had put his name to MacGregor's mandate in Washington. That was enough to dissuade the Spaniards from making any further attempt to recapture the island.

Aury was, in fact, a pirate, but for some time he had been operating under a letter of marque from the Mexican government, supposedly in support of the Spanish American Independence movement, but in reality to make his fortune. His descent in strength on Amelia suggests that his encouragement of MacGregor's invasion arose from an intention to take over the island himself once it had been subdued and, finding that the Scotsman had left, he lost no time in doing so. The original invaders were easily pacified when Aury paid them two months' back pay – in real money – which MacGregor still owed them.

At this point, however, another hidden agenda emerged in relation to the capture of Amelia Island. Aury's Mexican flag had flown over it for just three months when a new invader appeared in the form of an American naval battle squadron and 200 soldiers. In the face of such power, Aury had little choice but to surrender, which he immediately did, and Amelia became part of the United States. President Monroe justified this blatant seizure of the territory of a foreign nation in a brilliant piece of disingenuousness:

> Nothing unfriendly was manifested towards Spain, because the post was taken from a force which had wrested it from her. The measure, it is true, was not adopted in concert with the Spanish government, nor with those in authority under it, because, in transactions connected with the war in which Spain and her colonies are engaged, it was thought proper, in doing justice to the United States, to maintain a strict impartiality towards the belligerent parties without consulting or acting in concert with either ... It gives me pleasure to state that the governments of Buenos Aires and Venezuela, whose names were assumed, have explicitly disclaimed all participation in these measures.

So much, then, for the mandate MacGregor had received – with the approval of the American State Department – from the two Latin American revolutionary governments and Aury as the apparent agent of Mexico. Clearly, what had happened was that MacGregor had been used as a stalking horse by the Americans, who had long planned to take the Floridas from Spain but had no wish to go to war with her. By encouraging the revolutionaries to use MacGregor in what seemed to be their interest, the State Department had actually been pursuing its own design, helping to plot an illegal occupation it could later use as the excuse to gain its first foothold in Florida.

In fact, even as the flag of the United States was being hoisted in Fernandina, General Andrew Jackson was leading an American army towards Pensacola in the first part of a campaign to force Spain to cede Florida, which it eventually agreed to do in 1819.

Gregor MacGregor, meanwhile, ignorant of the power politics that had used him as a pawn, remained in Nassau, basking in the celebrity that the many newspaper reports of his capture of Amelia had brought him. These accounts were, of course, largely inaccurate, and there are suspicions that MacGregor himself was responsible for the information contained in some of them, claiming, for instance, that he had sold Amelia to Luis Aury for $50,000 – a plausible alternative to the truth of his shameful departure from the island, and a useful fiction for obtaining credit in the Bahamas.

The truth was that, although he had fled with what remained of the money he had raised from the gullible land speculators of the United States, he was still nowhere near acquiring the fortune he had believed that South American soldiering would bring him. His brief reign in Amelia had given him a taste of what life could be like for a successful freebooter, especially one who was in command, and he spent a good deal of time formulating plans to raise the sort of finance that would make him equal or, preferably, superior to the likes of the powerful Aury.

Much of this planning took place in concert with the man on whose ship MacGregor had escaped from Amelia. He was a captain of marines named George Woodbine who, after serving with the British army in the war of 1812 against the United States, had become a mercenary on the fringes of the Spanish American Wars of Independence. He was the man whose name would be forever linked with Poyais as MacGregor's deputy (though how much he knew about that is debatable), but at this time Woodbine's buccaneering had been less profitable than he might have hoped, and he was shrewd enough to see great opportunities for himself in the overweening ambition of a man such as MacGregor.

Playing the part of a loyal second-in-command, Woodbine encouraged the late ruler of Amelia to give full rein to his military fantasies, suggesting, among other things, that they might be more easily achieved if the troops on which they depended were drawn from the British Isles. The newspapers in the Bahamas were full of stories about regiments that were being raised in England, Scotland and Ireland for service in South America, usually financed through the London agents of the revolutionary governments, who seemed to be able to raise money easily from wealthy sympathizers and merchants willing to take substantial risks against potential profits. Given the degree of fame MacGregor had achieved through his exploits with Bolívar and in Florida, he should have no difficulty in attracting official support, or money, or men if he were to visit London on a recruiting drive. What the finances and forces he gathered might ultimately be used for was, of course, a matter entirely for him.

All this talk further inflated MacGregor's sense of self-importance. The 'glory' of Amelia Island was merely the beginning. What heights could he not reach on the South American mainland with a British force at his command, rather than the mercurial Creoles and motley collections of Europeans he had led so far? Full of enticing dreams, he sailed for home in the summer of 1818, taking Josefa and baby Gregorio with him.

They landed first, on 21 September, at Dublin, where, as Michael Rafter noted, MacGregor was 'announced very ostentatiously in the public prints, and where the arrival of the *celebrated* Sir Gregor MacGregor excited a considerable degree of interest, though most people were ignorant of the circumstances by which he had become famous; so easy is it to steal celebrity from the opinions of the multitude'. From Dublin, they crossed the Irish Sea to Liverpool, then travelled on to London,

> the theatre upon which he was to commence his career of dignity; and where his arrival was joyfully hailed by a number of adventurers, who foresaw, in this South American bubble, an opportunity for the exercise of their talents, and a new mode of filling their pockets, at the expense of those young men, possessed of more money than wit, with whom that capital abounds.

Bolívar was the name on everyone's lips at the time, since the Napoleon of Venezuela was enjoying considerable success against the Spanish, so it was the Venezuelan representative in London, Bolívar's friend Luis López Mendéz, to whom MacGregor presented himself shortly after his arrival.

Mendéz was delighted to see him, having naturally heard of the heroic retreat from Ocumare, and was able to pass on to MacGregor, at least verbally, the congratulations that Bolívar had tried to send him by letter. There was no doubt that the Commander-in-Chief would very much appreciate the return to his staff of such an able general.

In that case, said MacGregor, he would undertake to raise a substantial force for the Venezuelan service, and transport it to South America in chartered ships, if an advance of £1,000 could be made available to cover expenses. Mendéz had become accustomed to acting with extreme caution in financial matters – he had been duped before by unscrupulous adventurers, with the result that he had spent some time in debtors' prison. In this case, however, MacGregor's fame and the favourable opinion of Bolívar persuaded him to borrow the necessary funds and hand them to MacGregor.

It was a serious error of judgement. For MacGregor, the sophistication and luxury of life in London, where he had first enjoyed sweet, if short-lived, success as a socialite, remained as dazzling as they had ever been, and he squandered his advance in a matter of weeks, with not a soldier recruited or a ship engaged. A furious Mendéz sought MacGregor's arrest, but it was the Venezuelan who found himself in prison once more when the news spread that the loans he had raised had been dissipated. He was rescued by a mysterious gentleman identified only as Mr Newte, apparently a London merchant who interested himself in the liberation of South America, presumably with an eye to future trade there.

Mr Newte assumed responsibility for MacGregor's debt, allowing Mendéz to persuade his creditors that they would be repaid and so to be released from prison himself and to cancel the arrest warrant he had issued against MacGregor. In return, Mr Newte secured MacGregor's services for the independent government of New Granada, with whose London agent he had dealings. There was to be no further cash advance, but MacGregor was authorized to act on behalf of New Granada in assembling a fleet and an army for the purpose of helping finally to drive the Spaniards out of the country.

With no money to disburse, MacGregor was obliged to resort to more dubious methods in order to fulfil his revolutionary duty, and to this end he formed partnerships with some of the adventurers who had rejoiced at his appearance in London. The manner of their operations is described by Michael Rafter:

The great reductions which have taken place in the army, within the last few years, have thrown a number of young men, nearly destitute, upon the world; some of whom, unable to support the expensive habits they had acquired by a long intercourse with fashionable life, unfortunately, have had recourse to measures, which form a decided contrast to the honourable profession of a soldier.

Amongst these, three persons were particularly notorious, each assuming the title of colonel, acting independently of one another, and affecting to have authority, from the South American governments, to raise troops and dispose of commissions ... Colonel G— sold companies [i.e. the rank of captain] as high as £150 each, Colonel O— was more liberal and gave a lieutenant colonelcy for £150, a majority for £100, a troop for £55, a company for £50, and a lieutenancy for £35. Colonel M— still more generous, in consideration of a little ready money in London, would bestow a field marshal's baton in America, or the governorship of an El Dorado, for a trifling check on a Lombard Street banker ...

Numbers of young men, flattered at the idea of purchasing army rank, at so cheap a rate, crowded the levees of these adventurers, romance in their heads and money in their pockets, anxious to be invested in all 'the pride, pomp, and circumstance of war', and to exchange their paltry dross for the glorious prospect of, one day, rivalling, in the new world, the renown of a Pizarro or a Cortez.

These, then, were the methods and the sorts of people MacGregor used in organizing his new expedition. One of his most effective agents was Thomas Eyre, from Galway, whose family were prominent Irish landowners but who had no money himself when his service with the British army came to an end. Eyre sought out MacGregor in London and was rewarded with a colonelcy in the army of New Granada, together with the task of forming what would be known as the Regiment of Hibernia.

Back in Ireland, he bombarded the newspapers with advertisements offering for sale ranks from that of lieutenant colonel down to cadet, and he was overwhelmed with applicants almost desperate to fight for the pride of Hibernia. The measure of his success is shown in the accounts he submitted to MacGregor:

1 Lieutenant Colonelcy	£300
4 Majorities at 200*l.* each	800
80 Companies at 100*l.* each	8,000
50 First Lieutenancies at 50*l.* each	2,500
70 Second Lieutenancies at 25*l.* each	1,750
4 Cadetships at 15*l.* each	60
209	£13,410

About 12 commissions were given for a trifle less than the stipulated sum – say   410

£13,000

Out of this sum, Colonel Eyre used £7,000 to charter four small ships in which to transport his officers and men to England, which left a tidy profit in hand, presumably similar to that achieved by MacGregor's recruiters in London. But the money-raising was not confined to the sale of commissions. Some of the agents simply gave away honorary ranks to ingenuous young men they sought out in public houses and coffee shops, in return for loans that were 'guaranteed' by notes from the 'government' of New Granada, which promised a return of double the amount advanced.

As all this money was amassed, it must have been tempting for MacGregor to spend it on himself, as he had done with the much smaller amount borrowed by Mendéz – but with that debt unpaid, he was reliant on Mr Newte's good opinion so as to avoid going to prison, and Mr Newte was expecting a small army to sail for New Granada at the earliest opportunity. MacGregor had little choice but to see that the plan came to fruition – in addition to which, he remained firmly committed to his dreams of greater riches, not to mention glory.

As well as occupying himself with the lucrative business of attracting officers, MacGregor had to find soldiers for them to lead. In that endeavour, there was no money to be made; it was just a question of placing newspaper advertisements that appealed not only to the soldierly impulse but also to self-interest. An extract from one of them reads:

> Discharged effective soldiers and young men of spirit will do well to direct their attention to the uncommon advantages which are now offered them by entering this service [of New Granada], which is so infinitely superior to any other, that, after *five years*, they will be possessed of an ample provision for themselves and families *for ever*.

The whole exercise was completed in a remarkably short time. By 18 November 1818, MacGregor, his wife and child, and his fairly large headquarters' staff were able to set sail in a former naval brig – appropriately renamed *Hero* – on the first stage of their journey to South America. They were followed about a month later by the four other ships of MacGregor's fleet, carrying some fifty officers and more than 500 troops, 'their minds fraught with sentiments of honour; their hearts imbued with a love of freedom; and their ardour for military glory excited to the utmost', as Michael Rafter put it, remembering that his own brother, William, with the rank of Colonel, had been among them.

That they were all ready and willing to fight was obvious, even if the fighting ability of some of the so-called officers might be doubted, given that their rank depended more on their ability to pay for it, rather than any relevant experience. The problem was what they were going to use to fight with. Not one of the five ships carried arms or ammunition beyond those used by the sailors themselves. It was not an auspicious start to MacGregor's most ambitious military campaign.

THE ROAD TO POYAIS

If the lack of weapons caused dismay among the 'army of New Granada' assembled at Aux Cayes, it was as nothing compared to the effect of another oversight on the part of General Gregor MacGregor. Each enlisted man had been promised a bounty of eighty silver dollars upon arrival at Santo Domingo, and when the money failed to materialize, an ugly mood developed in the ranks which the officers had to work hard to prevent from developing into full-scale mutiny or mass desertion. As usual, MacGregor's extravagant promises were more real in their intent than in their fulfilment, so before he could bring any military skills to bear on the expedition, he was obliged to exercise his considerable ability to persuade people to give him money.

He had assumed that the government of Haiti, as an established native republic, would be generous in supporting his campaign to liberate the mainland, but when he travelled to the capital, Port au Prince, to see President Jean Pierre Boyer, he discovered that Haitian generosity was of the spirit only, with no financial element. The most President Boyer was prepared to offer was a schooner to augment the naval squadron. That might have been the end of the venture, but MacGregor was nothing if not determined, and his next approach was to a group of South American merchants in Port au Prince, appealing not just to their patriotism but also their desire to make profits.

One can imagine the grandiose terms of his exposition – the references to the freeing of subject peoples suffering under the Spanish yoke and to the riches that would become available with independence; the exaggerated descriptions of his motley army, which he had divided into corps, and even regiments with impressive names such as the 1st Lancers, the Rifles and the Guards. Fantastical and ridiculous as all this was, it was enough to convince the merchants, who supplied MacGregor with weapons, ammunition and gunpowder sufficient for all his troops, and who provided him with a line of credit that enabled him to pay the enlisted men and to feed them well.

Now properly equipped, and with the morale of his men restored, MacGregor would have done well to embark immediately on his campaign, but for some reason – Michael Rafter suggests 'imaginary ideas of new born dignity', and 'an amazing degree of indolence' – he wasted a whole month 'in trifling occupations'. It was not until he had reached the limit of his credit, and would therefore have been unable to continue feeding his troops, that, on 10 March 1819, he gave the order to sail. Even then there was more delay. While his fleet made for the island of San Andrés, just north of the isthmus of Panama, MacGregor himself went to Jamaica, ostensibly to find accommodation for his wife and son, but in reality to seek more financial support, having spent all the money he had borrowed at Aux Cayes.

At first, the Jamaican authorities refused entry to MacGregor's ship, since the British government had prohibited trade with Haiti. However, an appeal from 'Sir' Gregor to the Governor, the Duke of Manchester, finally resulted in permission to go ashore at Kingston. Lodgings were quickly found for Josefa and Gregorio, but MacGregor's attempts to raise money proved fruitless, succeeding only in making him deeply unpopular among a powerful section of the merchant class that profited from maintaining good relations with the Spanish authorities in South America.

Worse still, when MacGregor tried to leave Jamaica, his ship sprang a leak and was forced to return to port, where it was impounded after a search by customs officials revealed that it was carrying armaments. MacGregor himself only escaped arrest through the good offices of a merchant named Wellwood Hyslop, who had escaped with him from the siege of Cartagena. Hyslop was one of those traders who hoped to make money from a liberated South America, so he was inclined to help MacGregor, keeping him under protection in his house and eventually securing him a passage on a ship that would take him to San Andrés.

Undaunted by these setbacks, and by the hostility he had aroused, MacGregor left the merchants of Kingston a typically pompous address, which he arranged to have published in the local newspapers:

> Being about to recommence operations against the Spaniards on the main, and knowing, as I do, your connections with that country, and the sensations likely to be produced in this island; I hasten to assure you, that your property, as far as can be identified to be *bona fide* British, shall be respected. Unlike the violent rapacity pursued by Morillo [the Spanish General] against the British interests on his entry into New Granada, I pledge myself to secure you justice, and enable you to withdraw your funds with the least possible difficulty.

The army of New Granada, meanwhile, was quartered on San Andrés, wondering what could have happened to its Commander-in-Chief, and running out of provisions. Colonel William Rafter, elder brother of the future memoirist, Michael, had been entrusted with temporary command of the force, but there was little he could do with the troops in the way of training or preparation for battle, since he had no idea of what their ultimate military objective might be. A resourceful man, and a strong leader, Rafter called together the mostly British inhabitants of San Andrés, informed them that the island was now a dependency of New Granada, and carried out an impressive flag-raising ceremony. Having thus established his authority, he entered into a contract with the local farmers – believing he was acting on behalf of the government of New Granada – to supply his troops with food, then set the soldiers to work building a fort, a naval depot and a military hospital.

As the end of March came, however, and MacGregor had still not appeared, dissension began to spread through the ranks, as it had done at Aux Cayes. Many men wondered aloud what they were doing on San Andrés, and expressed doubts about whether they would ever see action or, indeed, receive the rewards they had been promised. Colonel Rafter was obliged to resort to brutal methods in order to maintain discipline, at one stage drawing his pistol and threatening to shoot any man who did not obey his orders.

The mood was ugly when MacGregor did finally arrive on 4 April, but he was able to restore morale by announcing that, the very next day, the expeditionary force would sail to attack the poorly defended town of Porto Bello, on the isthmus of Panama. To increase the enthusiasm of his troops, he made them all swear an oath of allegiance to New Granada.

'The capture of Porto Bello by MacGregor's troops', Michael Rafter would later write, 'is generally considered as the result of singular good fortune, assisted by cowardice and treachery on the part of the enemy; and little or no credit is attached to the captors.'

As with Amelia Island, MacGregor had chosen to

attack the Spaniards at one of their weakest points, but even so the invasion proceeded less than smoothly. To begin with, the commander of the naval squadron made an error in his navigation, and it was not off Porto Bello that the vessels dropped anchor on 7 April – it was at Rio Chagres, forty-five miles away. By the time the fleet did reach its objective, after two days of laborious sailing against the wind, the Spanish garrison was well aware of its presence, and the element of surprise had been lost.

When William Rafter went ashore with 200 men on 9 April, Good Friday, he found an equal number of Spaniards in a strong defensive position protected by palm and orange trees. Seeing that his soldiers would be cut down if they attempted an assault through the trees, Rafter turned his attention towards the little fort of San Juan, which guarded the town, and decided to approach it from the rear.

However, as the Colonel's brother reported, 'the country round Porto Bello is perhaps the most intricate, bushy and mountainous on the surface of the earth; displaying, at every step, almost impenetrable obstacles, consisting in huge rocks and close-woven thickets ... every yard of the advance affording admirable positions of defence'.

Fortunately, the enemy had not taken advantage of these positions, never imagining that the invaders would venture into such difficult terrain. After many hours of cutting their way through the brush and crossing steep ravines, Rafter's men finally reached hills above San Juan, where they almost collapsed from exhaustion. The plan was to camp overnight and assault the fort at daybreak, but when the Spanish defenders saw Rafter's campfires and realized the enemy had come so far, they slipped away during the night, leaving the assault force with nothing to do but march into San Juan, and then into Porto Bello itself.

Throughout the action, MacGregor had remained on his ship, with his friend and adviser, George Woodbine, now a colonel. The signal of victory from Rafter quickly brought him ashore, where he did what was becoming a habit with him – he issued a proclamation:

> Soldiers! The army of New Granada has covered itself with glory. Porto Bello, the most famous fortress in South America, could only withstand a few hours the valour of our arms. The Light Brigade, under the orders of the gallant Colonel Rafter, overcame obstacles and difficulties, which, only men, animated with your enthusiasm, could have attempted. The advance led by the brave Captain Ross attacked the enemy with such intrepidity, that they fled with fear and astonishment to their walls.
>
> The navy, under Commodore Hudson, in covering the landing, and in the diversion they made in attacking the Spanish forts in the harbour; did everything that their intrepidity gave me a right to expect from them. The Captains and seamen of the transports are deserving of every praise for the exertions they made in landing the troops.
>
> Soldiers! Our first conquest has been glorious, it has opened the road to future and additional fame. Panama

invites our approach, and the South Sea shall soon behold upon her shores the conquerors of the Isthmus.

Well, it had not happened quite like that, but the army of New Granada was entitled to enjoy its first success, and the mood of celebration lasted for several days. According to Michael Rafter, 'MacGregor spent many a precious hour in planning orders of Knighthood, and inventing rewards and distinguishing badges for different degrees of merit: the result ... was the institution of a Chivalric order, the members of which ... were to be decorated with a Green Cross.'

Apart from that,

A short period of the morning he gave to the ineffective consideration of military affairs; in the afternoon, reclined on a couch, he sunk into a lethargic slumber which continued until dinner called him from one enjoyment to partake of another; and the night was devoted to festive orgies, from which was sedulously banished the intrusion of all present cares and all future considerations.

MacGregor did have the energy, however, to send copious reports of the famous victory to the newspapers in Jamaica and in Britain, which

gained him in those places a degree of credit and a number of adherents ... In England, offers of men, money and ships succeeded one another with rapidity, and in Jamaica, the merchants hitherto so cautious, reproached themselves for their former mistrust, and determined for the future to take advantage of the opportunity of suddenly enriching themselves ... In the town of Kingston recruiting was carried on with considerable vigour, and six hundred men, principally disbanded soldiers, were raised in a very short time; several officers of respectability and rank were ready to start at a moment's warning; ships were provided, and Colonel Woodbine arrived from Porto Bello to hasten their departure.

What MacGregor intended to do with all these new recruits is unclear. William Rafter continually urged him to capitalize on the victory at the strategically insignificant Porto Bello and march on Panama, the capture of which would have been a serious blow to the Spaniards, but he does not appear to have formed any plans for susbsequent military operations. In the event, it was a decision he never had to make. Before George Woodbine could sail with his 600 men, the news reached Kingston that Porto Bello had been recaptured by Spanish troops – though the Commander-in-Chief had managed to escape.

In his customary fashion, MacGregor would later absolve himself from any blame for the disaster that overtook his army at Porto Bello. The full details of his self-serving explanation are given, in his own words, at the end of this book but, briefly, he claimed that he had been betrayed by a South American officer and that Colonel Rafter had let him down. The true story appears to have been somewhat different, at least as it was told to Michael Rafter and others by survivors of the debacle.

Within a few days of the victory, the troops were once more in a mutinous state, having again failed to receive a bounty they had been promised. They knew that large quantities of silver coins had been found hidden in the church, and they demanded their share of the booty. Most of them refused to obey orders, and spent their days drinking and fighting among each other, much to the anxiety of the townspeople, many of whom fled to Panama, where the Spanish authorities were very interested to learn of the disorder. MacGregor finally paid the men twenty dollars each, but by then it was too late to restore proper discipline.

The Spaniards, meanwhile, had taken advantage of the insubordination among MacGregor's men – including their reluctance to carry out patrols in heavy rain – and, early in the morning of 30 April, found themselves able to march on Porto Bello along an unguarded road.

Guided by a former Royalist official, the Spanish soldiers made for the main square, where they came upon MacGregor's Rifle Corps practising drill, and shot them down. Michael Rafter described what happened next:

General MacGregor was awakened by the mingled noise of the firing, the shouts of the victors, and the groans of the dying; and his aide-de-camp, Captain Colcough, bursting into his chamber, informed him that the royalists had attacked; upon which this gallant chieftain, whose courage and talent were to guarantee the freedom of America, without waiting to consider whether he might not by his presence retrieve the confusion of his affairs, jumped up and with a promptness and presence of mind which he had been little in the habit of displaying, he seized his bed and blankets, and throwing them out of the window (which was about twenty feet high above the beach upon which it opened) to break his fall, he jumped after them, and without an instant's hesitation threw himself into the sea and ... seizing a log of wood that happened opportunely to be floating near him, he endeavoured to propel it towards the shipping; but fright and fatigue overcame him, and he was picked up in a state of insensibility by Lieutenant Hodnet of the navy, who conveyed him on board the *Hero*, where having been blooded, he recovered at length the use of his faculties.

MacGregor subsequently admitted some of those details of his escape, but in his account, he boarded the ship, which he referred to as *El Macgregor*, and immediately took charge of the situation, raising his standard to let those on shore know he was safe and sending a messenger to Colonel Rafter – who had collected his forces in one of the harbour forts – ordering him not to surrender. In fact, it appears to have been Rafter who sent a messenger to MacGregor aboard the *Hero* obtaining, some little time later, a reply to the effect that he should hold out to the last man while the General organized the fleet to fire on the Spaniards. That, according to MacGregor, was what happened, while he himself, injured though he was by his leap from the building, made arrangements to be transported ashore in order to lead his troops, and would have done so had Rafter not disobeyed orders and surrendered.

The survivors' stories involved a rather different series of events. Safe in the fort, Rafter and 200 men kept up a barrage of fire on the enemy as they waited for the ships' cannon to be brought to bear. Instead of that, they noticed the *Hero* suddenly come about and make for the open sea, the rest of the fleet in her wake. Seeing themselves abandoned, Rafter's soldiers threw down their arms, leaving the Colonel with no option but to try to negotiate whatever surrender terms he could with the Spanish commander. He was no doubt unaware of a decree issued by the Spanish Court that 'all foreign adventurers taken with arms in their hands in our possessions beyond Sea, under the banners of the Insurgents; or who shall have furnished them with munitions or war, shall be condemned to death, and all the property which they possess within the territories of His Majesty shall be confiscated'.

The army of New Granada had lost eighty men dead and fifty wounded during the brief battle, and now more than 300 became prisoners. Seventy of the enlisted men were persuaded to join the Spanish army, others became servants to the officers, and a few who had been artisans in civilian life were allowed to practise their trades in the colony. Many others died of disease or malnutrition during a forced march to Panama City, or under torture. Colonel William Rafter and eleven other officers were summarily shot when the Spaniards discovered that they had been conspiring to escape from their prison camp. The remainder of MacGregor's unhappy force who had been taken prisoner were set to work on chain gangs, until those who survived were freed when the Spaniards finally withdrew from South America.

One man, however, a former Royal Navy midshipman named Mahary, did manage to elude the Spanish troops at Porto Bello and, after much hardship, reached Jamaica, where his story of how MacGregor had abandoned his army achieved wide currency in the press, and was subsequently reported in the British newspapers. It was to these reports that MacGregor was responding when, two years later, at the height of the excitement over Poyais, he published his own highly unreliable version of the events at Porto Bello.

In the early summer of 1819, though, MacGregor was safe on San Andrés, busying himself promoting Lieutenant Hodnet, who had saved his life, to the rank of Captain, and investing him with the Most Distinguished Order of the Green Cross. He also promoted the captain of the *Hero*, Commodore Hudson, to the rank of Rear Admiral of the White Squadron of the National Navy of New Granada, whatever that meant. But his obsession with ranks and titles was still matched by his thirst for conquest and, amazingly, he began to plan yet another invasion of South America.

During his short reign at Porto Bello, MacGregor had received a secret message from leaders of the independence movement in the town of Rio de la Hacha, on the north coast of what is now Colombia, inviting him to drive out the Spaniards and take possession of the place in the name of New Granada. This naturally appealed to MacGregor but, of course, he no longer had an army to commit to the operation. Reflecting on the success of his previous recruiting drive in Haiti, he decided to try his luck there again and, at the end of May, sailed for Port au Prince in the *Hero*, with Admiral Hudson and a handful of still loyal officers.

Unfortunately, news of the fall of Porto Bello had preceded him and, although the full details of his precipitate flight were not known, MacGregor was less enthusiastically received in the Haitian capital than he had hoped. Apart from anything else, he owed too many people too much money, which they now understood that they would never see. He was, however, heartened to learn that three ships and some 500 officers and men were waiting for him at Aux Cayes, dispatched by his successful Irish recruiter, Thomas Eyre, and one of the London agents of New Granada. That would certainly be a force large enough to capture Rio de la Hacha.

Before he could assume command of his new army, though, MacGregor had one problem to deal with. The newly created Admiral Hudson seemed to have become excessively troublesome since his elevation, arguing publicly with the very man who had granted him this honour, questioning his decisions and even ignoring orders with which he disagreed. The voyage from San Andrés had been marked by a series of rows, and MacGregor had reached the conclusion that he must somehow gain control of the *Hero* himself.

The opportunity came when Hudson became ill at Port au Prince. MacGregor had him sent ashore and took over the ship, renaming it *El Macgregor* and appointing as master a former British naval purser, with the rank of Commander in what had now become the 'Navy of the Federated Provinces of New Granada'. Hudson appealed to President Boyer for the return of the vessel, which he actually owned, but when MacGregor laid charges of drunkenness, insanity and mutiny against the 'admiral', Boyer refused to become involved, and simply ordered the ship to leave Port au Prince within forty-eight hours, which suited MacGregor perfectly.

He would not enjoy his prize for long, however. He did succeed in sailing the brig to Aux Cayes, though most of the crew had deserted as a result of MacGregor's appalling treatment of her owner, but when, a couple of weeks after his arrival, the vessel was seen to be dragging her anchor in the harbour, there were too few seamen aboard to right her, and the commandant of the port had to be summoned to take charge. This gentleman took a crew and beached the ship which, within a few hours, had been stripped of masts, rigging, cannon, anchors and everything else that could be carried off by the local population. All that remained was the hull, which MacGregor was fortunate to sell for 500 dollars.

Now styling himself 'Captain-General and Commander-in-Chief of the Land and Naval Forces of New Granada', MacGregor had an army, but no means of transporting it, the ships in which the men had travelled from Britain having sailed away when their charters ended and the captains realized there was unlikely to be any further payment for them. The situation improved shortly after the loss of the brig when Colonel Eyre reached Aux Cayes at the end of July, bringing two ships and 400 troops with him. A grateful MacGregor immediately promoted Eyre to the rank of General and awarded him the Order of the Green Cross.

The Commander-in-Chief had further cause for satisfaction in the middle of August, with the appearance of the schooner *Amelia*, named for MacGregor's 'triumph' in Florida and sent from London by the mysterious Mr Newte with a large quantity of muskets, pistols, sabres, gunpowder and a range of other military supplies. But although this meant MacGregor had all he needed for an invasion at Rio de la Hacha, he seemed reluctant to give the order for the operation to proceed.

His hesitation proved to be costly. To begin with, it had a devastating effect on the morale of his soldiers, many of whom – after weeks of inactivity, sparse rations and no pay – abandoned the enterprise and sailed for home on whatever vessel would give them passage. The second consequence was even more serious. Not long after the arrival of the *Amelia*, a British warship entered the harbour of Aux Cayes with orders to seize the schooner which, it appeared, had failed to heave to when challenged during its voyage across the Caribbean, and had actually fired at the naval vessel that had attempted to force it to stop for inspection. The Haitian authorities claimed jurisdiction over the *Amelia* and refused to hand her over, but when port officials discovered that she was loaded with munitions, and travelling on a false bill of lading that gave her destination as New Orleans, they impounded the schooner themselves and placed her under guard.

This seemed to be a fatal blow to MacGregor's plan – which, of course, he had announced in a flowery proclamation a few days after arriving at Aux Cayes – to drive the Spaniards out of the northern part of New Granada. Some of the officers recruited by Thomas Eyre, already disgusted by the lack of food and pay, and by the general air of confusion, fell into despair at the news of the sequestration of the *Amelia*. One night, they quietly boarded the ship that had brought them from Britain and sailed away, taking a large body of enlisted men with them.

The Commander-in-Chief appeared hardly to notice, as it was reported to Michael Rafter:

In the mean time Generals MacGregor and Eyre were living at Aux Cayes, surrounded by all the comforts of life, and studiously avoiding a contemplation of the miseries they had occasioned; the latter unfeelingly refusing even the slightest assistance to those starving officers, whose mistaken liberality had rescued him from the gloom of a prison, and placed him above the reach of want; and the former immersed in those indolent and sensual gratifications, in which he took every opportunity of indulging; now particularly enabled to do so, by the possession of five hundred dollars which he had received as a remuneration for the loss of the *Hero*.

It is difficult to avoid the conclusion that MacGregor,

although he sought glory and fame, would always put off the military adventures by which he might achieve those things until he had absolutely no choice but to act. He thoroughly enjoyed the preparation – which, of course, could also be profitable – and he loved to play the role of supreme commander, with all the privileges that accompanied it. But he could not bring himself to assume real command until he was in danger of becoming completely destitute and deserted by the troops without whom his privileges and his dreams could not have existed – and until, that is, he finally managed to combine all his fantasies in a single risk-free concept, the creation of Poyais.

As he idled away the weeks at Aux Cayes in the summer of 1819, hundreds of the disillusioned soldiers gathered there became ill with diseases such as yellow fever – of which many died – or simply drifted away to other parts of the West Indies and to North America in search of some reliable means of supporting themselves, all their hopes shattered. By the time MacGregor did make up his mind to sail for Rio de la Hacha, the 900 officers and men he had assembled for the operation had dwindled to fewer than 250.

What prompted him finally to act was the arrival in Haiti of yet another ship from England, the *Lovely Ann*, again sent by the London representatives of the government of New Granada. Aboard were sixty-one enlisted men and forty officers, among them Michael Rafter, who had purchased a lieutenant-colonelcy in order to reach South America so that he might help to rescue his brother, William, whom he believed was still alive and imprisoned in Panama after the calamity at Porto Bello.

These newcomers had been led to expect – on the basis of letters sent by MacGregor to his sponsors in London – that a large and well-equipped army would be awaiting them. When they discovered the true situation, fifteen of the officers immediately resigned their commissions, and the others could only be persuaded to stay by the promise of a speedy departure for battle. In addition, the *Lovely Ann* carried provisions enough to feed some 200 people for twenty days, and MacGregor was able to have these distributed among the remnants of his force on the understanding that the expedition would sail before they were exhausted.

There remained, of course, the problem of weapons, but when the Haitian President saw the prospect of all these troublesome foreigners departing, he agreed to release the *Amelia* and her cargo, so that MacGregor had no further excuse for delay. On 29 September, the *Amelia*, the *Lovely Ann*, and a single-masted cutter the Commander-in-Chief had somehow acquired, made sail and headed out of the harbour of Aux Cayes, on a south-easterly course that would take them to Rio de la Hacha.

'On board the *Amelia*', wrote Michael Rafter,

the Commander-in-Chief assumed, in its fullest extent, the dignity of his situation; which, in so confined a space, and under so many disadvantages, had the appearance of a burlesque upon grandeur; and was really productive of much inconvenience. The weather side of the quarter deck was always held sacred for the perambulations of His Excellency, while twenty officers and three ladies, huddled together on the lee side, gazed on the mighty man, whose thoughts were supposed to be pregnant with the destruction of armies and the fate of empires.

After an uncomfortable voyage of six days, in gales and heavy seas, the *Amelia* signalled to the rest of the fleet, 'The enemy's port in view,' and entered the harbour of Rio de la Hacha with the flag of New Granada at her masthead. Instead of the welcome he expected from a grateful citizenry, however, MacGregor was greeted by a volley from the shore batteries, and his ship was forced to turn tail. For the rest of the day, the little fleet floated uncertainly outside the harbour, while MacGregor and his officers argued about when and where to attempt a landing. Eventually, the vessels dropped anchor some three miles west of the town, and the soldiers were told to prepare to go ashore at midnight.

When the time came, MacGregor was asleep in his cabin and, woken by one of his staff, devolved command of the invasion force to Lieutenant Colonel William Norcott, one of Eyre's Irish recruits and an experienced soldier. Neither MacGregor nor any of his staff officers took part in the landing, which was unopposed – an extraordinary piece of good fortune, since Colonel Norcott discovered that some of the men under his command did not even know how to fire a musket.

For the next two hours, the little band – in units grandly named the Rifle Corps, the Guards and the Regiment of Hibernia – waited on the beach for the promised arrival of MacGregor to take charge of the assault on Rio de la Hacha. The Commander-in-Chief did not appear. The enemy, however, did: some 600 Spanish and Creole troops, who surrounded the invaders and killed or wounded twenty of them with their first volley from the woods bordering the beach.

In such an exposed position, Norcott's only means of defence was attack and, in a remarkable display of skill and courage, he and his men launched themselves at the enemy and drove them back to the fort that protected the town. There, the Spanish cannon opened up on the attackers, causing heavy casualties. Norcott realized that retreat would be suicidal, because he was so heavily out-numbered, so again he did the only thing he could. With Michael Rafter at his side, he led an all-out attack on the fort, which so shocked the defenders that most of them fled, and Rio de la Hacha was left in the hands of the army of New Granada.

MacGregor, meanwhile, was still at sea. He and his staff had attempted to land at about four o'clock in the morning, but had been fired upon and quickly retreated to their boats. Aboard the *Amelia*, they could hear the battle raging on shore. When the firing died away, while Norcott planned his attack on the fort, MacGregor assumed that his army had been wiped out, and ordered the fleet to position itself further offshore. The vessels moved in closer again when the fighting was resumed, but MacGregor refused to land even when the flag of New Granada was hoisted at the fort, believing that it must be a decoy.

It was not until later in the morning, when Norcott rowed out to the *Amelia* to report their victory, that the Commander-in-Chief could be persuaded to enter the harbour with his ships and drop anchor. And it was a full twenty-four hours before he could be induced to step ashore, 'fearful', as Michael Rafter put it, 'of encountering the resentment of his troops' at his absence during the battle in which some eighty of them had been killed or wounded.

MacGregor's fears were not entirely unjustified. When he did appear in Rio de la Hacha, many of the soldiers spat and swore at him, while others threatened to shoot him. 'Discouraged by such a reception he sought relief in another quarter, and collecting around him a few miserable, ragged inhabitants, some Indians and women, he wasted the day with them in fraternal embraces, in cries of "Viva la Patria!" and in drinking "healths five fathoms deep" to the success of the glorious cause of Independence.'

Then, as will now come as no surprise, he issued one of his bombastic proclamations. The text of this document has not survived, but MacGregor apparently signed it as 'His Majesty the Inca of New Granada'. Already his fantasies were reaching new heights. The title of Cazique of Poyais lay not too far away.

The proclamation was the summit of MacGregor's reign as Inca. As at Porto Bello, almost from the moment of his entry into Rio de la Hacha, the victory of his force began to be dissipated and the seeds of ultimate disaster were sown.

Michael Rafter observed: 'General MacGregor displayed so palpable a want of the requisite qualities which should distinguish the Commander of such an expedition, that universal astonishment prevailed amongst his followers at the reputation he had for some time maintained.'

They could only conclude that:

> The distance of Europe from the theatre of his exploits, and the garbled accounts of his achievements, which his partizans had found it in their interest to impose upon the public, are circumstances which materially favoured the cheat, and gave him a degree of celebrity which he was far from meriting. At Porto Bello, his indolence, his want of military talents, of decision and of courage, caused the loss of the place and the destruction of his troops; and instead of appearing to profit by experience, his proceedings at Rio de la Hacha were so palpably similar, that even the meanest soldier saw, and expressed his opinion of his incapacity, and with a melancholic countenance prophesied an equally fatal catastrophe.

Disorder and drunkenness rapidly spread among the victorious troops, who even began to fight and kill each other. Norcott and Rafter were unable to maintain discipline, because they were never supported by MacGregor. As at Porto Bello, soldiers refused or neglected guard duties, and most of the inhabitants of Rio de la Hacha abandoned the town, fearing both the depredations of the occupying force and the return of the Spaniards. It was a pathetic empire over which the Inca held sway. Nor was there any prospect of moving on. The Spaniards had substantial forces in the region, composed mainly of loyal Creoles, and the local Indians were almost uniformly hostile to the new invaders. Within less than a week of the victory, Norcott and Rafter saw the situation was hopeless, and decided to leave.

They had been fortunate enough to capture a Spanish schooner, which had unwisely entered the harbour, and on 10 October, along with three senior and two junior naval officers, and accompanied by twenty-seven soldiers and sailors, they boarded this ship and sailed away, leaving to their fate MacGregor and those foolish enough to stay with him.

The very next day, the Inca received news that a huge force of Spaniards, Creoles and Indians was massing to attack Rio de la Hacha. He called together his remaining officers and exhorted them to defend the town with their usual bravery, promising to lead them personally in the coming action and awarding them all promotions and Orders of the Green Cross. As soon as the ceremonies were over, however, MacGregor suggested to General Eyre that it would be best to send the general's wife and two children to one of the ships for safety – in fact, he would take them himself, and return with more men to assist in the defence.

What he actually did, of course, was place the Eyre family aboard the *Lovely Ann* then board the *Amelia* himself, and give the order to weigh anchor. As the ships sailed out of the harbour, the attack on Rio de la Hacha began. It ended with the deaths of General Eyre and every other man, woman and child who had been left there by Gregor MacGregor.

The news of Rio de la Hacha, and of MacGregor's conduct there, soon spread throughout the warring provinces of South America, and through the Caribbean. When His Majesty the Inca eventually arrived back at Aux Cayes, he was greeted with contempt, and the *Lovely Ann* was impounded by the authorities, forcing him to flee in the *Amelia* to avoid its sequestration. MacGregor's reaction was to write to the Kingston merchant Wellwood Hyslop and his colleague, Thomas Higson, thanking them in extravagant terms for the help they had given to the cause of independence, and conferring upon them the Order of the Green Cross.

In one respect, it was as well that he did so. Poor Josefa and Gregorio had long since been evicted from the lodgings in which MacGregor had left them, because they had no means of paying for them, and had taken refuge in the hut of a black slave. They were saved from destitution by Mr Higson, partly, no doubt, in gratitude at the honour bestowed on him by the Inca of New Granada.

MacGregor himself was in no position to take advantage of Higson's generosity and rejoin his wife and child. The British authorities in Jamaica had issued a warrant for his arrest on a charge of piracy, so the island was barred to him. Nor could he turn back to Simón Bolívar, although he had by now received the leader's congratulations for the Ocumare affair, and the letter promoting him to the rank of Major-General. After Porto Bello and Rio de la Hacha, Bolívar issued an order stating that if MacGregor should set foot on the South American mainland, he was to be arrested, charged with treason and hanged. Equally, he could not return to England, having so badly let down Mr Newte and with the threat of prison still hanging over him because of the unpaid debts incurred during his recruiting campaign.

Where he actually did go after his flight from Aux Cayes is unclear. What is known is that, in the early months of 1820, he was at Cape Gracias á Dios with the King of the Mosquito Nation negotiating, in the course of a drunken evening, the land grant that he would convert into the mythical state of Poyais.

The likelihood is that, on leaving Haiti, MacGregor headed for the island of San Andrés, where he had left a small garrison before the attack on Porto Bello. He had already circulated a story absolving himself from blame for the destruction of the Porto Bello expedition, and he concocted another fiction – which he would later publish in Britain – placing responsibility for the disaster at Rio de la Hacha on the 'desertion' of Norcott and Rafter, and accusing them of looting the town. Whatever was said about him, there were always those willing to believe MacGregor, and San Andrés was one place where he was likely to have found people with no particular reason to think ill of him.

It may be that, on San Andrés, MacGregor met up again with George Woodbine, which might explain why his name appeared in connection with the Poyais scheme, and it is possible that there he also encountered for the first time the Captain of the *Honduras Packet*, which was to become the first emigrant ship to Poyais. Both men would have known the trading port of Cape Gracias á Dios, and either could have suggested to MacGregor that there might be business for him there.

Whatever the sequence of events, and whoever was involved in it, the fact is that San Andrés was just a day's sailing from the Mosquito Coast, and it was there that, as his military career came to an inglorious end, Gregor MacGregor took the decision fully to embrace the profession of confidence trickster.

PART THREE

STATE OF CHAOS

FATAL SHORE

The true history of Gregor MacGregor was, of course, unknown to the unfortunate immigrants to Poyais in 1823, as they huddled, sweating, wet and – more often than not – hungry, in their tents and makeshift huts on the shores of the Black Lagoon, during the humid rainy season of the Mosquito Coast. In their ignorance, it was not the counterfeit and faithless Cazique most of them blamed for their increasingly desperate position, but the agents who had misled them, the merchants who had sold them short, the ships' captains who had deserted them and, in particular, the leader of the expedition, Colonel Hall, and the lazy, incompetent officers he had brought with him.

'We declare', a group of the eventual survivors swore in an affidavit to the Lord Mayor of London after their ordeal, 'that it is our true belief, that had Sir Gregor gone out himself, or if he had sent honest men there for managers, that the settlement would have gone on very differently from what it did.'

The men who signed that affidavit, however, were all hired labourers, ill-educated and with the low expectations and mulish determination of a class accustomed to abuse by their social superiors, and to a daily struggle for survival. They were not inclined to waste time in reflecting on the fact that there should have been an actual settlement there waiting for them, with land for the farmers and jobs for the labourers; there should have been a government, a civil service to help the settlers, an army to protect them, a bank in which they could deposit the Poyais dollars they had bought, or from which they could draw their wages. That, it was clear, had been just talk. What faced them now was reality, and what they wanted above all was for those placed in authority over them to recognize that, and to take charge of the situation so that the best could be made of it. Among such men, disappointment was a fact of life, something that just had to be accepted and overcome.

James Hastie, the Edinburgh sawyer who wrote a brief account of the Poyais settlement when he eventually made his way back to Scotland, observed:

I think it should have been evident to our governor, that the place where we were fixed, although it might be very well for a fort and a landing place, was neither a healthy nor a good place for final settlement, both owing to the lowness of the situation and the soil, which was mere sand, unfit for raising vegetables or pot herbs . . . Had we been on higher land a little farther up the river, where the soil was good, things might have been very different . . . And, in short, if things had been properly managed by our officers, we might have been comfortable enough, and doing well for our families; but our rulers never seemed hearty in the cause, or to go about it properly, and it seemed as if they had some separate affairs of their own to manage.

In fact, all that Colonel Hall, his 'officers', and the immigrants who had bought land sought to manage was a speedy departure from the place, to confront Gregor MacGregor and, if possible, to recoup at least some of the money he had tricked them into investing.

These were people unused to hardship and unfitted for pioneering. Many of those who had bought what they believed would become farms worked by native labour were elderly and, further weakened by the unhealthy climate of the Mosquito Coast, and by the diseases borne by the brackish water of the swamp and the mosquitoes that infested it, they had no chance of being able to build their own houses or clear land in order to cultivate their own food crops. Indeed, they were among the first to succumb to the fevers and other illnesses that would ultimately claim the lives of two-thirds of the passengers who had set out with such high hopes aboard the *Honduras Packet* and the *Kennersley Castle*.

As for Colonel Hall and the other supposed leaders of the expedition, they had come to Poyais in the expectation of assuming positions in an established administration or military structure not dissimilar to the ones they knew in Britain, which was what they had been told by His Highness the Cazique. In their minds, there had never been any question of having to assume responsibility for the creation of a new settlement in virgin land.

They had been led to believe that they would find homes in or near a great city that was essentially European in style, and peopled by men and women like themselves, including English and Americans. In the event, the only people they found living in Poyais, apart from the natives, were two eccentric Americans, named Murray and Windship, who had built themselves a farm in the hills behind the Black Lagoon a couple of years earlier. In was hardly surprising, then, that when the likes of Colonel Hall, the 'civil servants', the 'officer class' and the 'manager of the National Bank of Poyais' realized that they had been comprehensively duped, their first thought should have been to escape from the inhospitable wilderness in which MacGregor's deception had deposited them.

On the other hand, there can be no doubt that part of the tragedy of Poyais was the failure of the men who, through their social position alone, would have been regarded as the natural leaders of the group, to adjust to the uncomfortable and dangerous circumstances created by MacGregor's lies, and to show some of the capacity for leadership that might reasonably have been expected of them. Instead, when the conditions they found on their arrival did not correspond in any way to those promised, and under which they had embarked on the venture, they took the view that because the authority conferred on them by MacGregor was obviously as bogus as the country he had described, it was no business of theirs to try to compensate for his betrayal.

That was perfectly true in one sense. Colonel Hall, for example, was surely under no obligation to act as lieutenant governor of a province that had never existed, or as the nominated representative of a prince whose domain was clearly nothing more than a figment of his imagination. Yet, in purely human terms, he might be considered remiss for not paying more attention to the plight of those who felt that, in the natural order of things, they should be able to depend on him to make decisions and offer guidance. As James Hastie remarked:

> I do not wish to say anything rashly; but instead of attending to make us comfortable, it seemed as if every one was for his own hand; – even the boards and timber used for fitting up our berths in the ship were mostly sold, or delivered by Mr Goucher [one of the 'officers'] to Messrs Murray and Windship, instead of being, as was intended, put under our mattresses as bedsteads and bottoms ... Whether they acted fairly by us, or according to Sir Gregor's intentions, they will surely have to explain ... It is evident, however, that the determination of all parties in authority was to break up the settlement, and carry off the stores, at all hazards.

Whether Hastie was acting fairly in his criticisms is also a matter for debate, though. He gave Colonel Hall no credit for the positive actions he did try to take in order to extricate the hapless immigrants, while he and his friend, Malcolm McDougal, were under no more obligation to be led than Hall was to lead them. Had they been as determined to make the best of their situation as Hastie suggested in his account of the affair, they could easily have taken themselves off and built houses however and wherever they liked, and cleared as much land as they needed in order to survive, as the two Americans had done.

The truth is that, 'seeing nothing before us but confusion', as Hastie put it, nobody really knew what to do. The shock of finding themselves marooned in a hostile environment, when what they had looked forward to was a comfortable future in a well-organized land of plenty, must have been immense. It certainly led to one suicide. A cobbler from Edinburgh, who had left behind his wife and family to take up the appointment of Official Shoemaker to the Princess of Poyais, when he understood the awful truth of the settlers' predicament, lay down in his hammock and fired a pistol into his head.

Some of the braver souls among the gentlemen decided, after Colonel Hall's first fruitless visit to Cape Gracias á Dios, that if the natives would not help them, they must attempt to reach the British colony at Belize, 500 nautical miles to the north of them. Without the tools to shape timber sufficiently for the construction of proper boats, they set about making canoes from saplings and animal hides. Several men set out on the hazardous voyage, but their flimsy vessels barely carried them beyond the entrance to the lagoon, and when one man drowned, further attempts were abandoned.

There seemed to be some hope of relief, if not rescue, in the middle of April, when Colonel Hall had returned from another visit to Cape Gracias á Dios with the news that a ship named the *Skeen* was to be expected at any moment, loaded with supplies and money sent from England to sustain the settlers, and possibly also to evacuate some of those who wished to leave. But, though anxious eyes continually scanned the horizon, no vessel was sighted and, as the days went by, the condition of the party steadily worsened.

James Hastie remembered:

About the middle and end of April, sickness and despond-ency was so general, that few were able or willing to make any exertion; and I am sorry to have to add, that many of those who were still well, plundered instead of assisted their sick bretheren. And likewise plundered the public stores of any thing they could conveniently lay their hands upon.

Observing all this, he continued to be suspicious of the supposed leaders of the party, noting in his memoir that:

The medicine-chest was said to have run dry, although since I came home I found by inquiring at the druggists, that a full supply for 300 men for twelve months had been sent out with us. What became of these, and the cordials, and preserved provision for the sick, Dr Smith can perhaps tell; none of them, so far as I know, were given to the men, except a few dozes [sic] of salts, and similar medicine.

Thus far, the two deaths among the settlers had been the results of suicide and accident, but now the diseases borne by the water and the myriad insects of the swamp began to take their toll. Five men died during April, together with three children – one of them James Hastie's. Since the *Skeen* had not appeared as expected, Colonel Hall felt he had no alternative but to go back to Cape Gracias á Dios, to plead again with the Mosquito King for help and, with luck, to find either some message from England that aid was on its way or, better still, a ship with a captain willing to save the Poyais settlers from what was beginning to look like certain death.

When rescue did come, however, it was from a different and completely unexpected source. Two weeks or so after the departure of Colonel Hall for the cape, a schooner hove to off the entrance to the Black Lagoon – and it was flying a British flag. Was this the *Skeen*, which they had been expecting for so long? The settlers made frantic signals from the shore, then watched with mounting excitement as a boat was lowered from the ship and slowly made its way towards them. The two men who stepped from the boat were immediately surrounded by a chattering throng, demanding to know who they were, what their ship was and whether they had been sent to supply the settlement or to evacuate its inhabitants.

The vessel was not the *Skeen*. She was the *Mexican Eagle*, dispatched from Belize with gifts for the Mosquito King from the superintendent of the British colony, which carried on trade with the natives. Her passengers were the Chief Magistrate of Belize, Marshal Bennet, and his clerk, a Mr Westby, who were expecting to meet King George Frederic at the mouth of the Black River.

They knew nothing of any plans for British settlements on the Mosquito Coast, and had never heard of the Cazique of Poyais. So far as they knew, in fact, there was no such place as the Territory of Poyais, though they were aware that, sometime during the previous century, there had been a small British colony in the region, at a place called St Joseph, but it had long since been abandoned on the instructions of the government in London. They could well believe that King George Frederic, keen for support from Britain, might have made land available for settlement but, from what they knew of him, he would not have devolved its government. Indeed, there was no government to speak of. The King controlled only one of the tribes in the country, his authority was frequently challenged, and it was doubtful whether he had the power to determine the ownership of large tracts of land in the interior.

Mr Bennet listened sympathetically as the settlers told their tragic story. He could not say whether they were the victims of a gigantic fraud, since he did not know what had been the agreement between Gregor MacGregor and the Mosquito King, but he was sure that the British government would have had no hand in the settlement of the territory, because it had always resisted George Frederic's appeals that it should be declared a British colony. Nor could he be sure of the legal position of the people who had bought land, though it appeared they had done so under a false impression: that could only be determined back in London.

One thing the Chief Magistrate was clear about, however, was that the labourers who had been hired by MacGregor owed no duty to him because they had not received their promised wages, and there was equally no obligation upon those appointed to civil or military positions since, quite simply, no relevant authorities existed.

It was not up to him, Bennet said, to tell the deceived settlers what to do, but what he could say was that if any of the artisans in the party would care to return with him to Belize, they would be sure of finding plenty of work there, and at wages considerably better than those promised to them by this so-called Cazique of Poyais – which, of course, they were not going to receive anyway. Ominously, he added that the only piece of advice he could give them was not to stay where they were: if they did, they would surely die.

There was no great enthusiasm among the party for going to Belize. Most hoped that Colonel Hall would return with news that he had secured them a passage back to England, while James Hastie and some of the other labourers were for striking into the interior to find a healthier climate and better land where they would risk settling. The Americans Murray and Windship seemed to be thriving, and there was no reason why they should not do the same.

Their lives would certainly not be as comfortable and prosperous as they had imagined when they set out, but the possibilities remained more attractive than returning home to what amounted to a sort of serfdom in some grimy city. Surrounded by timber for building, an abundant supply of game and edible plants for the table, and every prospect of being able to grow their own crops, they would live free and, best of all, they would be their own masters.

A few days later, however, any decision was effectively taken out of the hands of the settlers. Colonel Hall arrived back at Black River, bringing with him King George Frederic and his tribal elders for their meeting with the representatives from Belize. Bennet and Westby came ashore and held a conference with the Colonel and the King, at the end of which Hall called the settlers together.

According to one of the eventual survivors of the expedition, Edward Lowe, from Pimlico in London, Hall announced that the King had now revoked the grant of land he had made to Sir Gregor MacGregor, angered by what appeared to be the latter's assumption of sovereignty over it. George Frederic had not given MacGregor the title of Cazique, and MacGregor had no more right to sell land in the Territory, or to raise loans against it, than he would have had in England. Consequently, any contract into which anyone had entered with the self-styled Cazique was null and void. Strictly speaking, the settlers were in the King's territory illegally, and they must leave – unless they were prepared to swear an oath of allegiance to George Frederic.

'Failing which', James Hastie added in his account, 'he would bring down a strong force and massacre every man of us.'

Colonel Hall went on to say that he was in no position to instruct the settlers to leave. From Cape Gracias á Dios, he had sent a letter to MacGregor resigning his 'offices' and informing him that he could take no responsibility for the fate of the party. Every man must now make his own decision. Mr Bennet had agreed to take with him to Belize as many as could be accommodated aboard the *Mexican Eagle*, and had undertaken, on behalf of the Superintendent of the colony, to send ships back to evacuate the rest.

For almost the entire group, there was no decision to be made. Hoodwinked, robbed of their savings, and cruelly abandoned, they could not wait to get away – many, in addition, wrongly believing that swearing an oath to the Mosquito King would mean renouncing their British citizenship. Only the old soldier James Hastie and some of his friends hesitated, doubting that 'the King could have got a sufficient number to join him to put his threats in [sic] execution' and being unafraid 'of all he could do if I had been one of fifty or sixty resolute men, with muskets in our hands'. But his closest companion, Malcolm McDougal, was now seriously ill, and 'seeing that it was the determination of all parties to break up the settlement at all hazards, I had no alternative but to do as others did'.

McDougal was among some forty people who were too weakened by malaria and yellow fever to be moved. Of the rest, the schooner was able to take just sixty, starting with those who, like Hastie, had wives and children with them. It was not a pleasant voyage.

The *Mexican Eagle* was too small to accommodate so many passengers in any kind of comfort, or even to give them shelter at this most inhospitable season of the year. The rescued settlers were obliged to camp wherever they could on deck, sweltering under the remorseless sun by day and soaked by the heavy rain that fell each night. They had brought with them an adequate supply of provisions from the storehouse at Black River, but they had neither the space nor the facilities for cooking, so they could not actually feed themselves properly during the three days and nights they were at sea. By the time they reached Belize, most were so weak from hunger, exhaustion and the illnesses that had been developing before they left the Mosquito Coast, that they had to be carried from the ship.

Nor was their salvation as complete as they might have imagined in their relief at escaping from the trap into which they had been led. At that time of year, the climate of Belize was even less healthy than the one they had left behind them, with the result that fevers and other diseases spread rapidly among people already seriously weakened by their ordeal. The small hospitals in the colony struggled to cope with this sudden influx of patients, and although the authorities and the residents offered as much help, medical care and emotional support as they could, the survivors of Poyais began to die in alarming numbers.

When a second shipload of settlers arrived, after a longer and even more difficult voyage than the first group, owing to bad weather, the situation became even worse, and the rate of deaths increased. Even those who had seemed to be recovering succumbed, often to maladies the doctors seemed unable to treat and, in some cases, could not identify. Others who had recovered, or who had never been very ill, joined the daily procession to the graveyard after poisoning themselves with excessive quantities of bad rum.

James Hastie lost another of his children, a little girl, and his friend Malcolm McDougal, in the hospitals of Belize, 'which are completely surrounded by stagnant water, emitting every morning, before the sea breeze springs up, a most pestilential smell'.

Meanwhile, as the schooner left Belize for the Mosquito Coast on its third and final mission of mercy, the Superintendent of the colony, Major General Edward Codd, announced an official investigation to 'lay open the true situation of the imaginary State of Poyais and showing the sufferings of the unfortunate emigrants to the Mosquito Shore'. He also advised his ministerial masters in London of the fate of the Poyais settlers, but his warning came too late to prevent the departure of five more ships bound for Poyais on the promises of Gregor MacGregor. Naval vessels had to be sent out to intercept them, and prevent an even greater tragedy.

But General Codd's enthusiasm to expose the Poyais deception began to wane somewhat when he received a complaint from MacGregor's agents in London – among them the innocent Major William John Richardson, who still had no reason not to believe in the existence of Poyais, and who continued to act as its chargé d'affaires. The petition sent to General Codd related to the disposal of the settlers' stores that had been carried off by the *Honduras Packet* and, it seemed, subsequently sold in Belize. There were questions, too, about the remaining property of the settlement brought back by the *Mexican Eagle* on its third voyage, which included, according to James Hastie, 'beef, flour, rice, and other provisions, tools, school-books, printing presses', all 'sold by auction for what they could fetch'.

In the first case, the merchants who had bought the cargo claimed that nobody had told them it belonged to Poyais, so they could not be held accountable. As for the goods sold from the *Mexican Eagle*, it may well have been a matter of the authorities in Belize doing what they could to recoup some of the £4,290 they had spent in rescuing, nursing, feeding and clothing the Poyais survivors. In the end, the report sent to London by General Codd was nothing more than a whitewash, absolving everybody of responsibility for everything.

To the survivors themselves, it hardly mattered. About 180 of them had died, either on the Mosquito Coast or, more tragically, in Belize after their rescue. The rest were in no position to take any action against guilty parties, even if guilt could ever actually be proved.

Some, including the man who had been appointed to take charge of the National Bank of Poyais, made their way from Belize to the United States, where they lived as best they could. Among the labourers, a few took advantage of the offer made by Mr Bennet and set themselves up as tradesmen in the colony. Of the original 250 or so settlers, fewer than fifty ever saw Britain again. Colonel Hall was not one of them. The available evidence suggests that, having remained in Belize for a time, he took himself off to Africa, where he was to spend the rest of his life.

James Hastie, his wife and his remaining child did live to see their home again. All suffering from malaria, they were tended mainly by the Belize magistrate's clerk, Mr Westby, and his wife, until 'we at last heard that we were to be sent home in the *Ocean*, Captain Whittle, to whose kind and fatherly care I attribute, under Divine Providence, the saving of my own life, and the lives of my remaining family ... that *good man* could not have been more kind to us.' Perhaps he was right to invoke Divine Providence, for a number of his fellow passengers, who had also been struck down by fevers on the Mosquito Coast, did not survive the final stage of their ordeal.

The ship left Belize on 1 August 1823 and, after a voyage of seventy-two days, docked in London, where the Poyais party almost immediately found itself swept up in an investigation by the Lord Mayor, William Heygate, into the activities of Gregor MacGregor and the circumstances surrounding his Poyais loan issue:

> Being sent for by the Lord Mayor, we found at the mansion-house Mr Prince, who I believe is somehow connected with Mrs Bennet of Belize, or his brother. A number of questions were asked us there, whether with a view of attracting the charitable attention of the public, or of implicating Sir Gregor, it is not for me to say ... When before the Lord Mayor, I was shaking so much with the remains of the fever and ague, that I could scarcely stand, or know the meaning of much that was said.

He certainly knew the meaning the following day, however, when the newspapers published colourful reports of the Poyais fiasco, full of details of the sufferings of the emigrants, and clearly suggesting that the whole scheme had been a fraud conceived and executed by Gregor MacGregor. Much of the information was attributed to the man from Pimlico, Edward Lowe – who, a week later, would publish his personal account of the 'Poyaise [sic] Settlers' in *The Times* – but Hastie was astonished to see himself and some of his fellow labourers quoted, 'statements which none of us had ever uttered, and which we found incumbent upon us to contradict upon oath'.

Hastie asked to see the Lord Mayor again and, on 22 October, went to the Mansion House with James Thompson, Thomas Burgess, William Mitchell, Archibald

Torry and Gregor Geddes, where all signed this astonishing affidavit:

> That it is true that they were at the mansion-house on Friday last, and not since, and made a statement before the Lord Mayor; but the statements published in the newspapers of Saturday and last Tuesday under the mansion-house reports, is [sic] not the statements that they made, but are false and unfounded in the greater part; and they feel themselves dissatisfied that any man should publish words as coming from them that they never spoke. Especially that part of the report which states that Sir Gregor MacGregor took money from us, it is false and unfounded; on the contrary, we ourselves received money, with many others, from Sir Gregor MacGregor. We had our passage free, as well as that for our wives and families, although it was at first understood that we were to pay for the same.
>
> We voluntarily swear that Sir Gregor MacGregor never told us, nor did his agents in Scotland, that we should find a theatre at San Joseph, nor a government house; but a young man named Picken, who afterwards made an affidavit at Belize, it was he that told us these falsehoods in our passage out in the *Kennersley Castle*, and in Leith Roads.
>
> We likewise swear and make known to the public, that from the best of our judgment we believe that Sir Gregor MacGregor has been worse used by Colonel Hall and his other agents than was ever man before; and that had they have done their duty by Sir Gregor and by us, things would have turned out very differently at Poyais, and we should have been now there doing well for

ourselves, instead of being in England without a shilling to support us.

And we further declare, that the first cause of discontent amongst the emigrants by the *Kennersley Castle*, was in consequence of the acting governor making a difference in the rations in favour of the emigrants by the *Honduras Packet*.

That these poor deluded souls should have so strongly defended the man who had brought about their downfall, and the deaths of so many of their companions in misfortune, must be a tribute to what we should now describe as the charisma of Gregor MacGregor, and must also help to explain how it was that he managed to play on human weakness and credulity to carry out perhaps the greatest confidence trick in the history of the City of London.

Hastie and his friends, now dependent upon the charitable donations organized by Mr Prince to procure medical treatment for them at St Thomas's hospital and, eventually, to send them back to their old homes, simply could not believe that a person with the obvious distinction of the man who had presented himself to them as His Highness Gregor, Cazique of Poyais, could have so little regard for other human beings as to send so many to their deaths, and to charge a large number of them for the privilege.

Back in Edinburgh, and having 'returned to the service of my old master', Hastie felt so strongly about the widespread criticism of MacGregor and the Poyais scheme, which was appearing almost daily in the English and Scottish press, that he sat down and wrote his memoir of

Poyais, taking every opportunity to repeat that he did not in any way blame MacGregor 'for the misfortunes which befel us'. He claimed that he had reflected coolly on what had taken place, but his capacity for reflection must have been severely limited. One thing that did not strike him, for instance, was the fact that, after all that had happened, Sir Gregor had not even been to London to commiserate with, look after and explain himself to the pathetic little group who were all that remained of the bright dream of Poyais.

'We experienced great attention and assistance from Sir Gregor's agent in London,' Hastie wrote, 'he himself being in Paris.' The agent to whom he referred was presumably the honourable and generous Major Richardson, who apparently still had faith in MacGregor, and who continued to carry out his duties as the Cazique's imaginary chargé d'affaires. Yet it is extraordinary that Hastie – and, for that matter, Richardson – drew no inference from MacGregor's absence at a time when he must have known that the survivors were on their way home, or from his failure to return to London when their arrival had been reported and he was being showered with what Hastie would presumably have regarded as unwarranted opprobrium.

Had Hastie and Richardson been minded to pay the slightest attention to all the evidence that was accumulating against MacGregor, instead of merely dismissing it as the libels of his enemies, they would have understood at once that he had done what he always did. When the course of events which he himself had set in train turned round to threaten him directly – just as at Amelia Island, at Porto Bello, and at Rio de la Hacha – he had fled, leaving others to suffer the consequences.

FRENCH LEAVE

The Poyais scheme, so carefully planned and so cleverly managed, had, in fact, begun to unravel even as the settlers aboard the *Honduras Packet* were making their way across the Atlantic ocean. Of course, it would inevitably have been in difficulty once news of what the colonists found on the Mosquito Coast filtered back to London, but by that time, Gregor MacGregor should have amassed a fortune from the subscriptions to his loan issue. Unfortunately, the instability and internecine conflicts of the new governments created in South America by Simón Bolívar and his colleagues prompted something of a panic on the London bond market in the early months of 1823, and the Poyais offering suffered from the growing fear that money invested in any South American loan might never be recovered.

MacGregor's cash flow virtually dried up in January,

when most of the people who had invested refused to sub-
scribe the second instalment required by the loan contract,
preferring to lose what they had already paid rather than
risking more money on what seemed like an increasingly
vain hope of a return. This left the Cazique in an awkward
position. His land sales had gone well – reaching, according
to his own account, at least 500 purchasers by the spring
of 1823 – but there were heavy expenses associated with
them. All the advertising had to be paid for; there was rent
for the land offices in London, Edinburgh and elsewhere;
chartering ships for the emigrants required payment in
advance, and not all the goods purchased for the expeditions
could be obtained on credit.

It had been to help meet such expenditure that the
loan had been floated but that, too, was not without its
costs, principally the generous underwriting fees offered to
Perring's bank. The contractor, John Lowe, also took the
usual commission on sales which, of course, applied even
to the dealing among insiders to which Lowe resorted in
an unsuccessful effort to maintain the price of the bonds.
All this meant that even if genuine investors could be
persuaded to buy at the knockdown price of fifteen, to
which the scrip had fallen by July 1823, the return of cash
to MacGregor was negligible.

At the same time, the summer brought the news to
London from Belize of the pitiful state of the Poyais
emigrants, and the turning back of the ships in which
new parties had embarked. MacGregor countered unfavourable press reports by claiming that he himself must

have been swindled – placing much of the blame on John Lowe, whom he accused of misappropriating funds that should have gone into the emigration programme – and by accusing jealous merchants in Belize of undermining an enterprise that threatened to reduce their own profits. He was obviously aware, however, that the game was very nearly up for, in October, when he knew that the surviving colonists were on their way home, he made another attempt to restore his fortunes by floating a second Poyais loan of £200,000.

It almost beggars belief that Sir John Perring again agreed to underwrite the issue. No doubt equally generous fees played their part in the decision, and perhaps the banker was further swayed by the expensively printed, multicoloured bearer documents with which MacGregor presented him as an indication of his confidence. The loan was to pay five per cent a year, the interest to be secured by a mortgage bond on 'all the revenues of the State of Poyais', guaranteed by 'Gregor the First, Sovereign Prince of the Independent State of Poyais and its Dependencies'. Redemption was to be underwritten by a sinking fund that would be opened with a deposit of £2,000 and augmented by payments of £1,000 in each of the thirty years to maturity, together with one-sixth of the proceeds from sales of land in Poyais over the same period.

The bonds were offered for sale at eighty, in denominations of 100, but even that discount failed to attract many takers. In the general climate of uncertainty, no other South American loans had been floated during that year, investors being more inclined to support Rothschilds' new issues for Austria and Portugal, which raised a total of £5 million. Some did stay in the South American market, buying Colombian bonds at little more than half their face value, on well-founded rumours that the British government had declared, through diplomatic channels, that it would officially recognize the new governments of the liberated provinces if there should be any attempt to reconquer them. There was, though, no benefit in this for Poyais since, as the Cazique had always proudly proclaimed, it had never been a Spanish colony, and the British government had no interest in recognizing it or otherwise supporting it. MacGregor's bonds soon became worthless.

Meanwhile, the ship *Ocean* was ploughing across the Atlantic, bringing back the remnants of the Poyais settlers who would expose the fabrications of the Cazique. It had already been reported in the newspapers that the Mosquito King had revoked his grant of land, and though MacGregor had been able to dismiss this as illegal, he calculated that it would be extremely difficult, if not impossible, to refute first-hand accounts of what had actually been found in Poyais. Turning to his still faithful chargé d'affaires, Major Richardson, MacGregor announced that his wife was unwell, and that medical advice was to take her to Italy before the English winter set in: the couple and their two children would leave immediately for Boulogne, on the first stage of the long journey.

That, of course, was another of MacGregor's lies. The family certainly went to Boulogne early in October 1823, taking with them what remained of the Poyais investors' money, but it was Paris, rather than Italy, that was their destination, and the reason for the journey was commercial rather than medical.

MacGregor had apparently prepared the way for his arrival in Paris by contacting the Compagnie de la Nouvelle Neustrie, a group of merchant adventurers with ambitions to become one of the leading trade organizations in the liberated countries of South America, whose formation had been reported in the English press. Ironically, it seems to have been MacGregor who had inspired the creation of the company, because its business plan – which consisted of raising finance for the settlement of French emigrants in Latin America, and taking profit from their subsequent commercial activities – bore remarkable similarities to his Poyais scheme. The difference between the two was that MacGregor had a grant of land, which la Nouvelle Neustrie did not. Here was an opportunity too good to miss, particularly at a time when England was becoming an increasingly uncomfortable base for the operations of the Cazique of Poyais.

The promoters of the French company, who included two leading lawyers, were extremely well connected, and within a few days of his arrival in Paris, MacGregor – as he later told one of his collaborators, at least – found himself being introduced to the Prime Minister, Monsieur le Comte de Villèle, on the ground that he was a visiting head of state. As always with MacGregor, we can never be entirely sure of the precise truth, but an account of what is supposed to have happened was compiled by Gustavus Butler Hippisley, former freedom fighter in Latin America, and the man almost certainly responsible for the establishment of relations between the Cazique and Major Richardson, who had become the Poyaisian chargé d'affaires in London.

In Hippisley's version, MacGregor spun the Comte de Villèle a complicated story about his need for French support in negotiations with the Spanish government with the purpose of obtaining a formal renunciation of any claims Spain might have to sovereignty over Poyais. He had, he said, taken part in preliminary discussions with Spanish envoys in London, as a result of which he had been encouraged to send an agent to Madrid. MacGregor was even able to produce a letter, purporting to be from a Spanish court official, in which he was recognized as Cazique of Poyais – though, curiously, the letter rendered the title as 'cacique', instead of using the actual Spanish word from which it was derived. 'Cacique' is the French version.

Regrettably, MacGregor went on, the Spanish government had been unable or unwilling to reach any decision about its future conduct towards the independent nations of South America, which was likely to cause difficulties for anyone contemplating the foundation of new settlements on the continent. In the circumstances, anything the French government could do to help would benefit not only Poyais, but also the Compagnie de la Nouvelle Neustrie.

It is difficult to be certain that the meeting described

actually took place. We only have Hippisley's word for it, and the sources of his information were MacGregor himself and a fellow Scotsman named Thomas Irving, whom the Cazique presented as his secretary. Hippisley seems to have accepted MacGregor's word without question, and his account is full of the inaccuracies, half-truths and downright lies that characterize almost everything MacGregor said about himself and his activities. It is quite possible, therefore, that what Hippisley was told about MacGregor's stay in France was, at one level, nothing more than a fiction designed to cover up the fact that the Cazique had fled from England, leaving Hippisley's future brother-in-law, Major Richardson, to deal as best he could with the impending exposure of the Poyais fraud.

If the meeting with de Villèle did take place, the Prime Minister could not have been aware that the concern about Spanish reaction MacGregor was expressing had not prevented him from arranging the departure of more than 500 emigrants to Poyais. Equally, de Villèle must have been ignorant of the miserable fate of the first two parties of settlers, though much of the story had already been told in the English press. Nor did it seem to occur to the Prime Minister that, because Poyais had never been a Spanish colony, it was extremely unlikely that the government in Madrid would wish to make any claim to it anyway.

In view of these inconsistencies, the fact of such a meeting must be seriously doubted, especially when it emerges from Hippisley's recollections that MacGregor used de Villèle as his excuse for not fulfilling the declared

purpose of his departure from England, which was to take
Josefa to Italy for the sake of her health. In the Hippisley
version, the Prime Minister asked MacGregor to remain in
Paris so that he might attend a conference called to consider
the affairs of the former Spanish American colonies, since
his advice could be useful and his ability to influence the
future of the new countries might be fully exploited.

'The Cazique', Hippisley faithfully recorded, 'replied
that, since the minister considered his presence might be
useful, he would remain at Paris in order to conform
himself to his wishes.'

Again, it is not easy to establish conclusively whether
there was any French plan for a conference to consider
the future of Latin America. Hippisley reported that:

> In consequence of these relations with the Count de
> Villèle, and with a view of forwarding the purposes
> which ought to have been the object of the congress,
> the Cazique was placed in report with the Marquis
> de Clermont Tonnerre, minister of the marine and
> colonies, and the Viscount de Châteaubriand, minister
> of foreign affairs, who highly approved of the plans
> which he proposed for the arrangement of the grand
> affair of South American independence. The projected
> conference, however, did not take place.

De Villèle, it is worth noting, was an ultra-conservative
Royalist, while Châteaubriand was the minister who had
done most to take France into war with Spain for the
purpose of restoring the Bourbon monarchy, so it is unlikely

that either of them would have had much sympathy for Republican movements. Indeed, it was the policy of Châteaubriand that had given rise to fears of a possible Spanish reconquest of the American colonies once the monarchy was restored in Madrid, causing the panic over South American loans in London. Though the French had been forced into an agreement with the British not to support any attempt at reconquest, they were no more anxious than the government in London to recognize the fractious new Republican regimes created in the wake of Simón Bolívar. Even if they did meet MacGregor, then, there would have been little hope of their enthusiastic support for his alleged cause.

The probability is that MacGregor either grossly exaggerated or entirely fabricated these contacts with the French government in order to legtimize his position as the man with the power to help la Nouvelle Neustrie to establish Latin American settlements. Unable, however, to cite any positive result from his negotiations, he made the next part of the story even more convoluted.

He told Hippisley that he had addressed his proposals to the Duke de San Carlos, the Spanish Ambassador in Paris, who had duly transmitted them to his masters in Madrid. The proposition, said MacGregor, consisted of an offer by him to pay to the Court of Madrid the sum of FFr5,000,000 (£200,000) as an indemnity for the abandonment by Spain of her claim to the territory of Poyais, in favour of the Cazique. Of course, the indemnity represented a substantial sum of money, but one of the leading banking houses in Paris had agreed to advance the money to MacGregor. The prospect of such a payment appeared to have attracted support for the proposal among some powerful figures in Spanish government circles, who argued that the relinquishing of any claim to Poyais might be considered as the first step towards an arrangement between Spain and her former colonies.

Poor, naïve Hippisley seems to have swallowed all this pretentious rubbish without a second thought. Yet it simply cannot have been true. To begin with, there was no such country as Poyais, so Spain could not possibly have had a claim to it. Why, then, would MacGregor have offered to pay £200,000 to the Spanish government as indemnity against sovereignty that could not exist?

Even if we give him the benefit of the doubt, and assume that what he was referring to was the territory known as the Mosquito Coast, the Spanish had never thought it worth their while to occupy it, so there was little likelihood that they would now assert sovereignty over it. In any case, since the Mosquito Coast had its own King, MacGregor would have had no right to sovereignty in the region, in the event that the Spanish government had accepted his bribe. If there were to have been any assertion of sovereignty, it would most probably have come from the British, on the basis of their settlements a century or so earlier, and on the desire of King George Frederic. The fact is that, at the time, nobody except MacGregor had any serious interest in the place that he called Poyais.

His suggestion to Hippisley that he had arranged with

a leading French bank to advance the money to pay the
indemnity seems equally mythical. He had been in France
only a few months, and had nothing like the reputation
there that he had created for himself in Britain. No doubt,
with the support of la Nouvelle Neustrie, he could have
presented the case for such a loan, but a bank would surely
have been wary of advancing the large sum of £200,000
against a very distant and uncertain prospect of a return. It
was very different from the risk taken by Sir John Perring,
with substantial fees to be earned and an immediate flow of
money from the public sale of bonds. Significantly, when
MacGregor did reach the stage of raising cash to launch
the Poyais scheme in France, it was in London that he
did it, not in Paris.

This story of tortuous negotiations with the French
and Spanish authorities – apart from being an example
of MacGregor at his most grandiose – may well have also
been a ploy designed to counteract the, by now public,
revocation of the Mosquito King's grant of land, upon
which the whole Poyais structure depended. MacGregor
knew, of course, that his legal position in regard to the
grant was, at best, uncertain. Any court proceedings arising from King George Frederic's rescinding of the grant
would have revealed that its registration by MacGregor
at the High Court of Chancery, on which his legal claim
relied, had not only taken place after he had actually sold
some of the land, but had also been based on a false
affidavit.

The document lodged with the court included the

following sworn testimony as to the signing and witnessing of the land grant:

> WILLIAM SMITH, of Clandon Street, in the County of Surry [sic], Mate of the Ship called the Honduras Packet, trading between Poyais and London, and now in the Port of London, maketh oath and saith, That he was present at Cape Gracias á Dios, and did see the Paper Writing hereunto annexed, bearing date the Twenty-Ninth Day of April, One Thousand Eight Hundred and Twenty, and purporting to be a Grant by GEORGE FREDERICK the Second, King of the Mosquito Shore and Nation, of certain Territories within His Kingdom, to General Sir Gregor MacGregor, signed by the said GEORGE FREDERICK, and that the Seal of His said Majesty was then affixed by His said Majesty to the said Paper Writing; And that he, this Deponent, did then and there also see WILLIAM BOGGS sign his name at the foot of the said Paper Writing.

Even if the contents of that oath were true – and there is no doubt that the King did grant land to MacGregor – it contained serious flaws. The swearing is recorded as having taken place on 14 October 1822, but the *Honduras Packet* had sailed from the Port of London, with the first party of emigrants, a month earlier. The statement, therefore, that the ship was 'now in the Port of London' was untrue. And if William Smith was the first mate, why was he not aboard the vessel when she sailed? If he had been the first mate in April 1820 and no longer held that position, why did his oath not say so?

The suspicion must be that William Smith was not the first mate of the *Honduras Packet*, or that the man swearing the oath was not William Smith, or that the 'witnessing' of the land grant had taken place after the event, with the cooperation of the ship's officers, or that MacGregor had simply made up the whole thing. The fact of the grant was never disputed, but we have only MacGregor's word that any document was signed.

In any event, lawyers would have made much of the inconsistencies had any disgruntled British investor sought to test, in court, the Cazique's right of possession over the land he had sold.

MacGregor was a fantasist and a liar, but he was not stupid. If he could obtain from the Spanish government recognition of his sovereignty in Poyais – or at least create the impression of having done so – that would effectively replace King George Frederic's now revoked concession, and appear to give MacGregor the right to continue selling land in the Territory and raising loans on its behalf. Hence the tale that he fed to the gullible Gustavus Butler Hippisley, who would later record that 'in consequence of the steps taken in favour of the Cazique', the Marquis de los Hermosos had written from Madrid, on 10 May, 1824, to the Comte de Colonne in Paris, to the effect that 'His Catholic Majesty refused to recognize the sovereignty of Poyais, but that M. MacGregor might obtain the title of Duke and the rank of grandee in Spain.'

Of course, the Cazique, as a man of honour, had immediately rejected the proposals of the Court of Madrid, 'which he communicated to the Count de Villèle, at the same time expressing his regret that his Excellency should so long have detained him at Paris in the expectation of an arrangement with Spain, who, with a blind obstinacy, refused to admit the only basis upon which an amicable arrangement could be brought about with the New American states'.

Hippisley noted that 'M de Villèle, who was well aware that the Cazique had remained in France, solely on account of his representations, promised to take care of his interests, and *le sort du Pays de Poyais lors de l'arrangement général des affaires de l'Amerique.*' With this in mind, he had invited MacGregor to communicate with the Baron de Damas, the Minister of Foreign Affairs who, he said, had received from him the necessary instructions relative to the affair.

According to the version of events given by MacGregor, he had been granted several interviews with the Baron de Damas, who had appeared to 'shew himself extremely favorably disposed; and shortly afterwards announced to him, that the government of his most Christian Majesty, had come to the resolution, of soliciting the court of Madrid, to accede to his recognition'.

This whole saga was carefully relayed to Hippisley when he arrived in Paris in March 1825, summoned from London by the Cazique on the pretext of discussing his possible appointment to the post of Poyaisian representative in the new republic of Colombia. The real reasons for the invitation are testimony to both MacGregor's effrontery and his cunning.

For one thing, Hippisley was a man of unimpeachable character and, having spent five years fighting with the revolutionary armies of New Granada, he knew a great deal more about the true state of affairs in South America than did MacGregor. The Cazique had had little or no contact with the leaders of the Independence movement on the continent since the scandal of his fund-raising visit to London in 1818, and had not set foot there – apart from his brief visit to the Mosquito Coast – after his ignominious departure from Rio de la Hacha. Hippisley's first-hand knowledge, and his very presence, would be invaluable as MacGregor sought to establish himself in Paris as one of the principal European promoters of Latin American independence. It would also be reassuring for the directors of the Compagnie de la Nouvelle Neustrie, with whom MacGregor was developing plans to send French emigrants to Poyais.

A second consideration in bringing Hippisley to Paris was his connection with Major Richardson. The Poyaisian chargé d'affaires in London had been valiantly defending the Cazique against the charges of deception and fraud that were being increasingly voiced by the British press, as well as doing his best to console and, in some measure, to try to compensate the returned emigrants. The extent of his efforts may be judged by the appearance of James Hastie's book, which completely exonerated MacGregor from blame for the fatal fiasco, and by the libel writs Major Richardson issued against some newspapers, on behalf of the Cazique.

However, MacGregor was still at risk from legal action by ruined investors and settlers, and from what appeared to be growing official interest in discovering the true facts about the Poyais affair. In the circumstances, it was essential that Richardson, and such other supporters as MacGregor still had, should continue to shield him – if for no other reason than that they might ultimately be made to appear responsible themselves if the truth did emerge. Thus, the Major had to be reassured that all was well in the state of Poyais. The idea that his friend Hippisley, who would later become his brother-in-law, would be appointed the Cazique's agent in Colombia, and might assist in obtaining the diplomatic recognition of Poyais, would inspire Richardson to continue to believe that the fictional state did exist, that MacGregor was acting selflessly in its interest, and that the allegations being made were baseless. That, no doubt, was part of the reason why the Cazique provided Hippisley with so much detail about his relationship with the leading members of the French government.

What Hippisley's motive was in accepting the invitation is more difficult to determine. He confessed himself flattered by the attention of the Cazique, but he had no real desire to return to Colombia which, he believed, had ill-rewarded his years of service to 'a glorious cause'. At the same time, he retained a strong interest in Latin American affairs, and perhaps he felt that an association with the apparently peaceful realm of Poyais would serve to ease the pain of the Colombians' ingratitude, and to give some meaning to the sacrifices he had made on behalf of the continent. On a more mundane level, he had little else to do, his health having been seriously affected by the hardships of his years of guerrilla warfare.

He was suitably impressed by the Cazique's way of life, with an official residence in the rue Louis Legrand and a large family home, Maison Villette, in the Champs-Élysées, 'where I was received with that marked urbanity of manners which even his enemies must admit, he in an eminent degree possesses'. MacGregor lodged Hippisley at an apartment in the rue Louis Legrand, which was normally at the disposal of his secretary, and 'personally directed every arrangement for my comfort'. He also lost no time in acquainting his guest with his own version of some of the events that were now being discussed in the British newspapers so that, within a month of his arrival, Hippisley was writing home to refute enthusiastically 'the bare-faced calumnies of a *hireling press*!'

Having presented a brief and largely fictitious biography of MacGregor, with a suitably dramatic account of his heroics in the service of Venezuela and New Granada, Hippisley went on to castigate 'the journalist who dared to designate him by the title of *"pennyless adventurer"*', in referring to the Poyais affair.

Large sums of money, he asserted, had been expended in attempts to settle this fertile country; but the cupidity of the agents employed, their 'malversation and disgraceful abuse' of the funds entrusted to their disposal, and the 'malignity' of the Belize merchants, had combined to disappoint the hopes and frustrate the intentions of the Cazique.

'I trust', Hippisley wrote, 'the period is not far distant, when the views of the Cazique, and the wishes of those sincerely attached to his interests, will be carried into execution.'

He went on to say that MacGregor's critics should be aware that commercial companies were being formed for the purpose of furthering his plans for the development of Poyais, and this time the Cazique would be more careful in choosing the people to whom he would entrust the responsibility of making sure his wishes were carried out.

'He has too dearly purchased experience', Hippisley concluded, 'to repose in future, unlimited confidence in the hollow professions of needy speculators, whose honesty has no better guarantee to offer, than that of their own assertions.' We, of course, can see that as a marvellous piece of unconscious irony.

Whatever it was costing MacGregor to maintain his visitor in some luxury in Paris, he was certainly getting his money's worth. Having fully exploited him as what might today be termed his 'spin doctor', he soon abandoned any pretence of sending Hippisley to Colombia, and instead involved him in what he continued to insist were serious discussions over sovereignty with the Spanish government. He also gave Hippisley a leading part in negotiations with the Compagnie de la Nouvelle Neustrie, which had 'a vessel at Havre [sic], nearly ready for sea, freighted with provisions, and every requisite implement of husbandry'.

Well, it had worked splendidly in Britain, and there was no reason why it should not do so in France. Clearly, la Nouvelle Neustrie, which was under the control of a certain Monsieur Lehuby, was as crooked as MacGregor was.

Hippisley spent the month of May 1825 attending meetings with Lehuby and one of his associates, Monsieur Valogne, concerning the Cazique's intention to cede exclusively to the company a large tract of land in Poyais, 'comprising two hundred and fifty-six superficial square leagues [that is, the surface area only, not to include any underground mineral rights], under the stipulation of paying to the Cazique, at the expiration of three years, after possession has been had of the same, one franc, per acre, per annum, upon all the land that may be in a state of cultivation'.

This was, Hippisley noted, 'a most liberal' concession on the part of the Cazique, representing about half a million acres, 'inasmuch as he receives no sort of immediate compensation: the advantages to be derived from it are only in perspective [i.e. prospect]: however, he will attain his principal object, that of cultivating a country, the fertility of whose soil will amply repay the labour bestowed upon it'.

It was also a very clever way of distancing himself from the settlement of Poyais which, of course, would expose the fraud from the moment the emigrants arrived, as had happened with the British parties. This time, instead of blaming dishonest merchants, MacGregor would be able truthfully to say that he had simply made the land available, and it had been la Nouvelle Neustrie that had taken charge of the emigration. What we shall never know is whether the innocent Hippisley was being used as a pawn in a stratagem agreed between MacGregor and Lehuby, or whether the Frenchman who sought to emulate the Poyais swindle did not realize how dangerous it was to deal with its inventor.

The terms of the concession, of course, meant that MacGregor would not be able to make money by selling land directly to the public, as he had done in Britain. That did not worry him, however, because he had another plan in mind. In August, he first published a new constitution for Poyais, converting it into a republic of which he was head of state – though retaining the title of Cazique – then, on 18 August, he issued a prospectus promoting a £300,000 loan offering two-and-a-half per cent interest per year, and secured against future revenues of Poyais from the working of a gold mine and the production of 'indigo, sugar, tobacco &c'.

Strangely, it was not a French bank underwriting the loan, in spite of MacGregor's earlier boast to Hippisley that one of the leading houses in Paris had been prepared to advance him £200,000. Nor was it Sir John Perring, whose Poyais dealings would contribute to his bankruptcy in 1826. This time, it was the relatively obscure London bank of Thomas Jenkins & Company that succumbed to the lure of MacGregor's lavish fees.

Jenkins was to have a lucky escape, however, for there is no evidence that the French Poyais bonds were ever issued.

Before that could happen, MacGregor's other boast, that he had the support of the French government, was also shown to be disastrously false.

While MacGregor had been busy organizing his loan issue, la Nouvelle Neustrie had been recruiting settlers for Poyais, requiring them for the privilege to buy FFr100 worth of shares in the company. Thirty of these adventurers obtained passports for their departure, but when thirty more applied, officials became concerned and began to question them about the nature of their proposed journey.

When it emerged that these people intended to travel to a country nobody at the Ministry had heard of, all thirty applications were refused, and the company's vessel at Le Havre was placed under an embargo preventing it from leaving port. This official action aroused suspicion among some of the would-be emigrants that all was not as it should be, and they demanded an investigation by the police into the background of the Nouvelle Neustrie company and the credentials of the man known as the Cazique of Poyais.

The unfortunate Hippisley described what happened next, in a letter dated September 1825:

On Sunday the 4th instant, at seven in the morning, I was disagreeably roused from my sleep, by the introduction into my chamber, of three agents of the police, who, scarcely allowing me time to dress, hurried me down stairs, where I found Mr Irving, the Cazique's secretary, in charge of an equal number of satellites: they conveyed us in separate coaches to the Prefecture de Police, where we were received in his office, by that prince of *mouchards*,

Vidoc,* who sent us to the Salle St-Martin, the depot for prisoners, prior to examination ... Orders have been given to arrest the Cazique, but I trust he will escape their researches.

It looked as if, at long last, the law was about to catch up with Gregor MacGregor.

---

* Eugène François Vidocq, the legendary criminal who turned police informer and became the first head of the Brigade de Sûreté in 1812. The word *mouchard* means 'sneak', 'grass' and 'informer': Vidocq was sacked from the Sûreté in 1825 for allegedly perpetrating many of the crimes he appeared to have solved so brilliantly.

BAD COMPANY

On Tuesday 6 September 1825, Gustavus Butler Hippisley and the Secretary to the Cazique of Poyais, Thomas Irving, appeared before an examining magistrate in Paris and were told they would be held in custody while the police investigated charges against them of conspiracy to defraud, and of the sale of titles to land they did not own. The two men protested their innocence, but were taken that evening to the prison of La Force, the former mansion of a duke where prisoners on remand were kept. Apart from the size of the rooms, there was nothing about the building to recall its past glories, as Hippisley reported in a letter to a friend:

> The prison is under the superintendance of a director, a brigadier, and several assistants, called *guardiens*, who are cloathed in a sort of uniform. The interior discipline

is vexatious in the extreme, even the use of a knife not being permitted to cut your meat. There are two rooms of common reception with iron gratings, which separate the prisoners from their visitants, at so great a distance, as to render it almost impossible to converse upon any subject, particularly when the apartment is crowded, which is generally the case. You are neither allowed to send, or receive any written communication, until the same has been perused at the *guichet*; in short, there is no species of annoyance to which you are not exposed; and here I must be permitted to notice the *mouchards*, who infest the prison, like rats in a barn, contaminating and destroying all the wholesome and invigorating germs of existence.

Hippisley and Irving were soon visited by Monsieur Valogne, one of the directors of la Nouvelle Neustrie, who told them that the Managing Director, Monsieur Lehuby, had evaded arrest and taken refuge in Belgium, while Gregor MacGregor had gone into hiding somewhere outside Paris. Hippisley expressed the hope that the Cazique would not be found by the police but, in one sense, his disappearance was bad news for the prisoners. Until he could be found, charged and brought before an examining magistrate, no arrangements for a trial could be made and, as Hippisley pointed out:

French justice is extremely dilatory at all times, and their laws so materially differ from ours, (indeed in many instances, they are incompatible with common sense) ... there is no specified time for the trial of an accused person, who is obliged to furnish proofs of his own innocence, and should he even be capable of so doing, if delay suits the purpose of the public prosecutor, a thousand excuses are made to impede the natural course of justice, and the prisoner may be detained *ad libitum*, or until *Monsieur le Juge d'Instruction* has collected information for his conviction from the four quarters of the globe.

Hippisley and Irving were allowed out of their prison for one day in order to witness the seizure of documents from the Poyais office and their apartment in the rue Louis Legrand, but that was the last they were to see of the outside world for quite some time, while the search for MacGregor continued and the authorities sought the extradition of Monsieur Lehuby from Belgium. Their confinement was relieved only by the dramatic escape of an officer charged with crimes against the state, who briefly shared their room, until he removed two bars from the window, climbed down to the courtyard below, and strangled a guard in whose uniform he disguised himself.

Otherwise, Hippisley passed the long hours in writing letters to friends – which he did not actually post for fear that his accounts of life in La Force would annoy the authorities – and in attempting to make contact with the examining magistrate and the Prefect of Police, neither of whom responded to his inquiries.

His health deteriorated as he began to suffer severe rheumatic pains, but he rejected the advice of the guards to move to the prison hospital, 'since its regulations would deprive me of many little comforts, which, at present, with money, I am able to procure; besides, I should be completely debarred from all exterior communication'. He had heard that a young man in the hospital, at the point of death, had been refused a visit from his father without a permit from the Prefect.

Two months went by, then three, with no developments in the case against the prisoners, who began to think they had been forgotten about. Then, on 7 December, Gregor MacGregor was brought to La Force. 'The myrmidons of justice had discovered his retreat on the 4th instant', and had lost no time in placing him behind bars. In spite of his blind loyalty, Hippisley was relieved, 'since, I conceive, the affair must now be speedily terminated'.

MacGregor apologized for leaving his colleagues in this uncomfortable position for so long. His inclination, he said, had been to surrender himself to the police as soon as he knew a warrant had been issued for his arrest. Artifice and evasion, he went on, were foreign to his character, and he refused to practise them even when threatened by great danger. However, he had been advised against trusting in justice by 'those whose counsel he had a right, in some measure, to make the guide of his conduct'.

Now that he had no choice in the matter, he was sure that the common justice of France would be fair, liberal and open, and that there was nothing to fear. He had, after all, obtained the support of the French government for his activities – indeed, the Minister for Foreign Affairs himself had declared that he saw nothing untoward in the contract between the Cazique of Poyais and la Nouvelle Neustrie. There could be little doubt that the charges laid against him and the others were political in nature, arising from some sudden change of policy.

It might well have been, MacGregor suggested darkly, that the new republican constitution he had created for Poyais had somehow fallen into the hands of the Spanish Ambassador and had enraged his masters in Madrid because of its commitment to freedom for the population, so different from the Spaniards' own despotic principles.

MacGregor said the case for their defence was being conducted by the lawyer who represented la Nouvelle Neustrie, Maître Merilhou. Hippisley and Irving told him that, not knowing what his position was, they had retained their own man, an English solicitor who worked in Paris and whom Irving knew. This man had provided them with the text of a letter, setting out the circumstances of the case, which they had sent to the British Ambassador, Lord Granville, together with an appeal for his intervention. They had high hopes that diplomatic pressure would resolve the matter.

Shortly after MacGregor's arrival at La Force, Maître Merilhou paid a visit to report that he had been summoned by Lord Granville and, after some discussion of the laws relating to the case, the Ambassador had expressed his intention of demanding that the Ministry of Justice should either release the prisoners or, at the very least, bring them to trial immediately. A week passed without a response from the Ministry, then Merilhou appeared again with the news that Granville had gone to see the Minister himself and made an official request that the trial of the three men should begin within seven days.

'Alas', Hippisley wrote, 'that period has elapsed, and

we are as far from the attainment of our object as ever. The only answer we can procure from that sapient magistrate, M. Lambert, to our almost daily applications is that the affair is not, as yet, sufficiently examined to make a report upon!'

As the delays and the excuses for them continued, MacGregor appeared to become ever more convinced that he and his associates were the victims of political persecution. Failing, or refusing, to see that what the Ministry of Justice was waiting for was the extradition of Monsieur Lehuby, in order to prove its charge of conspiracy between him and the Cazique, he told Hippisley that the Spaniards were the real villains, with the 'culpable connivance' of the French government.

But MacGregor knew what he must do. He must associate Poyais with the independence and the republican ideals of the new American states, which saw no reason why Spain should be compensated for losing the war they had fought for their freedom. With that in mind, he had decided to issue a declaration on behalf of Poyais, which would be presented at a congress of the new republics due to take place in Panama, with the object of forming some sort of federation among them. That would make the French and Spanish authorities take notice, and elicit much sympathy among the lovers of liberty.

The result was an excellent example of MacGregor's fantasising and bluster. Written in French, it announced itself as 'The declaration of General Gregor MacGregor, Cazique of Poyais, to the delegates of the United States of

Mexico, and the republics of Central and South America, gathered at the Congress of Panama', and it went on:

> General Gregor MacGregor, Cazique of Poyais, after two years of residence in France – where he was persuaded to go on the basis of negotiations relating to the consolidation of his country's independence – now finds himself, contrary to human rights, held prisoner by the French government for reasons of which he is not aware.
>
> Wishing to participate to the utmost in the conference of the New American States for the purpose of maintaining their common independence, and at the same time to retain intact the body of rights of the country which has given him the responsibility of its administration, the Cazique of Poyais believes it is his duty to set down in a public document, and bring to the attention of the whole of America, the sentiments which he is unable to express in person at the Congress of Panama because of the persecution he is presently suffering as one of the founders of independence in the New World.
>
> He protests to the world about his subjection to the violation of the rights which international law assigns to the head of an independent government, and to foreigners engaged in diplomatic activities.
>
> Since the territory of Poyais was never conquered by Spain, and since its inhabitants – as is well known throughout America – have always had the right to govern themselves, no Spanish decree, for whatever era, has the power to remove from those said inhabitants the right of self-determination. Former Spanish decrees being the acts of a usurping and tyrannical government, they can no longer constitute the titles of sovereignty, or

give authority to any such claim, or influence the new destiny of the American peoples.

In consequence, the Indian nations and other inhabitants of the country situated between Cape Delgado or Truxillo and the St John's River of Nicaragua have the same rights as Colombia, Mexico, Guatemala and all the New American States to enjoy independence and a government of their choice.

The Cazique of Poyais protests in the name of the said nations against the decision of the government of Colombia to lay claim to part of the said territory on the basis of a former Spanish decree, regardless of human rights, and to the detriment of American stability and the independence of Central America.

The constitution created by the Cazique on 4 July 1825 will remain in force, as a result of which the State of Poyais will assume the status of a republic, with its head of state continuing to bear the title of Cazique, as is customary among the chiefs of Indian nations.

Poyais is being placed provisionally under the protection of the government of the United Provinces of Central America, until such time as an assembly of its inhabitants, whatever their origin, may deliver a ruling on the question of whether the said republic remains independent, or whether it prefers to become, as a distinct state, an integral part of the union of Central America to protect itself against foreign aggression.

Given at Paris under the counter-signature of our Secretary General, and under our signature and seal, this 10th [day of] January, 1826.

What the disputatious delegates at the ill-fated Congress of Panama would have made of this nonsense, if they had ever seen it, can only be guessed at. The fact that the declaration was composed in French indicates that its real purpose was publication in the Paris press as an attempt to establish MacGregor's position as a head of state and thus to have the charges against him withdrawn. Unfortunately for the Cazique and his friends in La Force, the bluff failed. Monsieur Lambert, the examining magistrate, the Minister of Justice, the Prefect of Police, and the French government took no more notice of the declaration than its supposed audience in South America would have done. The incarceration went on.

For MacGregor, La Force was not so bad. The ever loyal Josefa, who had given birth to their second son, Constantino, at their home in the Champs-Élysées a little more than a year earlier, saw to it that her husband had every comfort in his prison room. And the Cazique always had his fantasy world for consolation.

Occasionally, Maître Merilhou brought the prospect of some resolution, either in the form of the dismissal of the charges or, at least, an early date for trial but, as January gave way to February, 'expectations of freedom proved fallacious', as Hippisley put it. In fact, at the end of February, they were suddenly removed from the relatively pleasant surroundings of the old mansion and taken, with 'about one hundred and thirty individuals, the very refuse of La Force', to the much grimmer environment of the Bicêtre prison on the outskirts of Paris.

'The air of this place is dreadfully cold,' wrote Hippisley, 'the corridor in which our chambers are situated being upwards of sixty feet above the tower of Notre Dame. I suffer severely from my rheumatism, and as there is no means of procuring a fire, I am obliged to lie in bed for the sake of warmth.'

MacGregor's main complaint was that it became more difficult to obtain his provisions from home, given the distance of Bicêtre from the centre of Paris. After not much more than a month there, however, came one of the events – even if the less desirable one – for which they had been waiting so long. Their trial was officially scheduled for Thursday 6 April.

'I am pleased that the government has thus afforded us an opportunity of publicly testifying our innocence,' Hippisley reflected philosophically. And he went on:

> Had we been placed at liberty, an unmerited stigma might have attached itself to our character; now, our honorable acquittal, for I anticipate no other result, must completely silence the tongue of slander, and will make us some amends for the persecution which we have suffered. The news has given me fresh spirits, and the whole of our companions in misfortune seem to rejoice, in the prospect of our triumph over what they do not hesitate to designate a cruel and unparalleled oppression.

He looked forward to the day of 'my appearance in that only land of freedom, dear England!' – but French justice had not yet finished with Gregor MacGregor and his associates, not by a long way.

The trial took place on the appointed day, before three

judges, 'dressed in black, with small forage caps, of the same colour, ornamented with a silver band', who sat in front of 'the picture of our Saviour upon the cross, by whose image the different witnesses were sworn'.

The case for the prosecution was that MacGregor and Monsieur Lehuby had conspired, with the participation of Hippisley and Irving, to defraud the public by means of the Poyais emigration programme, and that the basis of the swindle was land to which they did not have title under French law.

Witnesses described the negotiation and the details of the agreement between the Cazique and la Nouvelle Neustrie, and the prosecutor drew attention to the issue of MacGregor's loan prospectus, which had cited the company in relation to plans for the economic development of Poyais. Clearly, he suggested, there had been collusion between the Cazique and Mr Lehuby in the selling of shares in the emigration scheme and in the raising of a loan of FFr5,000,000, for a purpose that was not clear and a so-called government that was not recognized. He drew a parallel with the loan MacGregor had raised in London in 1822, pointing out that the government of Poyais had defaulted on its promised interest payments and it appeared that investors had subsequently lost all the money they had subscribed.

With regard to the contract between the Cazique and la Nouvelle Neustrie, the prosecutor said the only evidence that MacGregor had the right to cede land in Poyais to the company was a vague document which had no legal validity in France, and appeared to refer to a tract that did not extend to the 500,000 acres mentioned in the agreement. Indeed, a portion of the territory referred to in the document signed by the King of the Mosquito Shore now appeared to be, in reality, part of the neighbouring state of Colombia. He submitted that both the land concession and the loan prospectus were elements of a fraudulent plan created for the personal profit of MacGregor, Lehuby and their associates.

The prosecution was seriously hampered, however, by the absence of Lehuby, who remained in Belgium along with documents that were crucial to the case. This allowed MacGregor's lawyer, Maître Merilhou, to suggest that if there had been any wrongdoing, it had been on the part of the missing managing director. The Cazique had acted in good faith, with the best interests of his country in mind. He had not known Monsieur Lehuby, and had merely considered that a company properly constituted in France, and registered with the Tribunal de Commerce, must surely be a reliable partner in the economic and social development of Poyais. In this, the Cazique had been led to believe he had the support of the French government: Merilhou produced a witness who stated that the deed of cession had been shown to the Minister of Foreign Affairs and that no barrier to its execution had been remarked upon.

Why, then, Merilhou concluded, were the Cazique, his secretary, and his chief negotiator now on trial? Why had it suddenly been decided that a contract – which had previously received what amounted to official sanction – was an illegal document?

It was true, the defence counsel conceded, that French law did not recognize the validity of such an agreement under the signatures of foreigners with no official status in the country, but that obstacle had been overcome by having the *acte de concession* verified by a notaire. Perhaps some subsequent irregularities had been observed in the actions of la Nouvelle Neustrie, but these were not matters within the knowledge of the defendants, or over which they had any control. The prosecution had produced neither witnesses nor documents to prove that the three accused had committed fraud or been involved in any conspiracy, and the charges against them should be dismissed.

The prosecutor appeared to agree. In his closing speech, he admitted that he had no actual proofs of conspiracy or fraud, and that the Cazique had responded to the investigation with exemplary candour and fair-mindedness. In the circumstances, he was prepared to withdraw the charges against the accused – but with the recommendation that they be speedily deported from France.

The three judges concurred. They ordered that the defendants be taken to the Salle Saint-Martin where, after the completion of certain formalities required by law, they would be released the following day. It was, Hippisley recalled, 'a full and perfect acquittal'. But it was by no means the end of the matter.

Hippisley recalled bitterly:

Two days were suffered to elapse, without our receiving any intelligence: on the morning of the third, a friend of ours called upon the Procureur du Roi, to learn the cause of our detention, who informed him, that although the law allowed him ten days to appeal against the decision of the tribunal, he had no intention of profiting by his right, in the present instance, and assured him that we should be placed at liberty on the following day; on the afternoon of which, our friend again waited upon him: the learned gentleman had changed his note, and stammering some sort of an excuse, for the deception he had practised, stated that, in consequence of fresh documents which had just reached him, he had decided upon appealing against the sentence!

What had happened, in fact, was that the negotiations for the extradition of Lehuby from Belgium had suddenly turned in favour of the French authorities, and the Crown Prosecutor now believed he would have the opportunity to prove his case.

So MacGregor, Hippisley and Irving remained at the Salle Saint-Martin, where the Cazique was permitted to receive day-long visits from his wife and children, while the prosecutor awaited the arrival of Lehuby and the eventual report of the magistrate who would examine him. The three prisoners did not pass all their time idly, though. By the end of the first week of their new period of captivity, they had composed a letter to the President of the Royal Court of Justice.

We appeal to your authority [they wrote] in the hope

of securing the justice awarded to us by the district court which has now been suspended owing to the appeal against the verdict by the ministry of justice. We have been in detention for eight months because we are implicated in proceedings against an individual who is being pursued on the ground of his attempt to establish colonies in America. After an investigation lasting eight months, we came to trial on the 6th instant. Monsieur Pécourt, the lawyer acting for the crown prosecutor, declared that no case could be proved against us; he withdrew the charges, and, in a solemn judgement, we were all acquitted and ordered to be set at liberty.

We had reason to think that the ministry of justice would not seek to challenge what it had itself sought, and would comply with the order for our release; but we have learnt that it is now appealing against the judgement made on the basis of its own submission. We appeal to you, Mr President, to set an early date for a hearing of this appeal that serves further to suspend the liberty of which we have been deprived for so long.

Like their previous attempts to secure official intervention in the case, this one yielded no result – except that, a week after the letter had been sent, the prisoners were removed from the benign regime of the Salle Saint-Martin and returned to the considerably less comfortable conditions of Bicêtre. Whether they were ultimately to be found guilty or not, the authorities were clearly convinced, quite justifiably, that they had been part of a criminal conspiracy and were bent on punishing them.

At the end of April 1826 the extradition of Monsieur

Lehuby was finally completed, and he arrived at La Force on 6 May. As a result, MacGregor, Hippisley and Irving were given a new trial date of 20 May, but when the day came, the office of the Crown Prosecutor announced that it was still not ready to proceed. As it turned out, the delay was to be of benefit to the defendants: MacGregor used the time to work with Maître Merilhou on preparing a statement running to 5,000 words, setting out a highly inaccurate account of the Cazique's background and his activities in South America, and a passionate assertion of his complete innocence of any conspiracy or attempt to defraud.*

The questioning of Lehuby continued for another month, with the Crown Prosecutor showing no inclination to bring him to trial. It was obviously MacGregor that the Ministry of Justice had in its sights, and Hippisley began to think that the Cazique had perhaps been unwise to publish his declaration to the Congress of Panama, which 'will have naturally increased the political rancour' of the French authorities, so that 'it is difficult to say to what extent they may carry their hostility, if permitted to follow the bent of their own vindictiveness'.

As if to prove the point, their lawyer, Merilhou, was summoned as a witness for the prosecution, because of his connection with la Nouvelle Neustrie and therefore his knowledge of the background to the land transaction,

* A shortened and fairly literal translation of this entertaining document appears in the Appendix, starting on page 343.

which of course meant that he could no longer represent the defendants. However, Merilhou had completed his eloquent submission in defence of the Cazique, and he handed it to a trusted colleague named Berville, who proved to be equally skilful at delivering it when the case finally did come to court on 10 July. Indeed, it was probably at least partly owing to Berville's long submission that the hearing lasted for four days.

After picturing MacGregor as a selfless promoter of liberty in South America, falsely accused and improperly detained by the French authorities for what must be political reasons, the lawyer went on to deliver a detailed and almost completely fictitious account of his client's background.

As an aristocrat and chief of his ancient clan, he was related to many of the noble houses in England, as well as being a descendant of Scottish kings. As a soldier, he had been among the flower of the British army, the author of a book on infantry tactics that had drawn warm congratulations from the commander-in-chief – not bad for a man who had served just seven years, who had risen no higher than the rank of captain, and who had never taken part in a battle! His relatively lowly rank, incidentally, had to be acknowledged in court, since it was easily verifiable. MacGregor's failure to be promoted beyond it, in spite of his acknowledged technical brilliance, was attributed to the fact that he was a Roman Catholic, and therefore had been discriminated against.

Maître Berville then turned to the legends created by

MacGregor about his service in the armies of Venezuela and New Granada, including his resounding victories at Amelia Island, Porto Bello and Rio de la Hacha, which had played their part in driving the Spanish out of their former subject provinces.

> General MacGregor had accomplished the task he had set himself: a noble people had been delivered from foreign domination, and presented with the benefits of civilization. Since that moment, the existence of the new states has no longer been contested; and, today, the assent of Europe has given support to a result that was so long in doubt, and to the efforts demanded of the inhabitants of those once unhappy countries.

The small matter of the part played in this glorious liberation by Simón Bolívar and the other great figures of the South American Independence movement was, understandably, overlooked in this ardent address.

But it was to the history of Poyais that the advocate devoted the longest portion of his review of the career of General MacGregor, though he forbore from describing the circumstances that had brought the country into his possession, on the ground that they would take too long to explain. Suffice it to say that, seeking nothing for himself, he had been elected Cazique by the natives, who were confident that the qualities he had displayed during the revolution would guarantee their future. This election, it must be pointed out, was unconnected with the grant of land MacGregor had received from the King of the

285

Mosquito Shore and Nation, and which had endowed him with the rights of a sort of governor in the Territory.

It was important, Maître Berville emphasized, that the court did not confuse the responsibilities conferred by the grant of land with those attending the election of MacGregor as Cazique. Such confusion was largely to blame for the slanderous attacks by his enemies that had contributed to the charges he now faced and the unjust detention he had suffered.

The lawyer suggested that there was no connection between MacGregor's encouragement of emigration to Poyais, and his decision to raise money for the country in the form of publicly subscribed loans. The emigration related to his desire to develop the land ceded to him by the King, while the loans reflected his duty to secure the future of the people who had elected him as their Cazique. The only association between the two activities was an unfortunate one. In both cases, MacGregor, as an honourable man himself, had relied upon the honesty and integrity of others, and had found them wanting.

With regard to the loan issue, he had been caught up in events which he could not have foreseen and was powerless to prevent, but the judges should note the fact that he personally had received no complaints from subscribers, who had been shrewd enough to see where the real blame lay.

As for the emigration programme, he had become the victim of unscrupulous merchants in Belize, who, fearing that serious economic activity in Poyais would damage their own businesses, had lured away the settlers and had even persuaded them to seize the ship MacGregor had provided for them, and to sell it for their own profit. Some sympathy for the settlers had been expressed in the public prints, but it was surely difficult to feel sorry for people who had stolen a ship and had then betrayed the man who had paid them by taking their services elsewhere.

It was as a result of this series of events, the advocate said, that General MacGregor found himself in his present difficult position. Yet he had only remained in Paris at the suggestion of French government ministers, who had sought his participation in discussions on South American affairs being conducted by various European powers. In the light of such official interest, he had consented to negotiations with a French company that had approached him, as Cazique of Poyais, seeking to send its own emigrants to the country and requesting the concession of land for that purpose.

He declares upon his honour [Maître Berville told the court] that no condition other than those appearing in the agreement was ever discussed or demanded. The conditions offered and accepted as the principle of the negotiations consisted solely of the right on the part of the French to preserve the French language and French laws, and, in return, the payment of a rent of one franc per acre by each colonist after the third year of cultivation of the land.

He declares upon his honour that he never either sought or received, directly or indirectly, any sum of money in connection with this agreement, and that the only pecuniary clause that was ever agreed concerned the rent payable after three years.

He declares upon his honour that he met Monsieur Lehuby for the first time on the day of the signature of the agreement, that is to say the 4 June 1825, and that he has not seen him since then.

There were already many people who could have told the judges just what the word of honour of Gregor MacGregor counted for, but Maître Merilhou, as the author of the address the court had heard, and Maître Berville, as the actor who read the script, had done their work extremely well. The Cazique of Poyais was acquitted on all charges, and those against Hippisley and Irving were withdrawn and stricken from the record.

French justice contented itself with the subsequent conviction of Monsieur Lehuby, who was sentenced to thirteen months in prison for making false representations in relation to the sale of shares, and with the eight months the Cazique had already spent in jail on remand.

It was the only sentence Gregor MacGregor would ever serve, anywhere, for a fraud the like of which has never been seen again.

HOMECOMING

It would be reasonable to assume that the events in Paris were the last that anyone heard of the mythical land of Poyais, but Gregor MacGregor was not the sort of man to let a good idea wither away because of a few technical difficulties. Whatever the suspicions of the French authorities he had not, after all, been convicted of fraud, and, in some ways, the affair had actually enhanced his position.

The publication of the new Poyaisian constitution, and the pompous declaration directed at the Congress of Panama, while designed mainly to help establish MacGregor's status in France, also served to consolidate it among a British public that knew little or nothing about what was really happening in the chaotic new states of South America. Shifting alliances, sudden changes of government and uncertainty over which countries were which, as former provinces joined or left a succession of federations, led to confusion that militated in favour of the existence of Poyais – particularly as its supposed head of state was both visible and active in Europe.

The lesson MacGregor learned from his experiences in France was that the weakness of his original, fraudulent concept was the direct dealing in land in Poyais. He had attempted to avoid a repeat of the settlement catastrophe of 1823 by merely leasing the land he claimed to own to la Nouvelle Neustrie, but when that also led him into trouble, he resolved to confine his future operations to the issue of financial instruments. That would also remove any potential dispute arising from the revocation of King George Frederic's grant, upon which the first Poyais scheme had been founded. MacGregor was now promoting investment in the country on the basis of his alleged election as Cazique by its inhabitants, rather than as the beneficiary of the Mosquito King's generosity. It was a distinction he had been careful to emphasize publicly at his trial.

Having eventually been acquitted by the French Court of Appeal, he was spared the indignity of being deported, but he could not remain in Paris. His funds were running low after three years of expensive living, and there was now no prospect of his being able to derive an income there from the counterfeit persona upon which he had come to rely. In London, by contrast, the adverse publicity which had attended the return of the Poyais settlers had long since died away, and the market reports in the newspapers suggested that there was a new appetite for foreign investment.

There had been a serious financial crisis towards the end of 1825, following a sudden change of monetary policy by the Bank of England. Sir John Perring's bank had been one of almost a hundred institutions to collapse, and even Baring's had found itself in difficulties as a result of its attempts to maintain prices in the bond market. At least one leading City banker committed suicide, after losing all his clients' money. The bank failures led to the bankruptcy of hundreds of commercial companies, and perhaps thousands of individual investors. As for shares, the *Morning Chronicle* commented, 'no person thinks of mentioning their names, and thousands wish they had never had a name to mention'. South American bonds, of course, had become virtually worthless, as one new republic after another defaulted on its loans.

Strangely, there is evidence that, just before panic set in, some investors had sought to obtain a hedge against projected losses by subscribing to the Poyais loan MacGregor had arranged from Paris. He had taken the trouble to condense and republish Thomas Strangeways's so-called guide to Poyais as a forty-page booklet entitled *Some Account of the Poyais Country*. This concentrated mainly on the financial statistics and directed the attention of readers towards la Nouvelle Neustrie – along with eleven other, unnamed, companies – as an example of the confidence the country enjoyed in the business community. This time, the guide appeared under the name of W. R. Goodluck, an ironic touch that may or may not have been deliberate, but should certainly have aroused some suspicions. At any rate, the records of the Stock Exchange indicate that there was trading in the loan bonds, subscribers apparently believing Mr Goodluck's assertion that the previous loan had gone into default only because the funds raised had been 'misappropriated' by the contractor, John Lowe.

MacGregor calculated that if he could sell Poyais bonds in such unfavourable conditions, the recovery of confidence that began to emerge in the late summer of 1826 ought to make it easy to float the largest loan he had yet contemplated. This would be the financial coup that would ensure security and comfort for the rest of his life. So he closed down the Poyais establishment in the rue Louis Legrand, packed up his family home in the Champs-Élysées, and moved back to London – no doubt leaving behind him, as usual, substantial numbers of unpaid bills.

At first, it seemed he might well have cause to regret his decision. Shortly after his arrival, he was arrested and taken to the prison at Tothill Fields, in Westminster. The reasons for his arrest are unclear. No formal charges appear to have been brought against him, and he was released after only a little more than a week.

The most likely explanation is that a warrant had been issued against outstanding debts, perhaps stretching back as far as his recruitment campaign on behalf of New Granada. The debt of £1,000, it will be remembered – money squandered by MacGregor on his own pleasures – had been assumed by Mr Newte, who had subsequently lost a great deal more money in supplying a ship, arms and provisions for the expedition to Rio de la Hacha.

It would not have been surprising if, after some of the truth about MacGregor had emerged in the newspapers, and Michael Rafter had published his book giving details of the General's behaviour at Rio de la Hacha, Mr Newte had reached the limit of his patience. On the other hand, there were plenty of other people to whom MacGregor owed substantial sums of money.

Certainly, no criminal proceedings had resulted from the inquiry by the Lord Mayor of London into the tragedy of the Poyais settlers, and no evidence has come to light of legal action against MacGregor arising from the 1822 loan issue, or on the part of those purchasers of land who had never even reached Poyais, having been turned back by the British navy on the advice of the Superintendent of Belize.

The circumstances of MacGregor's release after such a short period of detention are also obscure: it may be that, if debt was indeed involved, he had enough money to repay it, or was able to persuade one of the adherents he still had in London to do so on his behalf. Whatever the details, he was again free to promote Poyais and thereby, he hoped, finally to make his fortune.

The Poyais legation in Dowgate Hill was long gone, and with it, presumably, the chargé d'affaires, Major Richardson. In any case, MacGregor now dropped any pretension to quasi-royal status, and there was to be no more scattering of titles, military ranks or honours. He also quietly set aside his 'knighthood', styling himself henceforward simply 'Cacique of the Republic of Poyais'

– the change from 'z' to 'c' in his nomenclature probably reflecting nothing more than the usage to which he had become accustomed in France. A new Poyaisian office, with no pseudo-diplomatic connections, was opened at 23 Threadneedle Street, in the City, not far from the Bank of England. This was strictly a business venture.

And what good business it was intended to be. Whereas the original Poyais loans had been for the relatively small sums of £200,000 and £300,000, the new issue was to be worth £800,000. Was this a case of wild over-confidence on MacGregor's part, an indication that he had fallen into the trap of believing his own lies? Or does the amount reflect a desire to make enough money so that he could put this whole Poyais nonsense behind him and retire?

Apart from anything else, the elaborate façade he had constructed, with the legions of agents, servants, secretaries, clerks, merchants and military 'officers', had swallowed up the greater part of the income it had been created to attract. For various other reasons, not all of them related to the fraud itself, the amount of that income had been rather smaller than the efforts made to achieve it might have appeared to warrant. One senses an air of weariness, almost of desperation, about MacGregor's last large-scale confidence trick.

Nevertheless, it was prepared with his usual attention to detail. Reflecting the current state of the market, the twenty-year bonds offered interest at just three per cent, which, for the first three years, might be paid in the form of warrants entitling the holders to land certificates. The now obligatory sinking fund was to be financed from future sales of land, the proceeds of which would be invested in British government securities rather than the unreliable foreign variety. In addition, the bonds themselves could be exchanged for land certificates, with the price set at five shillings per acre.

Thomas Jenkins & Company, having emerged unscathed from the Paris loan issue, once again agreed to act as brokers, and the bonds were produced at optimistic nominal values of £250, £500 and £1,000, sold at sixty per cent. But they failed to yield their promoters anything like the rewards that had been envisaged. For the time being, at least, it appeared that, while people did have money to invest, they had become more cautious, especially where South American countries were concerned. After the loan was announced in the early summer of 1827, the following handbill began to be circulated in the City:

Take care of your Pockets
Another Poyais Humbug

In August 1824, a plan was in agitation to catch the unwary again in the Poyais securities – suspecting at the time what was going forward I caused to be circulated some printed papers warning the public against the Trap laid for some and it so far had the effect as to cause those who had bought the Bonds to immediately sell them & prevented those who had not bought them from buying. The consequence was that they continued to decline till they were scarcely saleable at any price and what was given pounds for fell to shillings until taken up by a party who mean to turn their shillings into pounds again if they can gull the public to give Three pounds and upwards for a piece of paper (setting aside speculation) that would not be worth three farthing[s] & for this purpose they have sent forth an advertisement in the newspapers of a new scheme for the redemption of the old Bonds – but mark, they give you no money, all you [will] get will be a clean piece of paper for a dirty [one] with the promise of paying your Interest in land which if you do not like they will give you a shilling an acre for – therefore the inducement held out to purchase the new Bonds is that you will get one shilling back in the pound for the money you may lay out in them & no more.

Upon the coming out of the Spanish & Poyais Loans, I was, from the advantage held out in them induced to invest my money, and an intimate friend of mine who had from industry & care saved a comfortable independence embarked the whole of his property in the above & Colombian securities. The loss he sustained in them so preyed upon his mind as to send him to his grave about this time last year, the Bonds were sent into the market & sold & the produce arising from them laid out in an annuity for his Widow which is barely sufficient for her support, and her 3 daughters which were once comfortably off, have been obliged to seek their living by servitude.

Knowing these facts I think I am performing a duty in warning the public against such swindling concerns.

Interestingly, it was the failure of such bonds to deliver what they promised, or even to sustain the prices paid for them, that was seen as the swindle. Nobody thought to question the legitimacy of Poyais itself, the background of its ostensible head of state and the authority by which he could cede land and raise loans, or the existence of the assets allegedly to be employed for interest payments and redemption. Some investors had begun to understand that they were being fleeced, but almost none realized how comprehensively.

Still, there was enough wariness in the market to make the new bond issue a resounding flop, and MacGregor was extremely fortunate in being able to pass on the bulk of the unsold certificates, late in 1827, to a consortium of hardened speculators, though no doubt at a fraction of their discounted value. He made a little money, but nothing that came anywhere near reaching the retirement fund of nearly £500,000 the issue would have been worth if it had been fully subscribed at sixty per cent of face value. The actual proceeds could not have been more than a few thousand pounds, and MacGregor's continuing need for immediate funds was emphasized in 1828, when he resorted again to attempting to sell land directly.

Certificates entitling the holders to 'land in Poyais Proper', at a price of five shillings an acre, were issued against ready cash in blocks of as little as fifty acres, which would have yielded just £12.10s each. Even the largest parcel of land on offer, at 1,000 acres, would have netted MacGregor only £250. It was better than working for a living, but it was a sad decline from the days of large loan issues. His Highness the Cazique of Poyais had become the financial equivalent of a door-to-door salesman.

Yet there were enough gullible people with funds available who were willing to buy these worthless pieces of paper, so that it was not until December 1830 that MacGregor was obliged to refresh his product with the issue of new certificates for 'Poyais Proper and extensions':

> We, Gregor Mac Gregor, Cacique of Poyais, do hereby certify that the Bearer hereof is entitled to _____ Acres of Land in that part of the Poyaisian Republic called Poyais Proper. And we do hereby declare this to be a Certificate for a Special Grant of _____ Acres of Land, and that the Bearer hereof may take possession of the same in any unappropriated part of the aforesaid Territory (our Title to which Land in Poyais Proper being set forth in the foregoing Copy of the Original Grant,) or in any other unappropriated part of the Republic, on condition of paying unto us and our heirs the sum of one cent of a dollar per Acre annually, in the name of quit rent, on the twenty-fourth day of December in each year. The said quit rent, however, not to commence until possession of the said land is taken by virtue hereof. And we do hereby promise and bind ourselves and our heirs to make, execute, and deliver to the Bearer hereof upon request, at any time after the possession of the said land shall be had and obtained, a regular Title of the same to him and his heirs for ever. We hereby confirm the foregoing and do now extend the range of this Certificate to any other unappropriated part of the Republic.

Quite what was the point of the final paragraph it is difficult to see, save to make a difference between the new certificates and those MacGregor had issued in 1828.

This suggests that his need for cash was becoming acute. Shortage of funds, however, was not his only problem in 1830.

King George Frederic of the Mosquito Shore and Nation had died six years earlier – strangled, it was said, by one of his wives – and had been succeeded by his brother, Robert Charles Frederic. The new King, aware that his predecessor had revoked his grant of land to MacGregor, and conscious of growing interest in the country because of its virtually untouched timber reserves, began to offer for sale the same stretch of territory, and the thousands of certificates he issued competed directly with MacGregor's when they appeared on the London market.

The Cazique could respond to this challenge by drawing attention to his registration of the original grant at the Court of Chancery, fraudulent though that was, but his second problem could not be so easily dealt with. By 1830, people who had been foolish enough to invest in his 1827 bonds were beginning to complain that the promised interest payments had not materialized, and either threatened legal action or demanded their money back.

MacGregor had been clever enough to insert in the bonds a clause permitting the government of Poyais to convert the first three years' interest into land certificate warrants, but now that the three years were up, investors would not be satisfied with a mere promise. Almost at the same time as he was issuing his new certificates, therefore, MacGregor was obliged to produce similar ones to the value of the interest payments he owed. There was, of course, no money in this. Time was all he acquired in return, though, in a way, it was almost as precious as cash. With all these land certificates circulating, both from MacGregor and from King Robert, it surely could not be too long before the market began to wonder whether the boundaries of Poyais were infinitely expandable.

In fact, it has been calculated that of the eight million acres MacGregor allegedly acquired with his grant, he issued certificates covering half of that total – while King Robert produced documents in sufficient numbers to sell the same eight million acres several times over. Not only that, but other fraudsters were beginning to see the attractions of Poyais, and were setting themselves up to trade in any of the certificates they could get their hands on. Two men with the surname Upton, either brothers or father and son, opened a rival 'Poyaisian Office' in Pancras Lane, round the corner from MacGregor's, and offered for sale land debentures purporting to be based on King Robert's grants and verified by the 'Secretary' – though of what is not stated.

The debenture promised that '3,000 Acres of Land will be estimated as £1,000 Stock, or any other number in that proportion. Land, till occupied, will entitle the Holder of the Debenture to a proportionate share of the profits arising from the sale of the *produce of unoccupied Land*, and to a like share of half the *amount* received from the sale of *unappropriated Land*.' With that gobbledegook, it was clear that Gregor MacGregor had his imitators, and they were eating into his business.

How and where MacGregor actually lived during this period of twilight in his career of imposture and criminal deception is something of a mystery. It is inconceivable that, on his return to London in 1826, he would have been welcomed back to Oak Hall, the Wanstead estate of his former collaborator, Major Richardson. The Major had certainly remained loyal to him long after his flight to Paris in 1823, to the extent that, the following year, he had instigated an action for libel against the *Morning Herald* because of a defamatory article the newspaper had published about the Cazique. The journalists were convicted, because they had no verifiable proof of their allegations, but the amount of damages awarded was derisory, and costs were not awarded to the plaintiff.

Although MacGregor claimed not to have known anything about the case while it was proceeding, Major Richardson had obviously been given to understand that he was acting on behalf of the Poyaisian authorities, and that they would meet his costs. The strongest indication of this is that he refused to pay the fees of the lawyer he had engaged, which led to his being sued himself in June 1825. After that experience, it is highly unlikely that he would have wanted anything to do with Gregor MacGregor, let alone taking him back into his home.

Nor does Gustavus Butler Hippisley give any indication that he remained in contact with MacGregor after their release from prison. He certainly did make serious efforts to publish his letters of the period in book form, including his defence of a man of whom 'at the same instant that the

English journals were impugning his conduct, and casting unmerited obloquy upon his name, the inhabitants of a large portion of the Southern Hemisphere, were singing the praises of one of the earliest, and most intrepid defenders of their freedom!!' But the real purpose of his book – which, in any case, did not appear until 1831 – was to vilify the French government and system of justice and, like his future brother-in-law Richardson, he probably felt he had suffered enough from his association with the Cazique of Poyais, however much he might have admired him.

For the first time in many years, then, MacGregor seems to have known no one who was willing to provide accommodation for himself or his family. Doubtless he had managed to save some of the ill-gotten gains Poyais had brought him and, as has been suggested, some cash would have been forthcoming from the sales of his bonds and land certificates, enough to maintain him in London lodgings and put food on the table – though perhaps not of the standard he would have wished.

In 1831, he tried a new tactic, promoting 'Poyaisian New Three per cent Consolidated Stock', no longer as Cazique, but as 'President of the Poyaisian Republic'. Like all his post-Paris issues, the certificates were printed in both English and French, this one promising:

That the Bearer hereof is entitled to have this Stock Certificate exchanged for a SPECIAL BOND of **One Hundred Pounds**, of a new Stock, to be called 'THE POYAISIAN THREE PER CENT REDUCED STOCK,' and which said Stock is to be redeemable at par, at a certain date, to be therein named, and to bear Interest from the first day of May, one thousand eight hundred and thirty-two, at the rate of Three Pounds per Centum per Annum.

And furthermore, We hereby promise and engage to deliver or cause to be delivered to the Bearer hereof, in Exchange for this Stock Certificate, a SPECIAL BOND of **One Hundred Pounds**, of the Poyais Three per Cent. Reduced Stock as aforesaid, so soon as the same shall be prepared and ready for delivery.

So it had come to this, a brilliantly conceived and superbly executed fraud reduced to the level of a meaningless piece of paper offering something unknown at some unspecified time, and with interest that could not be calculated, because no redemption or payment dates were given. The mind that had been so creative in separating greedy people from their money had run out of ideas. Hardly surprising, then, that as his income dwindled, and the difficulties of 'selling' Poyais multiplied, he finally did what he had done before so many times, and in so many different circumstances: he retreated.

The year 1834 found him back home in Scotland, living in Edinburgh, and still besieged by disappointed investors in Poyais, since he was forced to issue a new series of land certificates as payment for unredeemed securities. Again, there appears to be no record of where he lived in the city, or how he supported himself, but the suggestion is that he depended at least to some extent on the financial help of his family. Some of his Poyais securities and land certificates were still circulating, and may have brought in some money, as evidenced by the fact that in 1836 he attempted to revive interest, as well as to distance himself from his rivals in Pancras Lane, by writing yet another new constitution, this time for a less extensive Poyaisian republic concentrated in the region of the Black River.

The world was changing, though, as the interests of businessmen and investors moved away from South America. One reason for this was that the new Republics owed British bondholders a total of nearly £27 million in unredeemed loans and interest payments on them – though that sum, of course, did not include the indebtedness of Poyais!

North America, which was rapidly industrializing, was a much better prospect, and throughout the 1830s, both federal and state governments found no shortage of takers for their stocks and bonds. The United States also became one of the favourite destinations for British emigrants, along with Canada, Australia and New Zealand, which were heavily promoted by a British government prepared to finance the foundation of settlements there as part of its creation of an empire.

Poyais had had its day, and so had the Cazique, or President MacGregor, as he now appeared in the documents he produced. His last recorded transactions on behalf of the country he had invented took place in 1837, with the sale of some land certificates. Thereafter, MacGregor might have passed the rest of his days not only in obscurity but in penury as well, had he not possessed the boldness and the determination to achieve one final 'score', as he might have put it if he had been a modern-day confidence trickster.

In May 1838, he lost the one constant element in his life when his wife died in Edinburgh. Josefa had endured a great deal during the twenty-six years of their marriage, not only the dangers and privations of war and of virtual destitution – the latter after being left by her husband to fend for herself and her children as best she might in Jamaica – but also the vicissitudes of his subsequent criminal activities. Whether she ever complained is, of course, not known, but her attachment to MacGregor was certainly 'until death us do part'.

Josefa must have been a very remarkable person. It is true that most of her adult life was spent thousands of miles from her native land, which would have made it difficult for her to contemplate leaving her husband, and especially with her children. On the other hand, she was obviously strong-willed and resourceful, and it would surely not have been beyond her capacity, had she so desired, to return to Venezuela, even before her cousin Bolívar had finally defeated the Spaniards in the former New Granada. Yet it is worth noting that, in his own way, MacGregor was as loyal to his wife as she was to him. He might have left her alone and unprovided for during long periods, but he always returned for her, and one has the impression that it was not just as an actor's prop that he involved her so closely in the construction of the image of Poyais.

The days of luxury and social superiority in London, as

the Princess of Poyais and, later, in Paris, must have provided some compensation for Josefa's previous hardships,
and there is every reason to suppose that she believed her
role was a genuine one. After all, she knew only what her
husband told her about his visit to the Mosquito Shore, the
grant of land by the King, and his election as Cazique by
the natives. Why would she not have believed it all? Plenty
of other people did. He had married her as a general in
Francisco de Miranda's army and also, apparently, as a
Knight of the Portuguese Order of Christ, and as the
Chief of a Scottish clan with royal blood in his veins. He
had proved himself a stalwart of the patriotic cause, and
had been Captain-General of the land and naval forces of
New Granada. If, towards the end of 1820, he arrived to
collect his family in Jamaica and announced that he had
become the leader of a small South American state, that
would not have been at all surprising to Josefa.

The alternative explanation, which is that Josefa knew
precisely what her husband was doing and was his willing
accomplice, seems an improbable one. MacGregor clearly
had the ability to charm women – he had earlier persuaded
his first wife, Maria Bowater, to become part of his fantasies
– and a corresponding inability to tell the truth. Any
scene in which he might have confessed all to Josefa and
sought her cooperation in the great deception is simply
unimaginable. She probably really did think that she was
the Princess of Poyais.

Without his princess, and with Poyais itself no longer
a potent force, MacGregor was bereft. In the early summer

of 1838, he was also virtually penniless, and it might be supposed that his relations had had enough of him. As he contemplated an increasingly bleak future, a thought struck him: he was still a major general in the Venezuelan army, given that rank by Bolívar himself, and in possession of a letter to prove it. Surely that must be worth something, at least the general's pay due to him, which he had not received for years. He was the hero of the retreat from Ocumare, one of the heroes of the siege of Cartagena. There had even been a proposal, back in 1819, that he should represent the island of Margarita at a republican congress. The new nation which had been built, at least in part, upon his efforts ought to be grateful. It should be willing to pay him a pension. He sat down at his writing table and began to compose a letter.

At that time, the President of Venezuela was one of the last survivors of the cohort of original revolutionaries. Simón Bolívar had died almost a decade earlier, in obscurity and disillusion as the Federal Republic of Colombia that he had established broke apart into separate and often warring countries, and Venezuela rejected him. Another of the old guard, General Antonio de Sucre, had led the country for a short time, before being assassinated. Now, General José Antonio Paez was *el caudillo*, a more or less benevolent dictator who had established a large measure of stability in Venezuela. His record went back to 1810, so he was a veteran of the Miranda campaigns, and Miranda's reputation had begun to be restored after the death of Bolívar. Later, Paez had been with General

Piar at Barcelona when the retreat from Ocumare had been celebrated, and he had heard Bolívar's expressions of admiration for the exploit.

When a letter from General Gregor MacGregor arrived at the President's office in Caracas, then, it awakened a flood of memories for Paez. Victory had erased the stains of Amelia Island, Porto Bello and Rio de la Hacha, and the country was in a mood to honour the great deeds of its revolutionary past. Paez instructed one of his staff to reply to General MacGregor, telling him that he would be most welcome to return to Venezuela and to benefit from what was certainly due to him.

No details are available of how MacGregor obtained a sea passage, but sometime in 1839 he appeared in Caracas, where confirmation of his former military rank was gazetted and he was awarded both his back pay and his general's pension. The money was sufficient to allow him to live in the capital in some style, and to indulge in one of his favourite pastimes, regaling all who would listen with dramatic stories of his military adventures, from the Peninsular War to the rout of the Spaniards at Rio de la Hacha.

MacGregor's children appear to have remained in Scotland, where his daughter, Josefa, is recorded as having died in 1872, leaving two sons, both of whom were childless. Of the lives of Gregorio and Constantino MacGregor, no details have as yet come to light.

Gregor MacGregor himself died in Caracas on 4 December 1845, just three weeks short of his fifty-ninth birthday.

He was interred in the cathedral, with all the pomp of a military funeral, and his name was inscribed on the monument of the Liberators, where it can still be seen today.

The memorials to what might be regarded as, in some ways, his most lasting personal achievement have been of a rather different order.

STRANGER THAN FICTION

While Major General Gregor MacGregor was enjoying a peaceful, comfortable and, it might be
thought, a thoroughly undeserved retirement in Caracas,
the Cazique of Poyais was becoming both something of
a figure of fun and a symbol of the human capacity for
delusion in early Victorian England. He appeared first
in this form in the Reverend Thomas Harris Barham's
popular series of highly irreverent comic poems entitled
The Ingoldsby Legends, which began to be published in the
magazine *Bentley's Miscellany* in the late 1830s. One poem,
'The Merchant of Venice', contains the following verse:

> The bulk of my property, merged in rich cargoes, is
> Tossing about, as you know, in my argosies ...
> One bound to England, another to Tripoli,
> Cyprus, Masulipatam and Bombay.
> A sixth, by the way, I consigned t'other day

> To Sir Gregor MacGregor, Cacique of Poyais,
> A country where silver's as common as clay!

The novelist Thackeray followed this up in 1841 with a reference in his satirical and moral tale *The History of Samuel Titmarsh and the Great Hoggarty Diamond*, which is all about greed, gullibility and fraud. In chapter ten, the eponymous hero of the story recalls an event from 1824:

> On Saturday, Abednego Junior left the office for ever, and I became head clerk with £400 a year salary. It was a fatal week for the office, too. On Monday, when I arrived and took my seat at the head desk, and my first read of the newspaper, as was my right, the first thing I read was, 'Frightful fire in Houndsditch! Total destruction of Mr Meshach's sealing-wax manufactory and of Mr Shadrach's clothing depot, adjoining. In the former was £20,000 worth of the finest Dutch wax, which the voracious element attacked and devoured in a twinkling. The latter estimable gentleman had just completed forty thousand suits of clothes for the cavalry of H.H. the Cacique of Poyais.'

The implications there are obvious, and they became much more so in a book published the same year by a prolific but now less well-remembered writer called Henry Cockton, who took what was known of MacGregor's incredible history and converted it into an entertaining comic novel entitled *George St George Julian, The Prince*. It followed the facts fairly closely, but some critics found it too fanciful and disliked its theme, which suggested that a gentleman could survive in modern urban society with his reputation intact, in spite of enriching himself by means of extremely dubious financial practices.

There was also evidence of some ambivalence towards the character on whom the story was based. One American reviewer conceded that 'the mysteries of speculation, the fluctuations of stock-jobbing, the disclosures of secret manoeuvres of brokers, are all plausible', and that 'the details of the Poyais colonization scheme will surely be well appreciated and relished by readers who are actually living in the midst of a feverish vortex, the California mania, which has never been surpassed, save, perhaps, by the excitement of the Mississippi, South Sea and Poyais emigrations'. However:

> One of the prominent actors in this work is the famous Gregor MacGregor. We regret to see that worthy figure in a manner so disreputable. If he really did perform in Europe the strange antics ascribed to him by the author, it only proves that men are strange compounds of contradictions. The history of MacGregor would be in itself a most interesting novel. He was one of the earliest, the boldest, and most adventurous of the champions of South American independence. His exploits in the Mexican war would fill a volume with improbable but authentic romance.

MacGregor, of course, did not take part in the Mexican war, so the romance of his exploits would definitely have been more improbable than authentic. What the writer's comment illustrates, though, is the lasting effect of all the stories MacGregor circulated about his background and his activities. They were still being accepted as fact a quarter of a century later, when the monumental *The Scottish Nation: The Surnames, Families, Literature, Honours and Biographical History of the People of Scotland* was published in Edinburgh. The author, William Anderson, summarized MacGregor's career as follows:

Sir Gregor MacGregor at one time rendered himself remarkable by his exploits in South America, and particularly by obtaining sovereign sway in Poyais, a fertile tract of land, on the Mosquito Shore, near the Bay of Honduras, with a capital of the same name. He was originally an officer in the British army, and served with distinction in Spain. In 1816 he was very active in the Venezuelan Revolution, and in 1817 he took possession of Amelia Island, on the coast of Florida, then belonging to Spain. In 1819 he attacked Porto Bello, which he captured, but was soon after surprised in his bed, and obliged to escape out of a window. Some years subsequently he settled among the Poyais, a warlike race of Indians, who had maintained their independence, and having gained their confidence he was chosen by them as their cacique. In this capacity he encouraged commerce, founded schools etc. In 1824 as Cacique of Poyais he procured a loan in London from respectable houses. Strangeways, his aide-de-camp, published at Edinburgh in 1822 *A Sketch of the Mosquito Shore, including the Territory of Poyais*, in which there are many interesting particulars regarding this enterprising member of the house of MacGregor.

313

That little tribute might have been written by MacGregor himself, and in a sense it was. William Anderson had clearly based his research on documents the Cazique had produced to establish his reputation, and to distort the historical record for the purpose of disguising the extent of the fictions he had created. So successful was he that even now, the *Dictionary of National Biography* contains an only slightly more sceptical assessment of him. It notes that he 'called himself' Cazique of Poyais and that he was 'said to have served' in the British army, yet at the same time it attributes to him without comment the knighthood to which he had no entitlement. Of his remarkable confidence trick there is no mention, other than that he 'failed in his schemes for colonizing the Mosquito Territory'.

That is a remarkably kind epitaph for a cruel fraudster whose cheating directly caused the deaths of some 200 people and contributed to the ruination of many hundreds more.

Posterity, which is often a poor judge of character, tends to bestow undue respect on evidence that is available in writing. Too little attention is paid to the reasons why documents were produced and to the personalities and motivations of the people responsible for them. When one reads MacGregor's proclamations, his letters to newspapers, his reports of his military victories, and the defence he composed for his trial in Paris, it is not difficult to accept his characterization of himself as a man of honour, integrity and altruism who became the innocent victim of circumstance and betrayal by others. It is only when one reads between the lines, and delves into the background, that something like the truth emerges.

For example, MacGregor explained away the tragedy of the Poyais settlers by accusing them of stealing and selling one of the ships he had provided for them, and of allowing themselves to be lured away from the territory by the unscrupulous merchants of Belize. However, apart from the fact that justifying one's crimes by blaming the victims is a well-tried technique, the story stands up neither in logic, nor in historical context.

The fact is that if the settlers from the *Honduras Packet* really had stolen the ship, they would not have been waiting in the swamps of the Black River when the second party arrived in the *Kennersley Castle* – and yet we know they were, because the eyewitnesses James Hastie and Edward Lowe have told us so, and they had no reason to lie.

Equally, while it is true that the Chief Magistrate of Belize arranged for the removal of the settlers to that colony, his actions were not directed towards the prevention of settlement on the Mosquito Shore. At that particular time the merchants of Belize would have been actively in favour of colonization of the territory that became known as Poyais, because the timber reserves on which their business largely depended were being rapidly depleted and they knew they would have to find new resources to exploit. It would have been in their interests to have Europeans willing to work on the Mosquito Coast, as proved by their efforts to promote logging settlements there just a few years later.

But if all that is so, and MacGregor's excuses were false, why was no action ever taken against him by the British authorities? The Superintendent of Belize, General Codd, had seen with his own eyes the results of the Cazique's deception, and the colony had significantly depleted its treasury in rescuing and trying to care for the poor settlers.

The answer is simply that the deception could not be proved conclusively, and that no one – not even victims such as James Hastie – could actually believe that a man who had gone to so much trouble and expense would have done so on the basis of a lie.

MacGregor was an extremely skilful confidence trickster and, like all such men, he understood the value of the printed word and the official-looking document. Thus, when he needed tangible evidence to support the concept of his fraud, he merely produced the documents himself, knowing that, no matter how implausible, they were likely to be accepted at face value.

In that respect, his masterstroke was the famous guidebook, *A Sketch of the Mosquito Shore*, to which William Anderson referred in approving terms. Nothing would have been more calculated to encourage belief in Poyais than a 300-page, leather-spined volume replete with descriptions, quotations and statistics and the sort of detail that only one who knew the country intimately could have provided. If nothing else, the cost of having it printed would have attested to its authenticity. And yet it was a complete fake, written either by MacGregor himself, or by someone he paid to do it, since no trace of a 'Captain Thomas Strangeways' can be found.

Most of the information in the book was more than half a century out of date, being reprinted wholesale from a report relating to the British settlements on the Mosquito Coast, written by Colonel Robert Hodgson, who had been superintendent of the colony during the 1750s. Some material, in fact, had no connection with the area at all, coming from books written about the West Indies and about other parts of Honduras. The examples of crops grown and the profits they yielded were drawn from places such as Jamaica and even the southern United States, if they were not entirely made up, while the earnest discussion of commerce seems to have little relevance to anything more than the imagination of the writer.

As for the supposed author, he could not have been an officer in the '1st Native Poyer Regiment' because, as we know, there was no such military unit, or, indeed, a Poyaisian army of any kind. The name Thomas Strangeways does not appear among the lists of officers, or enlisted men, for that matter, who accompanied MacGregor on his various ill-fated expeditions in South America. Nor has it so far been noted on the, admittedly incomplete, roll-call of the thousands of British and Irish volunteers who fought at various other stages of the conflict, and in different regions. Was Strangeways, then, one of the dubious characters MacGregor engaged in London to help him promote the Poyais scheme? He could hardly have been an innocent dupe, like Major Richardson, because he would have known that the book he was producing was, at best, misleading.

It is interesting that Strangeways is one of the names contained in the first of the fraudulent papers MacGregor circulated, his 'Proclamation to the Inhabitants of the Territory of Poyais', which purported to give some impression of his status and to explain his reason for visiting Britain. Another name quoted in the document – which was probably printed in Edinburgh, long after the event it was supposed to record – was that of George Woodbine, allegedly in charge of the Poyaisian administration while the Cazique was abroad. Woodbine never appears again in the Poyais story, except in parentheses as a prop to support MacGregor's claims of government, so it may be that Strangeways was just such another former acquaintance whose name came in useful, and that neither man had any actual part in the fraud.

Alternatively, there is a case for linking the name Strangeways to that of Mr Goodluck, who was credited with the authorship of the second Poyais guidebook in 1825. Both have connotations that may reflect the devious mind of Gregor MacGregor, perhaps enjoying a tasteless private joke at the expense of the people whose trust he found it so easy to abuse.

MacGregor was not in the habit of taking anyone completely into his confidence: his experiences among the South American revolutionaries had taught him the dangers of being too trusting. Neither was he particularly renowned for actually paying the people he persuaded to work with him, preferring instead either to appeal to their vanity, by bestowing meaningless ranks and titles upon them, or to let them pay him for the privilege. The likelihood must be that he himself was responsible for the guidebooks and, if that were so, it might help to explain how he occupied himself between rejoining his wife in Jamaica, which he must have done at some time during 1820, and his arrival in London the following year. All the materials he required for fabricating the book would have been easily available in Kingston.

There is no doubt that, for a man described by his former subordinate, Colonel Michael Rafter, as lazy, self-indulgent and dedicated to the pursuit of pleasure, MacGregor expended what would seem to be an uncharacteristic amount of effort in constructing his great fraud. Yet, as Rafter also revealed, his was a mind which, apparently from his youth, was obsessed with small details so that, once he had decided the Poyais scheme was worthwhile, it was his natural inclination to fill up every corner of the picture he set out to paint. Not only did this give MacGregor satisfaction, but it also helped to make Poyais so believable that it was many years before some people finally accepted that there was no such place – even if they had realized long since that it had been associated with a huge swindle.

The Mosquito King's grant of land and the map MacGregor embellished, together with the guidebook, would almost certainly, in themselves, have made Poyais utterly convincing to the British public at a time when so much attention was being paid to South America. Such things are necessary tools of the confidence trickster's trade, but in the case of MacGregor, they served to inspire a romantic imagination that seemed to be unlimited.

There was the coat of arms that adorned his land and bond certificates, with its heraldic symbols and Latin mottoes. There were the flag, adapted from the green cross of Florida, and the order of chivalry that went with it; the complex constitutional arrangements involving three representative chambers and a professional civil service; the multifarious elements of the army, for each of which the Cazique had designed uniforms down to the last button and strip of braid; the sophisticated commercial, economic and banking systems – including, of course, the national currency. Later on, as the political climate changed, there were the various new constitutions.

It is fascinating to consider how MacGregor went about inventing all these things. Did they occur to him on the spur of the moment, as potential collaborators or journalists asked questions about Poyais, or did he arrive in London having worked through and written down the whole structure? He was obviously, like all good con men, a fluent talker, but where others floated fake companies and sold shares in spurious commercial ventures or engineering projects, MacGregor was selling an entire country.

Did he base his creation on the political structures he had seen emerging during the South American revolutions, or on books he had read? We know that for at least one of his constitutions he employed the services of a lawyer

– Maître Merilhou, who represented both MacGregor and the Compagnie de la Nouvelle Neustrie in Paris – but there is no evidence to suggest that the others were anything but his own work. And did Merilhou know he was writing fiction, or had MacGregor persuaded him that it was a real state he was describing?

In a way, though, it was MacGregor's overactive imagination that prevented the Poyais scheme from being as financially rewarding for him as it might have been. He had learned in America, when he was raising money for the invasion of Amelia Island in 1817, just how easy it was to play on people's greed and optimism. There he had managed to sell land in Florida that he clearly did not own or control – indeed, it was actually held legally by a foreign power – raising a substantial amount of cash in a matter of weeks. How much more he would have earned if he had simply repeated the Florida technique with Poyais, offering straightforward scrip against millions of acres for which he could at least make some sort of legal claim to ownership, and then disappearing, as he had done in America.

He was correct in thinking that the selling of Poyais would require rather more substantial evidence than he had produced for the Florida operation. British investors would generally be better informed and more worldly than those in the American South, given the status of the London capital markets. However, along with his map and the guidebook, the mere 'registration' of his land grant at the High Court of Chancery would surely have been sufficient to overcome any doubts against the background of the rampant speculation that was sweeping the City in 1822. And yet it was almost as an afterthought that MacGregor did register the deed, following his sale of a great deal of the land to which it apparently referred, and when the first party of colonists was already on its way to the Mosquito Coast.

In the meantime, his imagination had run almost out of control, leading him to promote Poyais to such an extent that he had found himself organizing the ambitious programme of emigration that would ultimately undermine his whole project, and turn what would have been an inspired hoax into a cruel and deadly one.

For the purpose of making the fortune he desired from his invented country, MacGregor had absolutely no need to retain the hundreds of people he purportedly made soldiers, government officials, civil servants and the like. In fact, the hiring of labourers and household staff, with cash advances against their wages, was positively counter-productive, especially when many of them received free passages for their families aboard ships MacGregor had paid to charter and even refit. It is often said that money has to be invested in order to achieve a truly successful large-scale fraud, but MacGregor was taking that principle to extremes, and seriously diminishing his profits in the process.

The conclusion which suggests itself is that he had been, in some measure, seduced by his own pretensions. Fantasist that he had always been, he may have fallen into the trap of believing that he could become Cazique of Poyais in fact, as well as in name, if he really could establish viable settlements in the territory.

There is even some evidence to support this idea. MacGregor had, after all, established himself as the head of a government on Amelia Island, and it was said that, during his brief occupation of Rio de la Hacha, he took the title of His Majesty the Inca of New Granada. In both cases, there were real communities over which he could rule: the Cazique of Poyais, by contrast, signified nothing much in practical terms. Then there were the roots of his undoubted attachment to South America. A desire to emulate the celebrated General Miranda, along with a desire to make money as a soldier of fortune, have already been discussed, but there was more.

It is recorded that MacGregor was fond of referring to the disastrous Scottish attempt to colonize Darién in the late-seventeenth century, and proud of the fact that one of his ancestors had displayed the enterprise and courage not only to join the expedition, but also to survive its disastrous conclusion. But it was also rumoured, as Michael Rafter reported, that the Darién MacGregor had 'formed a marriage (the world is perfectly well aware of the nature of such marriages) with a native Princess of the country, from which has sprung our hero, a lineal and legitimate descendant of the "Children of the Sun"'.

If that rumour were true – and Gregor MacGregor did have an unusually dark complexion – it might go some way towards explaining his behaviour in relation to Poyais.

MacGregor first suggested that his status as Cazique accompanied the grant of land by the King, and later that he had been elected to the position by native tribesmen – largely, he claimed, because of their attachment to the British who had once settled the region. Neither of these ideas really bears examination. The Mosquito – or Miskito – Indians were indeed heavily influenced by the British, but they had had their own system of political and social organization for nearly two centuries, and it was based on kinship, not election.

Research has shown that between 1641 and 1894, there were no more than three accepted lines of succession for Mosquito kings, and after the 1750s there was only one line and two regional leaders who were subordinate to the kings, in theory at least. The regional leaders were known, for some reason, as 'the general' and 'the admiral', and a series of local chieftains called 'captains' were subordinate to them. The idea that a 'cazique' should have been superimposed on this well-established and essentially stable system, either by royal influence or the choice of the population, is ridiculous. For one thing, such a position would have seriously distorted the traditional structure of power and, for another, the Mosquito would never have departed from the custom of relating their hierarchy to English titles.

Much more persuasive is the thought of MacGregor awarding himself the title for the sake of fulfilling a fantasy arising from the fact that he was descended, or *believed* that he was descended, from native South American royalty. He would have heard the term 'cazique' from the Spanish-speaking native troops he had recruited and commanded years earlier in New Granada, and not from the Mosquito at all.

Similarly, his decision to embark on the extremely risky strategy of directing emigration towards a country that did not exist, or at least not in anything like the form he described, may well have been influenced by the Darién connection. One obvious pointer towards such a conclusion is MacGregor's insistence that the bulk of the settlers should come from Scotland. With the Darién venture, the Scots had shown their willingness to take risks in unknown territory, and their endurance in trying to make a new settlement work against all the odds. If part of MacGregor's fantasy was somehow to compensate for the Darién fiasco by actually establishing a colony in Poyais, those were just the sort of people he would need. But in order to attract them, he had to make Poyais seem much more developed than it was, and he was wise enough to see that he needed English capital to finance the project – unlike his Darién predecessors, who gambled the economic future of Scotland on their expedition, and in consequence helped unwittingly to bring about the union with England.

The underlying tragedy of MacGregor's Poyais, aside from the death and financial ruin it wrought, is that a serious programme of British emigration would have been perfectly feasible and was likely to have succeeded. Had MacGregor been able to set aside his fantasies, and the prospect of acquiring great riches very quickly by means of deception, he might easily have helped to create a thriving little territory as productive and wealthy as the West Indies.

The economic and social conditions of Britain in the 1820s and 1830s, as the population increased steeply and the industrial revolution gathered pace, were such that emigration was seen as both desirable and necessary, so much so that the government supported it financially in many cases. It would not have been difficult to persuade people of all classes that the virgin territory of the Mosquito Coast offered bright hopes for their future, as it could well have done. If only Gregor MacGregor had told the truth. He might have changed the course of history and made himself the kind of fortune that the Poyais fraud failed to produce, largely because of his own inability to restrain himself.

We can never know whether it was a self-induced retreat from reality that prompted MacGregor to push his confidence trick well beyond the point at which it might have succeeded, or whether it was just a matter of overwhelming greed and something approaching contempt for his intended victims. It is, perhaps, a measure of his character that he never showed remorse for the deaths of the settlers who had placed their trust in him, suggesting instead, during his trial in Paris, that they had only themselves to blame. That does seem to indicate a remarkable lack of sensitivity.

His 'unfeeling heart and callous disposition' were noted by Michael Rafter, writing before the Poyais fraud and basing his observations on the way MacGregor had abandoned so many of the soldiers in his care.

It was melancholy to record, Rafter went on, that 'since the affair of Amelia Island, eleven vessels amounting to 3102 tons burthen and mounting 43 guns, have been chartered by MacGregor's agents and have conveyed to South America 329 officers, 1601 soldiers, 101 women and 40 children, amounting in all to 2071 individuals, who, with a few exceptions, have been rapidly swept from the earth.'

Such a display of disregard for human life made MacGregor 'an object painful to contemplate', a man who now wept 'not for the ruin he has caused, but, for the disappointment of his ambition and the blight of his hopes.' As a young man, Rafter suggested, he had 'dared to deny the existence of God'. Self was his ruling principle and 'he has frequently asserted that he did not know what it was to love'.

Yet at the same time, even Rafter felt it necessary to concede that 'no man perhaps, in a similar situation, was ever so remarkable for extreme carelessness in pecuniary matters', adding that MacGregor probably found it 'incompatible with the dignity of the rank to which he aspired' to indulge in the sordid pursuit of money.

That, of course, could not be said about his attempts at self-enrichment through Poyais. Or could it? In spite of its simple brilliance, and the effort MacGregor devoted to it, the Poyais fraud was spectacularly unsuccessful if its aim was only to line the pockets of its creator. The fact that MacGregor was still trying vainly to sell bonds and certificates sixteen years after he had first presented Poyais to the world is a measure of the shortcomings of the hoax as a money-making venture. Was it, then, something other than pure greed that drove him to construct such a comprehensive framework of make-believe?

Michael Rafter reflected that 'the human mind displays an enigma which has baffled in all ages the researches of the most acute philosopher'. The contradiction in MacGregor's character between 'the intrepidity which marks his early career' and the behaviour 'which has rendered his later years contemptible' could only be seen as 'one of those inconsistencies that we must admire without being able to comprehend'.

Gregor MacGregor himself left no clues as to his innermost thoughts and deepest feelings. Probably he was not a man much given to introspection. He was too busy pretending to be the person he would like to have been to spend time considering the sort of man he really was. So thick was the cloak of lies, half-truths and distortions with which he covered his life that much about him remains mysterious, enigmatic and subject to dispute.

When he died in 1845, and the President, government ministers and military chiefs of Venezuela marched behind his coffin, the obituaries in the Caracas newspapers concentrated on his 'heroic and triumphant retreat' from Ocumare to Barcelona, describing him as 'a valiant champion of independence'. There was not a word about Amelia Island,

Porto Bello or Rio de la Hacha, and there was no reference to the Cazique of Poyais.

It was almost as if the man they buried was not the one who would ultimately take his place in history as an exotic footnote in the long and sorry saga of fools and their money.

APPENDIX

THE MACGREGOR VERSION

Following reports of the disasters at Porto Bello and Rio de la Hacha, and the publication, in 1820, of Colonel Michael Rafter's book about him, Gregor MacGregor wrote to the *Edinburgh Courant* to 'set the record straight'.

The letters reproduced below were published in the newspaper in September and October 1821 when, of course, MacGregor was promoting the Poyais scheme and could not afford to allow unfavourable publicity to go unanswered. The spelling, grammar and punctuation are as they appeared in the originals. As for the content, readers now familiar with Gregor MacGregor will be well aware of what credence may be attached to the idea that he acted always with the best of intentions, and from the highest motives, and that his misfortunes were entirely the fault of others, who betrayed his trust.

GENERAL MACGREGOR

The following letter from this celebrated officer is in self-vindication: we therefore make no apology to our readers for inserting it:

Sir,

The failure of the expeditions against Porto Bello and Rio de la Hacha was announced many months ago in all the journals of the Old and New World; nor should I have now troubled you on the subject, had the accounts then given been anything more than mere fabrications.

The events, however, connected with the equally extensive and important revolution in South America, and the motives and conduct of those who have been conspicuously concerned in it, are a matter of history; and were I less interested than I am, I should deem it incumbent on me to correct, when in my power, any statements inconsistent with truth, which involved the reputation of any of those, who co-operated in that grand struggle for the emancipation of the finest portion of the habitable globe.

But the enterprizes above mentioned were under my command, and I have been denounced as the sole cause of their disastrous termination; I am, therefore, bound by every tie to give the real exposition of these transactions.

Let me notice, that as soon as I could, I transmitted the details to Europe; but the same influence which turned our success into defeat, prevented their publication; and the unfavourable impression so artfully made and so industriously kept up, acquired strength by assertions of great authority in Britain and in North America, that I acted without sanction – in short, that I had no commission; while it is well known – indeed, it scarcely required to be stated, that I am, by my Commission, dated 16th May, 1812, the oldest General of the revolution, and that no one adhered more strictly to instructions or exerted himself more ardently to fulfill the designs of those who gave them. The very expeditions to Porto Bello and Rio de la Hacha, were under the orders of the Government of New Granada, of which state I had been a General Officer, ever since the year 1813.

With these preliminary remarks, I proceed, first, to the particulars of our expulsion from Porto Bello, which happened on the 30th April, 1819.

Being well informed with respect to the force and position of the Spanish army, I had stationed strong guards on all the roads by which they could approach, and had taken all the precautions necessary for the security of the town. What then was my surprise, about ten minutes before day light in the morning, when part of the regiment of Catalonia entered, and the rest surrounded the government house, in which I was! Treachery was apparent, though I knew not the traitors.

The house had a balcony about twenty feet high; beneath it a party of Spaniards were placed, and were firing at one of the forts, which occupied their attention, and having no alternative, I leaped from the balcony clear of them – fell, but recovered myself in an instant, and made for the mole [pier], when I plunged into the sea, pursued and fired upon by the enemy. In the water, I stripped, and tied up my clothes and cap, and sent the bundle away from me to deceive the enemy, and attract his fire. I was a full hour in this predicament, when a boat picked me up, through the sides of which, three shots passed before I reached the brig of war, *El Macgregor*, at anchor in the outer part of the harbour. The moment I got on board, my flag announced my safety, and I began to think of the means of regaining what we had lost; with the view, therefore of convincing my troops that I did not give up the contest as hopeless, I ordered the brig to be warped in, in order to bring her broadside to bear upon the town.

At this time I was nearly naked, and suffered severely from a pain in my side, occasioned by my fall. I went below to get my body bandaged, the surgeon at the same time requiring that I should be instantly bled. I was but a few minutes in the cabin, when the firing on shore ceased, and a boat came alongside with a Spanish officer and one of my aides-de-camp, Cornet Sempill, just made prisoner. The officer was dispatched by the Spanish General, with the consent of Colonel Rafter, who commanded in Fort San Geronimo, for the purpose of proposing to me a capitulation, and to sanction the suspension of arms, to which both parties on shore had already agreed. In order to gain time, I told the Spanish officer that he must return and treat with Colonel Rafter, declaring, however, that with respect to the surrender of the squadron, it was ridiculous and absurd to propose it. I also sent two officers to Colonel Rafter, one of them a surgeon, to explain my situation. These gentlemen had written and verbal instructions, authorising him to act as he thought for the best, but warning him that no faith could be put in the promises of the enemy. I exhorted him earnestly to defend the forts, and endeavour, with the assistance of the squadron, to drive out the enemy; for, even if our efforts should fail, there was no necessity for capitulating, as we could still evacuate the forts and bring the troops in the boats of the different vessels on board the squadron. Lastly, I assured him, if he would recommence hostilities, I should cause myself, enfeebled as I was, to be carried on shore. In about a quarter of an hour, to our astonishment, the independent colours were hauled down, the Spanish hoisted, and a heavy fire commenced from the batteries upon the squadron. While this was passing, we were warping the brig close in shore, and I had already sent two boats, loaded with dressed provisions, to each of the forts. These boats escaped back to the brig, and brought the report, that part of the troops had refused to fight any longer, and that, in consequence, Colonel Rafter had been obliged to capitulate. The only thing that could now be done, was done; I brought away the garrison and ammunition of one of the forts, that was situate in the opposite side of the harbour, and saved the squadron.

This occurrence was to me altogether mysterious: no noise, no alarm, and the house in which I was, entered and environed by the enemy. Soon afterwards, however, I obtained the most satisfactory explanation. An officer, under my command, had engaged to the Duke of San Carlos, in London, to seize the earliest opportunity of delivering me into the hands of the Spanish. He had obtained my confidence, and was advanced. This person had the command of all the advanced posts in the morning of the assault. He ordered them to retire, and according to a preconcerted plan, two divisions of the enemy, of six hundred men each, were conducted into the town, just as the day began to dawn. This very man entered Fort Gloria arm in arm with a Spanish officer, and assisted in hauling down the Patriot standard.

The account of the affair of Rio de la Hacha, I shall

endeavour to send you in time for insertion in the next number of your paper.

I am,

Sir,

Your humble Servant,

GREGOR MACGREGOR

Edinburgh, September 25th, 1821.

This second letter was published the following month:

To the Editor of the Courant

SIR,

According to my promise of the 25th ultimo, I proceed to give you a sketch of the affair of Rio de la Hacha.

After the capture of this place on the 5th of October 1819, I called a meeting, or Junta, of the inhabitants, a great many of whom assembled late in the evening at the house of the Cabildo [leader of the municipal council], whither I proceeded, accompanied by General de Lima and an aide-de-camp. The troops were stationed in the fort, upwards of a mile distant. I stated to him that it was my wish that they should elect a Governor, and the other persons necessary for the administration of the province, as also officers to organize a corps of national troops, adding, that I now deposited the civil authority in their hands, and would confine myself solely to the command, naval and military. The election took place accordingly; a merchant of the place, named Valverde, became Governor, and the command of the national troops was intrusted to a native of the town, called Rodrigues, on whom, in vitue of my authority, I conferred the rank of Colonel.

The new Governor invited me and the whole of the multitude to his house; and upon our arrival, we were shown into his store. Valverde left us to give the requisite orders to his domestics, for not knowing that he was to be elected Governor, he had made no arrangement for our reception.

It was night, the room in which we were was large, and contained at the moment about three hundred persons of every hue and description. Just three days before, some of them had fought against my troops, and not a few of their relations and friends lay wounded at that very moment in the town.

We had been but a few minutes assembled, when by some accident, the light was put out, and we were left in perfect darkness. My situation was critical! I immediately addressed them as follows:– 'Citizens, I am MacGregor, my objects and my name are familiar to you all, but three days ago, most of you fought against me; if you are more attached to the Spanish Government than to the independence of your country, you have now a safe opportunity of revenge; it is dark, my troops are far off, the hand that strikes will not be known, and thus with impunity will you be freed from me for ever.' I was answered by a general shout of 'Long live our General, long live our country, you are as safe here as amidst your own troops, there are none here but friends.' – The shouts brought the Governor and his servants with candles, and the evening was spent with the greatest harmony and enthusiasm, and afterwards all present accompanied me to the fort.

I have been the more particular in relating this occurrence, that it will the more clearly show the disposition of the inhabitants, and how easy it would have been for me to keep possession of this province; but, if treachery excite avarice and the lower passions into mutiny, what general is safe? What enterprise can succeed?

The inhabitants of some of the nearest villages presented themselves, and voluntarily sent us supplies of cattle. Great numbers of the Indians also came in, as well as their chiefs, some of whom had not been in the city of La Hacha for the last thirty years.

I had now organised and armed a body of national troops, whose principal duty consisted in patroling the town, in order to prevent the depredations of the European troops, who, from the first moment were intent upon plunder.

The evening before the catastrophe of Rio de la Hacha, I had made arrangements with a partizan leader of the enemy, who had his troops already encamped within a mile of the town. He was to march in the next morning, and take the oath of allegiance to the Patriot Government. I was likewise to have had that same morning the accession of a squadron of cavalry, with abundance of cattle, a voluntary gift from the inhabitants of the town of Camarones. Thus reinforced and supplied, I designed to march into the interior of the province to the Valle de Dupar, whither the Spanish Governor had retired, and was concentrating his forces.

Waiting this increase of means, contrary to my custom, I slept that night in town. The Rifles under Colonel Rafter (brother to the officer of the same name at Porto Bello) were ordered to patrole during the night the outskirts of the town.

I retired to rest at an early hour, in the hope that the following day I should find myself at the head of a native force, sufficient to enable me to reduce to subordination the European troops, who, with the exception of the native bravery, were the most unfit class of men that could possibly have been selected for such a service.

About two o'clock in the morning, I was awoke by Captains Grant and Smith, who had come on shore to report that they had been boarded by an armed force under Colonels Northcotte and Rafter, who, after taking several articles from them, had repaired with their party on board of a Spanish schooner, and stood out to sea with her. This vessel was a rich prize recently taken, and committed to the charge of Colonel Northcotte, the commander of my own Guards! Upon farther inquiry, it appeared that the Rifles had that night plundered several houses and stores, and conveyed the property on board the prize, nor had they even spared the effects of their own companions; and finally, that almost the whole of the sailors, as well as the mate of one of the transports, had gone off with them.

Being informed of the desertion of these troops, amounting to nearly a third of my European force, and having ascertained the extent of the pillage they had made, I dispatched the Chief of my Staff, General de Lima, to the Governor and Colonel Rodrigues, to let them know what had taken place, and that it was my intention, in order to prevent any thing of the kind happening in future, immediately to re-embark the remainder of the Europeans, and then send them to the garrison island of San Andres. I directed him farther, to request them to communicate this determination to the inhabitants and national troops, that it might be the means of appeasing their resentment. I then proceeded to the quarters of General Eyre, the Commander of the European troops, and requested his immediate attendance at the fort.

Upon my arrival there, I ordered the troops to be drawn up on the parade, and told them briefly of the desertion of their comrades, and added, 'that the Creole troops were much enraged at the enormities that had been committed; that they were well aware of the repeated complaints made against them by the inhabitants; and that their numbers being now much diminished, the citizens would no longer be intimidated, and in a word, the only means that I could now adopt for their safety, was to embark them aboard the transports.' I farther admonished them that 'the most serious consequences were to be apprehended, if any man should leave the fort and go into town.' General Eyre and his men pledged themselves that they would strictly obey my orders.

I was now joined by the Governor and Colonel Rodrigues, who assured me that my promise to send off the Europeans, had in a great measure restored tranquility in the town, and satisfied the national troops.

During the embarkation I was solicitous about many things, but particularly that the sick and wounded should be well taken care of. I visited the ship destined for the hospital; along side of her I saw several canoes full of large Spanish boxes, and boats receiving a still greater number piled up on shore. I immediately sent Ensign Gibbons of the Guards, a most steady and confidential officer, with orders not to allow any more of the packages to be put into the boats, and learn who had sent them.

A few minutes after, my attention was called by the sound of musketry, and taking my glass, I saw several of the European soldiers flying towards the fort from all directions, pursued by the national troops.

The men in the fort turned some of the guns upon the town, and a brisk fire for a short time, was kept up on both sides; when, horrible to relate, the fort blew up, and only a few persons were saved by swimming to the different vessels.

The troops, most of them without arms, had sallied out of the fort, *en masse*, declaring that before they embarked, they would plunder the town, but Colonel Rodrigues, with the national troops, assisted by the Indians, compelled them to fly back to the fort, which they had scarcely reached, when a soldier, in a state of intoxication, discharged his musket in the magazine; hence the tremendous explosion.

Let us now follow the deserters: they made the best of their way to the island of Santo Domingo, and came to an anchor in Flemand Bay. Their leaders went ashore to Aux Cayes, where they waited upon the Governor; said they were sent from me, requesting him to deliver up to the said officers such soldiers as, belonging to the expedition, had remained behind – They at the same time purchased a large quantity of provisions. During the absence of these officers, Dr Nuchet, a Frenchman, who had been carried away against his inclination, got ashore, and informed the Governor how matters really were. Orders were immediately issued to arrest them, and detain the vessel, but they got intelligence of it in time to escape on board of the schooner, leaving their provisions behind.

The object of these marauders, it is stated, was to man and provision the vessel, and proceed on a cruise up the Mediterranean. This plan was frustrated, for, being short of water and provisions, they had no alternative but to put the vessel before the wind, and make for the island of Jamaica, where they accordingly arrived. Here they at first endeavoured to present themselves as belonging to a national vessel of New Granada, but fearing detection, they resorted to the artifice of publishing a declaration against me, by which means they obtained the protection of the merchants hostile to the cause of South American independence, and were thus screened from inquiry, and ultimately assisted in leaving the island.

Deserted by one part of my force, and obliged to send away the remainder, every one will perceive the predicament in which I was. I had obtained no status among the inhabitants, and when the Spanish influence and Spanish troops resumed their activity, how could I calculate by my single efforts to retain the command of the place, or even to repress the bloody commotion which was to be dreaded between those who had lost and those who had recently obtained the ascendancy, between the partizans of the old and the partizans of the new order of things.

I had resolved, however, at any hazard, to avert such calamity; my design was to place myself at the head of the Creole troops, and that if I could gradually establish my authority, I would recal the Europeans from San Andres; or, if I should find my situation untenable, I would endeavour to effect reconciliation among the parties, and depart; but the same evil genius that had actuated the deserters, incited to madness their comrades who remained. The irruption made by them upon the town, had induced the Creole leader to call to his assistance the Spanish force; thus at the same instant the fort blew up, and the Spaniards had possession, and instead of returning to, I had under the necessity of using the vessel, in which I was, to carry me with all possible speed from Rio de la Hacha.

I am, Sir,

Your humble Servant,
GREGOR MACGREGOR
Edinburgh, 17th of October, 1821.

This next piece of 'Gregoriana' dates from 1826, when MacGregor was imprisoned in Paris on charges of fraud, following the collapse of his attempt to repeat his Poyais scheme in France. For his trial in July, he had his lawyer, Maître Merilhou, compose a highly coloured and misleading account of his life and activities, in order to convince the judges of his good character and altruistic motives.

Merilhou produced a brilliant piece of 'spin', but was unable to present it himself in court because he had suddenly been called as a witness for the prosecution. However, it was delivered with equal brilliance by another lawyer, Maître Berville, and the effect of both its content and the manner of its delivery is evident in the subsequent acquittal of MacGregor.

A heavily abridged version of this long and almost entirely inaccurate document, which was entitled 'Submission on behalf of General Sir Gregor MacGregor, Cacique of Poyais, in Central America', is reproduced here in translation from the original French:

Sir Gregor MacGregor, from a family that has given Scotland some of its kings, and chief of a Scottish clan known in history under the name of Clan-Alpin, was born in Scotland, at Edinburgh. He is a Catholic, like his ancestors, and it is well known that the ancient houses of Scotland are all faithful to a religion which, in Great

Britain, excludes its adherents from public office and does not allow them to aspire to the higher ranks in military service. Related closely to several branches of the English peerage, notably the Duke of Northumberland, General MacGregor, destined from birth for the profession of arms, was at the age of eighteen, a captain in the 57th Regiment of Foot – that is, the highest rank a Catholic could obtain. He served with honour in the British army in Portugal. During that period, he achieved some renown as a military theorist: the publication of his work on the formation of closed columns brought him to the attention of his government, attracting particular praise from His Royal Highness the Duke of Kent, one of the sons of King George III, and flattering letters from His Royal Highness the Duke of York, who then directed military affairs in England.

In 1811, Europe began to turn its attention towards the efforts of South America to free itself from its colonial master; Sir Gregor MacGregor saw in this struggle that there was glory to be gained in the defence of a just cause: he travelled to Venezuela to offer his help in achieving American independence.

As the commanding general of the Venezuelan cavalry, Sir Gregor MacGregor also became second-in-command of all the country's forces, under the celebrated Miranda, who was their generalissimo, who later became a prisoner of war, and who has recently died in a dungeon in Cadiz. From that time until 1820, General MacGregor never ceased to be a commander-in-chief, whether it was of the Venezuelan armies or those of New Granada. Always faithful to the cause of American liberty, in good times and in bad, he presided over its birth, did as much as he could to ensure its success, and often made good the setbacks that were inevitably occasioned by such a vast territory and such a varied chain of command.

It was he who, in 1816, took charge of the famous retreat of the American army to the Orinoco, who dashed the hopes of General Morillo, and deprived him of the momentary superiority the use of European tactics had given him. It was he who organized the army with which Bolívar liberated the island of Margaritta and captured the Spanish squadron blockading it.

In 1815, Morillo's triumphant army had invaded the greater part of the new realm of Granada. General MacGregor was charged with raising the siege of Cartagena, one of the most memorable events in the history of American independence. After a blockade of four months on land, and numerous assaults by sea, General Morillo used starvation to make himself master of the place. That victory earned him the title of Count of Cartagena; General MacGregor, leading the remnants of his garrison, was forced to retreat under fire from Spanish artillery. Soon afterwards, going back on the offensive, he drove the Spaniards out of Amelia Island, and seized the capital of Florida.

In 1819, appointed captain-general of the naval and land forces of New Granada, he set himself the task of reconquering from the Spaniards the country to which he had confided his fate: he travelled to England, organized an expedition of army and naval forces, and Porto Bello and Rio de la Hacha soon fell into the hands of his victorious armies; the territory of New Granada was liberated from the presence of the Spaniards. That period of triumph for the American armies ended with the treaty signed at Angostura on 21 December 1819, by which the states of Venezuela and New Granada were united in perpetuity to form a single state under the name of the Republic of Colombia.

The gratitude of the Americans was marked by the calling of General MacGregor at the first session of the federal congress, as the representative of an important province. It was a worthy reward for the blood he had spilt in the cause of emancipation.

Thus was completed the task which General MacGregor had set himself; a generous people had been liberated from foreign domination and given the benefits of civilization. Since that moment, the existence of the new states has no longer been contested; and, today, the assent of Europe has given support to a result that was so long in doubt, and to the efforts demanded of the inhabitants of those once unhappy countries.

Here we turn to a new series of events which are more closely attached to the pretext for the current incarceration of General Sir Gregor MacGregor.

Circumstances which it would take too long to rehearse here brought to General MacGregor the possession of the territory called Poyais, about which his enemies have increasingly spread the most crude fabrications. This country, also known as Mosquitia, is situated in the peninsula of Central America, of which part once bore the name of the kingdom of Guatemala: the territory of Poyais, or Mosquitia, is north of Colombia, separated from it by the isthmus of Panama ... This country, separated from the kingdom of Guatemala by a mountain range, and from the republic of Colombia by the Bay of Chiriqui, had never been conquered by the Spaniards, according to the celebrated Bryan Edwards, in a report prepared for the English government in 1773. Inhabited by independent natives, and by several European families, the remnants of an old British settlement abandoned following the treaty of 1786, this territory is destined one day to become a place of considerable importance. The abundant life of its rivers, the fertility of its soil, the beauty of its ports, long ago attracted the attention of the English government, through the commissioners it sent there, as a prospective colony, which could replace the lost Antilles . . . [and] the Indian tribes there have always been notable for their attachment to and boundless confidence in the English . . . General MacGregor was chosen by the Indians as their chief, under the title of cacique, in an election which took place at Rio Secco in April 1821, following the customs of the native population. This was announced by a proclamation, inserted in all the newspapers of the day, in which General MacGregor declared his acceptance of the nomination. An account is also given in the English book *A Sketch of Poyais*, by Mr Strangeways.

From even before that date – in fact, on 29 April 1820 – the king of the Mosquito tribe, George Frederic, had made to General MacGregor a grant of land situated by the Plaintain river, along with the power, among others, to make laws, to levy customs duties, and to make all necessary arrangements for the protection, the defence and the prosperity of that territory.

Since some confusion has arisen between the rights bestowed on General MacGregor by this grant, and those arising from his appointment as cacique – and has permitted his enemies to make allegations against him – he now wishes, in responding to those charges, to make clear the importance of the grant of land.

This grant has been authenticated in every manner required by the law of England. It was verified by an affadavit sworn before the authorised official of the High Court of Chancery in London, and transmitted in the same form by Henri-Joseph Durieux, the notary royal in London, with further certification by Messrs Sundius and Barber, also notaries there. It need hardly be said that such a legal document cannot be the subject of argument.

During this trial, reference has been made to the subsequent revocation of the grant by the Mosquito king, but that assertion is a falsehood circulated by the enemies of General MacGregor, against which he protests most strongly. Without even considering the question of the point up to which revocation of such a grant might be possible, he contests the existence of any authentic legal instrument relevant to his position, and, on that point, he undoubtedly has a right to be believed equal to that of his anonymous accusers.

General MacGregor felt that the most important element of his possession of the territory was the advancement of the native civilization, which was already greatly superior to that of other American tribes. After taking some provisional measures to establish peace and good order in the country, he felt it his duty to travel to Europe ... The object of his visit, in 1821, was to find farmers, artisans and their families willing to emigrate to his country and to become landowners there, so as to contribute to the development of the native civilization ... That is what all the new American governments are doing ...

Much has been said about a loan raised in London by the general, for the purpose of financing the settlement of Poyais; but, although events outside the control of the general, and which he could neither foresee nor prevent, made that operation less than successful, it is enough today, for the benefit of French justices, to say that no one with an interest in the loan has expressed the smallest complaint or the slightest regret. They know the circumstances surrounding the matter too well not have placed the blame upon those who deserve it.

An expedition of four or five hundred Scottish colonists left English ports in 1822 to establish agricultural undertakings in Poyais. General MacGregor found it impossible to direct this operation in person, and that has provided a pretext for a great deal of criticism. The main object of the Scottish colonists was to have been the cutting and exploitation of the dye-woods that grow in abundance on the northern coast of the country, but this was not to the liking of English merchants in Belize, whose entire business consists of cutting wood on the Poyais coast and who saw that, as the colonists sent by General MacGregor began to prosper, their own resources would disappear. Consequently, every possible means was employed in order to break up the colony on the banks of the Rio Tinto; emissaries were sent to persuade the settlers to move to Belize, with the bait of a better future; threats and promises were made by turns, and soon, the workers had not only been brought to Belize, but had also been persuaded that they could take with them General MacGregor's ship and sell it for their own benefit. What could General MacGregor – living in Europe – do against a body of merchants in the Bay of Honduras? In vain did he attempt to reclaim his ship and her cargo; the response was a campaign of defamation in the newspapers ...

One can hardly be moved to pity at the fate of the Scots who have stolen one's ship ... If some subjects of the English crown have complaints to make against General MacGregor, the English courts are certainly open to them; that being so, the complete silence that has been maintained on the matter in England suggests that Sir Gregor must be utterly irreprochable ...

If General MacGregor had known, for a single moment in his life, the need for gold, which so often lies behind dishonest behaviour, how often he would have had the opportunity to satisfy it by departing from the path of honour! But, being a soldier as disinterested as he was intrepid, he never saw in his battles anything but the glory of attaining his great result that was his ambition, and of doing his duty. From 1810 until the end of the war, he served as a general officer at his own expense, without receiving a salary; he himself paid the greater part of the costs of the expedition he organized in England in 1819 as captain-general of the naval and military forces of New Granada ...

Yet it is to such a man that people are imputing, on the basis of the weakest proof, acts that are contrary to the course of honour!

SELECT BIBLIOGRAPHY

Byrne, Thomas J: 'The Four Brothers', *The Glencorbry Chronicle*, Vol. 1, No. 2, Glin Historical Society, 2001.

Chancellor, Edward: *Devil Take the Hindmost – A History of Financial Speculation*, Farrar, Strauss & Giroux, New York, 1999.

Davies, Glyn: *A History of Money*, University of Wales Press, Cardiff, 1994.

Dawson, Frank G: *The First Latin American Debt Crisis*, Yale University Press, New Haven and London, 1990.

Ducoudray-Holstein, General H. L. V.: *Memoirs of Simón Bolívar*, S. G. Goddrich & Co., Boston, 1829.

Eastment, Winifred: *Wanstead Through the Ages*, Wanstead.

Fairbridge, Edith: *Lady Anne Barnard at the Cape 1797–1802*, Oxford, 1924.

Hastie, James: *Narrative of a Voyage in the Ship* Kennersley Castle *from Leith Roads to Poyais*, printed for the author, Edinburgh, 1823.

Hippisley, G: *A Narrative of the Expedition to the Rivers Orinoco and Apuré, in South America; Which Sailed from England in November 1817, and Joined the Patriotic Forces in Venezuela and Caracas*, London, 1819.

Hippisley, Gustavus Butler: *Acts of Oppression Committed under the Administration of M. de Villèle, Prime Minister of Charles X, in the Years 1825–6*, Alfred Miller, London, 1831.

Hippisley, Gustavus Butler: *The Siege of Barcelona, a Poem in Three Cantos*, London, 1842.

Hippisley, Gustavus Butler: *Hours of Idleness*, London.

Jones, I. Fitzroy, *The Hippisley Family*, Taunton, 1952.

Lambert, Eric: *Voluntarios Británicos e Irlandeses en la Gesta Bolivariana* (3 vols), published with the cooperation of the British Embassy in Venezuela, British Petroleum, The British Council, and the Venezuelan Ministry of Defence, Caracas, 1993.

Lenta, Margaret & le Cordeur, Basil: *The Cape Diaries of Lady Anne Barnard*, 2 vols, Capetown, 1999.

Massingberd, Hugh: 'A More Than Likely Story', *Spectator*, 25 May 2002.

Michie, Ranald: *The London Stock Exchange: A History*, Oxford University Press, Oxford, 1999.

O'Leary, Simon: *Memories of Jerome O'Leary Published by Order of the Venezuelan Government Under the Auspices of the President Guzman Blanco.*

Quennell, Peter (ed.): *Diversions of History*, Allan Wingate, London, 1954. (Article *The Prince of Poyais*, by Victor Allan, reprinted from *History Today*).

Rafter, Michael: *Memoirs of Gregor M'Gregor*, J. J. Stockdale, London, 1820.

Sinclair, David: *The Pound: A Biography*, Century, London, 2000.

Smout, T.C.: *A History of the Scottish People*, William Collins and Sons, Edinburgh, 1969.

Strangeways, Thomas: *A Sketch of the Mosquito Shore*, William Blackwood, Edinburgh, and T. Cadell, London, 1822.

Thorning, Joseph F.: *Miranda: World Citizen*, University of Florida Press, Gainesville, 1952.

Trevelyan, George Macaulay: *British History in the Nineteenth Century and After, 1782–1919*, Longmans, Green and Co., London, 1937.

Manuscripts in Glin Castle archives:

Letter from the late Eric Lambert to the Knight of Glin on Col. Hipp senior, 16 January 1974.

Action by Lt. Hippisley against Lt. Amory PRO WO/71/108.

Letters from H.G. Burrard and Sir Gerald Burrard to the Knight of Glin, 1955.

Letters from Geraldine Burrard and the Countess of Munster to Lady Rachel FitzGerald, 1900.

Acknowledgements (foreword): Graham Viney, Basil le Cordeur, William Laffen, Giles FitzHerbert.

INDEX

COAST OF POYAIS.